MARC MÁRQUEZ

MARC MÁRQUEZ

EVERYTHING OR NOTHING

Stuart Barker

First published in the UK in 2025 by Blink Publishing
An imprint of Bonnier Books UK
5th Floor, HYLO,
103–105 Bunhill Row,
London, EC1Y 8LZ

Owned by Bonnier Books
Sveavägen 56, Stockholm, Sweden

Hardback – 9781789468298
Ebook – 9781789468304
Audio Digital Download – 9781789468311

A CIP catalogue of this book is available from the British Library.

Designed by Envy Design Ltd
Printed and bound by Clays Ltd, Elcograf S.p.A.

1 3 5 7 9 10 8 6 4 2

www.bonnierbooks.co.uk

Special thanks to Livio Suppo

CONTENTS

Chapter 1: **Three Kings Night**   1

Chapter 2: **The Ant from Cervera**   15

Chapter 3: **Double Vision**   31

Chapter 4: **The Rookie**   53

Chapter 5: **Dominion**   81

Chapter 6: **The Good, the Bad and the Ugly**   101

Chapter 7: **Invincible**   125

Chapter 8: **Maximum Risk**   139

Chapter 9: **Monster**   157

Chapter 10: **Fame**   175

Chapter 11: **Pandemic**   193

Chapter 12: **To Hell and Back**   217

Chapter 13: **Breaking Point**   235

Chapter 14: **Phoenix**   259

Chapter 15: **El Retorno Del Rey**   281

Appendix: Marc Márquez Grand Prix Results,
2008-24   299

Endnotes   311

Bibliography   323

CHAPTER 1

THREE KINGS NIGHT

'YOU HAVE TO GO AND SEE THIS KID FROM CERVERA – YOU'LL BE AMAZED.'

Jaume Curcó

The little boy with the dark hair, olive skin and brown eyes was almost four years old when he wrote his letter to the three kings and waited, excitedly, to see if his wish would be granted. Sleep did not come easy in the run-up to Three Kings Night, for that was when the boy would discover if his wish would be granted.

Three Kings Night falls on 5 January, and festivities carry through to the following day – Three Kings Day. A European tradition dating back to the 14th century, Three Kings Day is also known as Epiphany, and the kings in question are known in other parts of the world as the Three Wise Men who, according to Christian tradition, visited the infant Jesus bearing gifts of gold, frankincense and myrrh.

Once a year, children all over Spain – and in several other Latin and Hispanic countries – write letters to these legendary bearers of gifts, asking if they too might be favoured, in much the same way that children in other countries write to Father Christmas.

Of course, the Spanish also celebrate Christmas, but the festivities are extended until 6 January, with Three Kings Day being the culmination of the festive season; street parades provide a riot of music and colour in villages, towns and cities all across Spain, as families get together, bake special Three Kings cakes, exchange gifts and celebrate the occasion as has been done for centuries.

As children from Bilbao to Marbella excitedly tore open their presents on Three Kings Night in 1997, a gift from those kings to a small boy in Cervera would prove to have profound consequences. It was a mini motorcycle, a Yamaha PW50, and the brown-eyed boy couldn't believe what he was seeing. It was magical: his wish had come true; the Three Kings had delivered.

Tearing off the last pieces of wrapping paper, the boy threw a leg over a motorcycle for the first time, his Joker-esque grin lighting up the humble little dwelling in Cervera that he called home.

His name was Marc Márquez, and now he had a motorcycle. 'I asked for it in a letter to the Three Kings, and they brought it,' he explained when he was ten years old. 'I thought that they were real.'

It might have been Julià and Roser Márquez who spent their hard-earned money on the PW50, but in Marc Márquez's young mind, it was the Three Kings who had made his dream come true. Maybe they had also blessed him with powers to ride a motorcycle like no one had ever done before, because Marc Márquez would one day change the face of motorcycle racing and become the highest-paid rider on the planet, as well as one of the most successful of all time. The Kings had played their part on that cold and fateful January night in 1997 – the rest was up to Marc Márquez.

o

Cervera is the capital of the Segarra region in the province of Lleida, which itself forms part of the Catalunya region of north-east Spain.

Founded in 1026, Cervera is some 60 miles north-west of Barcelona and home to around 9,000 people. A pretty hillside town, topped by the Gothic bell tower of the Basilica of Holy Mary and framed by its medieval walls, the town boasts a university and no fewer than eleven monuments of national interest amongst its ancient architecture.

Cervera is off the beaten tourist trail and remains a very traditional Spanish town: a pleasant place to be born and raised in, and a town that has raised not one, but two multiple motorcycling world champions. Marc and Álex Márquez's astonishing careers and achievements are documented in a permanent exhibit at the Museu Comarcal de Cervera in the centre of town.

The brothers are celebrated throughout the town and the local residents are fiercely proud of them. Flags and posters bearing Marc's number 93 and Álex's favoured number 73 are omnipresent; they hang over balconies, in bars, from lamp posts, and in shop windows. Near the centre of Cervera is the MM93 official merchandise store and, as well as doing a brisk trade with visiting fans, the store seems to be responsible for clothing many of the locals. There's even a sign on the outskirts of Cervera, proudly proclaiming it as the birthplace of Marc Márquez.

Just as nine-time world champion (and future rival) Valentino Rossi has Tavullia, Marc Márquez has Cervera. Both communities have guarded their favoured sons well, and have provided stable environments amongst lifelong friends to help keep their respective superstars' feet firmly on the ground.

The beautiful Catalonian spring had not yet arrived, and the mists that often shroud Cervera had not yet retreated as Julià (Catalan for

Juliàn) Márquez and Roser Márquez Alentà awaited the birth of their first child in early 1993 (the year of Marc Márquez's birth would later inspire the choice of 93 as his race number). The pair had met in the Big Ben nightclub in Mollerussa, some 18 miles east of Cervera, in 1987. They were married in 1991 and, according to Spanish newspaper, *El Correo de Burgos*,[1] their first child was conceived amongst the euphoria that followed Barcelona's victory over Sampdoria in the European Cup final the previous year. It was the first time Barcelona had won the championship, and the first time any Spanish team had won it since 1966. Like most other people in the Catalunya region, Julià and Roser Márquez were ecstatic, but unlike most, they celebrated by conceiving a child. Were it not for Ronald Koeman's winning goal for Barcelona at Wembley, Marc Márquez might never have been born.

'There we were, Julià and I, a year after getting married, sitting on the sofa in our house in Cervera, jumping for joy at Barça's historic victory,' Roser explained in *El Correo de Burgos*, 'and, the truth is, we enjoyed that final so much; so much so, that we looked at each other and we asked ourselves, "But what are we doing here alone? Come on, Julià, let it be whatever God wants!" And, you see, soon this wonderful little devil appeared!'

The 'little devil' appeared on 17 February, nine months after the championship final, and the young couple named him Marc Márquez Alentà (Spanish women traditionally retain their maiden names as part of their married names and children inherit both names). The world would come to know him more simply as Marc Márquez.

He was taken home to a very modest household and raised to believe in hard work, respect for others and the importance of family; in this case, a working-class family: Marc Márquez was not born with a silver spoon in his mouth. His mother worked as a secretary and, before the financial crisis in Spain in the mid-1990s left him temporarily unemployed, Julià Márquez had been a construction worker, operating a heavy digger. He soon gained a reputation as the go-to man for difficult jobs. 'Anyone can operate it,' Julià explained, 'but to actually work with one is different. Like a motorcycle – easy to ride, but hard to ride to the limit.'

Julià Márquez's affinity with machinery would be inherited by his son, as would his love of motorcycles. Although he never raced, he was a keen road rider and would often ride to Jerez in southern Spain and Assen (a round trip of over 2,000 miles to the Netherlands and back) to watch races. Márquez senior also acted as race controller and flag marshal at local enduro and motocross events at the Rufea circuit, run by Moto Club Segre, and would often take Marc along with him, exposing his son to motorsport from a very early age.

The circuit – which lies 38 miles west of Cervera – offers motocross, dirt track and flat-tracking facilities, and it would become like a second home to Marc Márquez as he trained there on a regular basis throughout his childhood and subsequent career.

While Julià taught his son about flag marshalling, Roser kept herself busy making sandwiches and snacks, not only for her son, but for all the other riders too: she was a mother to the whole paddock. Roser would also make special drinks for her tiny son. 'Marc was so small that we had to make fruit shakes to help him grow.'

Marc Márquez still looks back on those early years with great fondness. 'Rather than the times on the track, I remember the times *off* the track. We'd go spend the weekend, and our motorhome would turn into the Sunday lunch spot for all the riders. Tito Rabat and the Espargarós (Pol and Aleix – Márquez's future rivals in Grand Prix racing) would come by and have lunch too. That was motorcycling; it was more than motorcycling, it was passion.'[2]

On 23 April 1996, when Marc was just over three years old, he gained a younger brother with the arrival of Álex. The two would become inseparable, and their continued support for each other would play a huge part in their later success.

Given his father's love of bikes, and his regular attendance at enduro events, it didn't come as any great surprise when Marc Márquez wrote a letter to the Three Kings asking for one in 1997. 'When I was three years old – almost four – I asked for a gas bike for jumps,' he explained. 'I think because my parents would take us to Bell Puig (a dirt track 50 miles from Cervera) with the Segre Moto Club. When I was a kid, they'd sit us up on the mountain and we'd watch bikes all day long and, if you watch them all day long, you want one.'[3]

Once he had his Yamaha PW50, Marc Márquez needed to learn how to ride it. At first, his father took him to a nearby industrial estate, or a friend's field, to get used to riding the bike, which he had fitted with stabilisers. 'When we started, with the help of a friend, we attached these little wheels, because he didn't know how to ride,' Julià explained. 'We went by ourselves – him on his motorbike and me on mine – around Cervera, around the roads. It was one of those moments between father and son that felt really good.'

Crucially, Julià Márquez never pushed his son during those formative years on two wheels. He encouraged him and advised him, but never pushed him – he had seen too many children burnt out too young because of domineering fathers almost forcing their kids to get results. 'When Marc first rode, I told him, "This is your toy – play with it,"' Julià later remembered. 'When I see parents pushing or shouting at their kids at a racetrack, I tell them, "YOU get on! YOU ride the bike! Your kid's not going to make it, because of what you're doing to him."[4]

Marc Márquez's childhood was a happy one, and Cervera proved to be an idyllic place to grow up. 'One advantage of living in a small town is that everybody knows each other, so even young children can play in the street or the park without anyone having to look after them too much,' he said of his formative years. 'I remember when I was little, I would go to the promenade in front of my school and spend the afternoons there, with my brother and my friends, playing all sorts of games or riding our bicycles.'[5]

According to his mother, Marc Márquez was never shy of taking chances. 'Marc has always taken risks,' she confessed, 'even from an early age. He doesn't think about it. He always playfully pushed the limits. If he was on the sidewalk, he wanted to walk on the edge.'[6]

A risk-taker by nature, the young Márquez found an outlet for his inner daredevil on two – and sometimes three – wheels. According to Roser, 'When he was little, he was always running around on his toy bike and his tricycle. He was very excited with anything that had wheels.'

When his mother and father were in work (both temporarily lost their jobs during the Spanish recession), Marc spent a lot of time being looked after by his paternal grandparents, Ramón and Sole. His parents would drop him off at school on their way to work, then he would go to his grandparents' house after school and wait to be picked up in the evening.

Marc became particularly close with Ramón. In later years, when he was racing in MotoGP, the first thing he would do on returning home to Cervera would be to visit his grandfather to assure him he was okay, and to update him on how his racing weekend went.

Ramón had nothing but fond memories of Marc as a child. 'Marc has always been a good kid,' he said before he passed away in 2024. 'We've never had to get cross with Marc – never! He's always been easy-going.'[7]

Don Ramón played a huge part in guiding his grandson through his formative years, both literally and metaphorically. Márquez remembered one incident in particular when his grandad came to the rescue. 'My grandfather really liked walking in the countryside and, when I was little, I used to accompany him on my motorbike. One day I had the idea of entering a cornfield; the problem was that the stalks were so high, and the field so big, that I got lost. My grandfather guided me with his voice. I tried to pull my motorcycle, but I couldn't get out. I was very scared, but now it's a great memory from my childhood!'

Just one year after getting his Yamaha PW50, a five-year-old Marc Márquez started racing – complete with stabilisers. He wanted to race motocross but was too young, so had to enter 'Enduro for Kids' races instead. This proved to be no bad thing as, in enduro, Márquez could take his time to learn how to ride without permanently stressing about lap times as he would have done in shorter motocross races.

The following year, 1999, Julià Márquez bought his eldest son a second-hand 50cc pocket dirt bike which Marc raced in both enduro and motocross events. Right from the start, Márquez was like a sponge, absorbing everything that was going on around him; desperate to learn, desperate to become faster. Julià said his son would even eavesdrop on conversations, hoping to pick up scraps of information. 'When he was a child and we went to the races, when parents and mechanics were talking – while the kids were playing around – he was always there by our side. Depending on the conversation topic, I used to say, "Be careful – he's around!" The parents answered me, "He's just playing," but it wasn't true – he was listening!'[8]

Another trait the young Márquez displayed from the outset was bravery: he had no fear of crashing, as his father has testified. 'I remember once with a friend in Vic (a circuit 60 miles from Cervera) when Marc was still a kid. I told him, "Marc, at this corner, try to do it full throttle – I think you can do it." He said, "It's not possible, but I will try it." He did it – he entered full throttle, and we had to pick him up from the tyre fence! He looked at us and said, "See? It wasn't possible."'[9]

Continuing to race in both disciplines in 2000, Márquez finished fourth in a local enduro championship and, more impressively, was runner-up in the Catalan Motocross Championship. The following year, he would win it – his first title.

Already, Márquez was impressing others with his intelligence and innate abilities. 'He was a bright kid,' recalled Márquez family friend Luis Capdevila. 'He had fast reactions and eyes that took in everything. If you gave him advice, he absorbed it immediately.'[10] The young Márquez was so versatile he would often stand on the podium in three different disciplines – enduro, motocross and speedway.

By this point, Álex Márquez was five years old and had been attending races with his brother for as long as he could remember. Wanting to become more involved, in 2001 he hatched a plan to be Marc's mechanic in future. 'He was just a spectator at first,' Marc explained, 'and he came up with the mechanic idea so as to have something to do at the track.'[11] Rather than becoming a mechanic, however, Álex Márquez would soon start racing himself and would discover that Marc wasn't the only talent in the family.

Marc Márquez started road racing in 2002, although he continued to also race in motocross events during that transitional season. He made his road racing debut with the Mataró-based ProCurve team on a 50cc Conti Copa RX in the Conti Cup, a series for riders aged seven to nine and organised by the Catalan Motorcycling Federation. Designed as a relatively cheap way for youngsters to gain racing experience, the series charged a flat fee which covered everything from the bike to leathers, helmet, boots, gloves and racing licence.

One of Márquez's rivals in his first year of racing was a seven-year-old rider called Maverick Viñales who, in 15 years' time, would find himself racing against Márquez in MotoGP. Márquez remembers the chilled-out atmosphere in the Conti paddock from that year. 'After the races, all the kids got together to play football and ride their bicycles and skateboards,' he said in an early Spanish television interview when he was just ten years old: the real rivalries would come later.

In that same 2002 interview, Márquez also revealed the nature of the balance between his schooling and his racing life. 'I'm doing well with my lessons,' he said, 'so my teacher lets me out to practise.'

Márquez attended the Jaume Balmes school in Cervera between the ages of 5 and 12. One of his teachers there, Roser Atienza, claims he was always very focused, despite his tender years. 'Even as a little boy, he had very clear ideas,' she said. 'He was very impulsive, and you noticed that on track, because he makes decisions in milliseconds and is rarely wrong. He was already like that at school.'[12]

Because he often missed Fridays at school while travelling to race meetings, Márquez would ask Roser Atienza to prepare his homework for him and he would take it to the races. 'On Thursdays, he asked me to prepare his work for the weekend,' she said, 'and, when Monday came, the first thing he did was take out his work and put it on the table.'[13]

Atienza noted Márquez's intelligence and drive before he was even in his teens. 'He was an impressive student. He wasn't satisfied with a nine – it had to be a ten. He was very good.'

In a later interview with CNN, Atienza sang her famous pupil's praises even more. 'This child could have been whatever he wanted, from a doctor to an architect – anything he wanted,' she said. 'He had a personality that I only saw in a few children.'

Márquez knew exactly what he wanted to be and wasn't shy in stating it. In his 2002 television interview he revealed his ultimate intentions and named his racing hero (who would later become his teammate). 'I want to be a professional bike racer, like Dani Pedrosa,' he confidently told the reporter. Few ten-year-olds know their minds like Marc Márquez knew his.

After finishing third in the Conti Cup, he moved up to the six-round Open RACC (Royal Automobile Club of Catalonia) 50 Championship in 2003, riding a 50cc Rieju RS1 for the ProCurve team. The championship was held on three circuits – Montmeló, Calafat and Can Padró – and Márquez stunned everyone with his performances. Racing with the number 35 plate (he wouldn't start wearing his now traditional 93 until the following year), Márquez absolutely dominated – sometimes winning races by over 20 seconds – and collected his first road racing championship title by season's end.

That championship win was enough to earn Márquez a ride with the highly professional RAAC-Impala racing team. Being supported by a professional team was crucial if Márquez's career was to go any further. His parents were working class, and while they sacrificed family holidays and other luxuries to help pay for Marc's racing, there was only so far that they could take him – he needed outside assistance. So, when he was offered a ride with the RACC-Impala team in 2004, it was a real lifeline. He would be riding a full-size motorcycle for the first time (a Honda CBR125R) and they were much more expensive to run than the 50cc Mini GP bikes he'd been riding previously.

Speaking of his parents' contribution to his career, Márquez said, 'Neither of them earned a huge amount, so they could only make a limited investment in my career in absolute terms. In relative terms, though, it was substantial.'[14]

His teammate in the Impala team was another talented young Spaniard called Pol Espargaró who, like Maverick Viñales, would later become a rival in MotoGP. Two years older than his teammate, and with more racing experience, Espargaró won the championship, but Márquez finished second.

Remaining with the same team (although now rebranded as the RACC-Caja Madrid team) for the 2005 season, Márquez's career got a major boost when he was taken under the wing of Emilio Alzamora, the 1999 125cc Grand Prix world champion. Alzamora would act as Márquez's manager and mentor for the next 18 years. At the time, he was working for Monlau Competición Technical School and scouting for young talent; with the creation of the new Estrella Galicia team that ran in the 125cc Grand Prix world championship, Alzamora's aim was to find promising riders at a very young age and shepherd them all the way up the racing ladder to the world championships. He had previously been manager and coach for Spanish world rally champion Carlos Sainz, so was in a perfect position to guide Márquez's career.

Márquez had been brought to Alzamora's attention by a patron of the Moto Club Segre, Jaume Curcó, who had told him, 'As soon as you get a chance, you have to go and see this kid from Cervera – you'll be amazed.'

Alzamora did. And was. 'From the first day I saw him, I had the feeling that I was in front of someone very special,' he would later say. Right from the start, the former champion was also impressed by his young pupil's maturity, manners and dedication. 'I was always surprised by his attitude in the garage,' he said, looking back on that first year. 'You wouldn't have believed he was just 12. At that time, racing in the 125cc Spanish Championship, he weighed only 35kg. It was really tough, but he learned a lot that way.'[15]

'Tough', because Márquez was in fact so small and light his team had to add weights to his bike in order to meet minimum combined rider and bike weight regulations, meaning his bike would have handled differently to the others. By learning to adapt, he was being forced to explore his versatility, and discovered it wasn't lacking.

Emilio Alzamora is from Lleida, just a few miles from Cervera, so he and his young protégé had much in common from the outset, and the pair would become firm friends as well as enjoying a hugely successful professional relationship. Julià Márquez had taken his son as far as he could with the limited contacts and funds available to him; it now fell to Alzamora to progress Marc's career and to steer it all the way through to world championship level.

The next step on that journey was completed when Márquez won the 125cc Catalunya Championship in 2005. He also won the 85cc class in the Catalan Supermotard Championship, proving he had lost none of his dirt-riding skills. In 2006 he won the 125cc Catalunya Championship for the second year in a row, and also made his debut in the CEV championship – Spain's national motorcycle racing series, and a proven breeding ground of future MotoGP riders. Because it acts as the most effective stepping stone to Grand Prix racing, the championship attracts some of the best young talent in the world, so it was a huge step up from the regional Catalunya championship.

After finishing eighth overall in his debut year, Márquez returned to the CEV championship in 2007, this time switching his Honda CBR 125R for a KTM RRF 125 with Team Monlau Competición. He was fast, but he also crashed a lot, meaning he only finished ninth by season's end. He did win a race at Jerez, however (his only race win in the CEV series), and his raw speed was not in doubt.

Just before the final round of the CEV championship, due to be held at Valencia, Emilio Alzamora took his young protégé to the same circuit to watch the final Grand Prix of 2007. Márquez was thrilled to be inside a world championship paddock and was of the understanding that he was there to pick up any tips and to learn anything he could ahead of his own final championship round. But Alzamora knew better and sprang a surprise on his young protégé by revealing that this paddock was to be Márquez's new home: Alzamora had secured him a seat with the Repsol KTM team in the 125cc Grand Prix world championship for the 2008 season.

The team had been watching Márquez in the CEV championship and realised his potential, if only he could reduce the number of crashes he had. It had long been understood in the Grand Prix paddock that you can teach a fast rider to stop crashing, but you can't teach a slow rider to be fast. Márquez had the speed – everything else could be worked on. By that point, he already had six years of racing experience behind him yet was still only 15 years old. He was a rough diamond, ready to be polished in one of the most fiercely contested motorcycle championships on earth: Marc Márquez was going Grand Prix racing.

CHAPTER 2

THE ANT FROM CERVERA

'IN THOSE FIVE RACES I TOOK RISKS, AND I WON ALL FIVE OF THEM.'

Marc Márquez

For Marc Márquez, one of the best things about graduating to the Grand Prix paddock was the chance to finally meet his racing hero. Posters of Valentino Rossi adorned the walls of Márquez's bedroom, and models of the Italian superstar's famous racing bikes crowded the shelves. Márquez was a superfan.

At the Catalan round of the championship, he persuaded Spanish photographer Jaime Olivares, and journalist Emilio Pérez de Rozas, to introduce him to Rossi and to capture the moment in a photograph.

The end result is a picture of perfect happiness; the superstar and the budding young rider all smiles; Rossi with his arm around the diminutive Márquez, who's beaming with pride. Rossi stands a good foot taller than his young fan, and graciously accepts his gift of a model Subaru Impreza rally car from Márquez. According to Pérez de Rozas, Rossi said, 'So, you're the brave Marc – great!

I hope they're treating you well in the world championship. You just let me know if they don't – I've got a bit of influence around here!'[16]

With seven world titles to his name at that point, Rossi did have a 'bit of influence' in the Grand Prix paddock and, for many years, his relationship with Marc Márquez was a good one, but that would all change. The old master and the young protégé were set on a collision course that would reach a climax in 2015, with one of the most controversial races in the history of Grands Prix.

But that was all in the future. Before the two could clash horns, Márquez had a lot of learning to do. The Catalan round was the seventh in the series that year, and it hadn't been an easy debut season for Márquez up to that point. Every rider needs time to adjust to the pace and pressures and tactics involved in riding at world championship level (or, at least, most do – Pedro Acosta pulled off a miracle by winning the Moto3 championship at the first attempt in 2021) and Márquez was no exception.

His first race was at Estoril in Portugal – the third round of the championship. He had missed the opening two races after fracturing his right arm in pre-season testing. There was no fairy-tale beginning to Márquez's Grand Prix career; he qualified in 26th place and finished the race outside the points in 18th. But it was a start, and, given that he was only 15 years and 56 days old when he made his world championship debut, there was plenty of time to learn.

He proved to be a fast learner; in only his second Grand Prix – at the Shanghai circuit in China – he took 12th place and netted four points. He was on the ladder.

Following a crash in France, there was a lowly 19th at Mugello, but Márquez picked up more points for tenth place at his home round in Catalunya – the same event where he met Valentino Rossi for the first time. Then came the British Grand Prix at Donington Park.

In what was just his sixth race, the Spanish teenager made history by taking third place and becoming the youngest ever rider to get on to the podium in a world championship race. He was 15 years and 126 days old. In the same race, British rookie Scott Redding also made history by becoming the youngest rider ever to win a Grand Prix. He was 15 years and 170 days old.

Márquez had been running in sixth place at Assen before crashing out and being unable to take the grid in the restarted race. A ninth in Germany was followed by another crash at Brno in the Czech Republic before he took his second-best result of the season with fourth place at Misano.

Despite battling so fiercely on track, Márquez was still just a boy, as evidenced in the Misano paddock. His mother, Roser, explained that, 'He was 15, and in the Misano race of the world championship – I don't know if it was Friday or Saturday – he lost a baby tooth. He said to me, "Mum! My tooth has fallen out!" but we didn't say anything to the journalists, because if a guy who's racing in the world championship loses a baby tooth, they'd laugh at him.'

Márquez was so small he became known as 'The Ant from Cervera' and an ant would form the basis of his helmet design throughout his career; small, tough and hard-working, an ant was a perfect spirit animal for Márquez.

During the first practice session at the penultimate round in Malaysia, Márquez crashed and was run over by French rider Cyril Carrillo. Both his legs got trapped between the rear wheel and swinging arm of his KTM, and he suffered a dislocation of the cartilage of his right tibia. He had to endure 15 minutes of agony as race marshals tried in vain to free him from his machine. Eventually, his team were called out to remove the rear wheel from Márquez's bike so that he could be freed.

It was enough to rule him out of the last two races of the season at Sepang and Valencia. Of the 18 races in the 2008 season, Márquez missed four due to injury and crashed out of another four. Given that he only saw the chequered flag in ten races, an overall championship position of 13th could be considered a reasonable return. But it was the flashes of brilliance – the podium at Silverstone and fourth place at Misano – that pointed towards a brighter future: the speed was coming, but the crashing had to stop if results were to improve.

Márquez's performance over the 2008 season compared favourably with that of his Repsol KTM teammate, Esteve 'Tito' Rabat. A fellow Spaniard, Rabat had three years' Grand Prix experience under his belt, but finished the season in 14th place, one position, and 14 points, behind Márquez.

It was a strong debut season, and it was enough to gain Márquez promotion to the official Red Bull-backed KTM team for 2009, alongside rookie Cameron Beaubier – the American rider fresh from spending two years in the Red Bull Rookies championship. KTM had downsized its involvement for 2009, fielding just two bikes, as opposed to the nine bikes on the grid the previous year. It would also prove to be the Austrian firm's last involvement in Grands Prix until the four-stroke Moto3 class replaced the two-stroke 125cc championship in 2012.

The KTMs were no match for the host of Derbis and Aprilias on the grid, and Márquez would be forced to ride even harder than his rivals to secure good results. That would later prove to be a blessing when he finally got to ride a more competitive bike. As a rule, when riders have to ride below-par machinery for any length of time, then find themselves on a more competitive bike, they find it relatively easy and don't need to ride quite so much on the limit.

After qualifying ninth for the first race in Qatar, Márquez was first to fall victim to the conditions when lightning struck, and heavy rain caused him to crash out. He never made the restart after the original race was red-flagged.

Damp and changing conditions also affected the Japanese Grand Prix, but this time Márquez stayed on, taking a more encouraging fifth place after qualifying tenth.

From fourth on the grid at Jerez, he finally started to show what he was capable of, battling for the lead throughout the race and eventually finishing second to Sergio Gadea, after the crashing Jonas Folger affected his run out of the final corner.

At Le Mans in France, Márquez took his first ever pole position in Grand Prix racing, but, having turned 16 three months before, he just missed out on being the youngest rider in history to do so. Marco Melandri's record from 1998 still stood, where he set pole at the German Grand Prix at 15 years, 11 months and 10 days old.

That pole position showed Márquez's one-lap pace was as good as anyone's, and his race pace in damp conditions was impressive too. He was battling for second place when Joan Olivé overtook him, crashed right in front of him, and ended both riders' races at the end of lap six. Nil points again to Márquez; this time through no fault of his own.

Fifth on the grid translated to fifth in the race at Mugello, but at least it meant points, and Márquez moved up to sixth in the championship.

Another fifth in his home race at Catalunya didn't do justice to

Márquez's pace: second to sixth places were covered by less than three-tenths of a second, proving that Márquez had the pace to be in contention for the win.

Things didn't go so well at Assen in the Netherlands. After qualifying tenth, Márquez was battling a group for sixth place in the race when he punted Pol Espargaró into the gravel trap at the chicane and dropped to tenth at the flag.

With no 125cc race being staged at the Circuit of the Americas, the next outing was at the Sachsenring in Germany but, despite starting from a strong third place on the grid, the race was a disaster for Márquez. He had been battling for third until the last corner when he clashed with Joan Olivé and was highsided off his KTM. He remounted and finished 16th, just outside the points.

The crashes may have been disappointing, but they were necessary for Márquez to learn. He had to know where the limits were, he had to know how to fight in a pack, he had to learn how to look after his tyres, and the occasional crash was inevitable. So long as he was learning from his crashes, Márquez and his team weren't unduly concerned; they had never expected to be fighting for the title, so as long as Márquez kept learning and progressing, everyone was happy. He was, after all, on an underpowered bike, and was having to compensate by riding it on the absolute limit. These formative years in the 125cc championship would help define Marc's 'everything or nothing' style, and he would never quite shake it off.

There was more learning to be done at Donington Park. Not for the first time, rain interrupted the British Grand Prix and, after another front-row start, Márquez led the restarted five-lap race for three laps before succumbing to the wet conditions and crashing out at the chicane. Crash and learn. Crash and learn.

Starting from a lowly 20th on the grid at Brno after suffering problems in qualifying, he had a strong ride in the race to eighth place before heading stateside for the Indianapolis Grand Prix. Starting from ninth on the grid, he made up three positions in the race to finish sixth and retain his seventh place in the points table.

Unlike fellow Spaniard Pedro Acosta in 2021 (who was second in his Moto3 debut, won a race at the second attempt and went on to become world champion as a rookie), Márquez took time to learn his trade; it was only after his two foundation years in Grand Prix racing that he started to look like something special. In 2009, he showed occasional glimpses of brilliance but was hampered by too many crashes and mistakes as he figured out the puzzle of how to ride fast but consistently.

At Misano he converted a seventh place grid start into a fourth-place finish and in Portugal he was lying second (after qualifying fourth) when he crashed out on lap 12. A ninth place was the best he could do in Australia, meaning he dropped to eighth place in the championship.

With a pace half a second quicker than anyone else, Márquez took his second pole position at Sepang in Malaysia but once again crashed out of the race and failed to bring home any points as the MotoGP circus headed to the final round of the championship at Valencia in Spain.

From fourth on the grid, Márquez found himself in a desperate eight-man scrap for fourth place. While he led the group on to the last lap, the fight became so frantic that he was pushed off-track by other riders and, while he recovered, could only manage 17th place to end his second season of GP racing in eighth overall.

Márquez had mixed feelings about the 2009 season; he had clearly been expecting more but felt he had done as good a job as he could with a relatively uncompetitive bike. 'I've made some mistakes I shouldn't have made,' he admitted, 'but I've done my very best with what I had . . . I personally believe that I had a good level, and we all thought that the bike would accompany us more. At the end of the season, the KTM was closer to the Aprilias and we did expect a podium or two that I think we could have achieved.'

Eighth place might not have been quite what he had been hoping for, but it was a significant improvement on his 13th place from the year before and, crucially, Márquez felt he had learned a lot. 'This year, above all, I've learned to battle hand to hand, because in 125cc almost all races are ridden in a pack and there is always a lot of battling,' he told crash.net at the end of the season. 'Furthermore, fighting with a bike that had a few weaker points, I had to learn to make the most of the turns – to come out fast and reach the next braking point close to the other riders, etc. Another important aspect, which Emilio Alzamora has helped me with, is managing practices.'

The fact that Marc Márquez was the only non-Aprilia rider to finish in the top 22 of the championship (there were Derbis in there too, but they were merely rebadged Aprilias) shows how well he rode. The only other KTM in the standings was his teammate, Cameron Beaubier, who finished in a lowly 29th place with just three points to show for his season's work.

Márquez had grown, physically as well as mentally, during the season and no longer needed to carry ballast on the bike to meet the minimum bike and rider weight limits. As his body filled out slightly, he felt he could muscle the little KTM around more and make it do what he wanted. It all helped.

Reflecting on his 2009 season, Márquez was fully aware of his shortcomings and knew what he had to work on in 2010 if he was to be a genuine championship contender. 'I think that my weakest point is consistency,' he admitted. 'It is important to finish races because that's where you gain experience, and it allows you to win and opt for the title. You also have to constantly polish your riding style a little.'

With KTM withdrawing from the 125cc class in 2010, Márquez would find himself riding a Derbi (although, as pointed out, it was actually an Aprilia, with Piaggio owning both brands). That would at least create a level playing field and put him on a par with his rivals in 2010, and he could expect to be a championship contender, even though he was only 17 years old.

He couldn't have joined a better team either. Niki Ajo's Red Bull-backed squad had won the 125cc title in 2008 with Mike Di Meglio, and Ajo had a reputation for getting the best out of young riders and nurturing them to become future stars. Everything seemed to be in place – Márquez had two years' experience under his belt, a bike as competitive as any other, and a hugely experienced team and team boss. Even so, nobody could have predicted the utter dominance the young Spaniard would display in 2010. After two years of mixed results, the world was about to see what Marc Márquez was truly capable of.

o

Marc Márquez started the opening race of the 2010 season in Qatar from pole position and it would prove to be prophetic. He didn't have it all his own way in the race, however, and found himself mixed up in a seven-rider scrap for supremacy. He led on occasion but was eventually beaten back to third place behind Nico Terol and Efrén Vázquez. But it was a podium to kick off his campaign and he clearly had the speed to win; he just needed to put everything together, perfect his racecraft and the wins would surely come.

Starting from pole in Jerez, as he had done in Qatar, this time Márquez didn't last a lap; he crashed out when his exhaust fell off and slipped underneath his rear wheel, causing him to fall and dislocate his right shoulder.

Now three races into the season without a win, Márquez was beginning to doubt his championship credentials. 'The first three races made me think about if I was perhaps not quite ready to fight for the title,' he later admitted, when looking back on the 2010 season. 'I think the distance between the leader and myself was 32 points, more or less (it was, in fact, 33), which was already a lot.'[17]

At least the race calendar played out in his favour: with three weeks until the next race in France, he had time to recover and managed to put his Derbi in fourth place on the grid. A last lap collision with Bradley Smith sent the British rider wide and Márquez sneaked through to claim third place and move up from eighth to fifth in the championship standings.

It was at Mugello where Marc Márquez took his first Grand Prix win, and he did it in swashbuckling style. At one point in the race, he was three seconds behind the leaders, but he worked hard to pass Bradley Smith and then closed the gap to Pol Espargaró and Nico Terol. Smith followed and brought up the tail of a four-man fight for the lead.

From that point on, the race was anybody's and, while each rider took turns leading, it was Márquez who finally broke free and led over the line to achieve his long-held dream of winning a world championship race. It was the third closest finish in the history of the 125cc class, with just 0.16 seconds covering the top four. The 25 points Márquez took for the win saw him climb up to third in the points table and, with the pressure of needing to win finally off his back, the 17-year-old Spaniard embarked on a winning streak rarely seen in the smallest class of Grand Prix racing, where there tends to be a different winner in almost every race.

The 125cc world championship had been in existence since 1949 when it was the smallest of the four original classes of Grand Prix racing – 500cc, 350cc, 250cc and 125cc. Later, 80cc and 50cc classes would be introduced, then dropped, meaning that in 2010 the 125cc class was once again the smallest capacity category. That meant the bikes weren't as ferociously fast and intimidating as MotoGP bikes, and they were much lighter machines too, meaning riders could physically boss them around the track. Because the bikes are easier to ride, more riders are capable of winning in the 125cc class, so much of Márquez's job in 2010 was to focus on racecraft – to put himself in the right position, at the right time, to slipstream or outrun his rivals to the chequered flag. He had possessed the speed for some time, but it wasn't until he perfected his racecraft that he managed to put together a winning streak that stunned the Grand Prix paddock. Finally on a more competitive bike, after two years of having to ride over the limit on an outpaced KTM, Márquez made it look easy as he romped to five consecutive wins in Italy, Britain, the Netherlands, Spain and Germany.

Starting the Silverstone race from pole (his second in succession), Márquez fought a ferocious battle with fellow Spaniard and friend Pol Espargaró before Espargaró ran off the track and left Márquez to win by 2.5 seconds.

Pole position at Assen was almost expected and Márquez didn't disappoint, posting a lap over half a second faster than his closest rival. He was just as dominant in the race, leading from start to finish to win by 2.33 seconds. Still too young to be presented with champagne on the podium, Márquez was riding like a seasoned veteran, and he carried his domination of the class through to his home round at Catalunya, where he set yet another pole position and led the race from the second corner all the way to the chequered flag. His fourth win in a row saw Márquez take the lead in the championship for the first time. He led Pol Espargaró by a single point, and also became the youngest rider ever to win four Grands Prix in a row.

Márquez would later say his win at Catalunya meant the most to him because 'I was at home, in front of the fans, of my fan club, and at the circuit closest to my house. To race in front of your fans and win, do the lap of honour in front of your people, even more after a near-perfect race, leading from start to finish, is very special. It's every rider's dream: to win in your country and, in this case, at Montmeló, which is the one we have closest and is a circuit where, since I was little, I went to see my idols.'[18]

Once again setting pole by over half a second from his closest rival in Germany, Márquez started the race cautiously due to the damp conditions. As the track dried out, he upped his pace and fought a titanic duel with Pol Espargaró before Espargaró ran wide, touched the grass and was thrown violently from his bike with just three laps remaining. Márquez then cruised to the flag some 17.5 seconds ahead of Espargaró, who had managed to remount and finish the race, still in second place – a measure of just how far he and Márquez had been in front of the rest of the pack.

That fifth consecutive win was significant as it proved that Márquez had the maturity to race in tricky, damp conditions, as well as being blindingly fast in the dry. He was becoming the complete package. 'In those five races I took risks, and I won all five of them,' he said of his winning streak. 'That was key to the championship as it gave me the lead in the standings and helped me in a big way in the second part of the season. With a good position in the table, you can approach races differently.'[19]

Márquez's magnificent run suffered a blip at Brno in the Czech Republic when he dislocated his left shoulder during practice (he had already dislocated his right shoulder at the second round at Jerez). As painful as it was, he still managed to qualify in fourth and struggled through the race to gain some valuable points for seventh place. It was enough to retain his championship lead over Espargaró by 15 points.

Normal service was resumed at Indianapolis where Márquez started from pole position yet again. The race, however, didn't go to plan. Pulling away from the rest of the pack, safely in the lead, he then slipped off his Derbi. After remounting, he sliced through the field back up to fifth place, gaining three positions on the last lap alone. But it was all to no avail; after the event he was judged to have taken a shortcut when rejoining the race and was handed a 20-second penalty which dropped him to tenth place in the corrected results.

Márquez retook control of the championship at Misano with another perfect pole position and race win, this time after passing Nico Terol and then pulling two seconds on him in the closing stages of the race.

He was not so fortunate at MotorLand Aragón. Once again taking pole by over half a second, Márquez was wiped out by Randy Krummenacher in the very first corner. It was a decisive moment: with no points scored, he lost the championship lead to Nico Terol. 'I knew that, after Aragón, if I wanted to win the championship, I had to react straight away,' Márquez later said. 'And what better way than to get three pole positions?'

Not just three poles, but three wins too, in Japan, Malaysia and Australia. And then came Estoril, and the most dramatic race of Marc Márquez's career to date.

With practice and qualifying being severely disrupted due to bad weather, he set off from a lowly 11th place on the grid. The first attempt to run the race lasted just eight laps and saw ten riders crash out when rain once again started to fall.

During the warm-up lap for the restarted race, Márquez touched a damp patch and crashed. 'I pushed quite a bit on that lap, and the only wet spot on the track, I couldn't see, because of my dark visor. I went into the turn as usual and crashed. Just as I fell, I held on to the bike and didn't let go.'[20]

His team went into full panic mode, thinking their championship charge was all but over. Márquez managed to get his bike back to the pit box for some extremely rushed repairs. There were only ten minutes until the race was restarted and Márquez's bike needed new bodywork, a new exhaust, the handlebars needed straightening, and all the gravel had to be tipped out of the little Derbi. 'In the pit box, everyone was quite nervous, but I decided to pit as I saw the bike needed more of a fix than would have been possible on the grid, with a broken exhaust etc.,' Márquez explained. 'They fixed it very quickly. There were mechanics from other teams helping us, as well as some friends from the paddock – everyone was helping. I got to go and race with a bike that was not perfect, and I was starting at the back. I said, "Oof! Last!"'[21]

It was a maximum stress situation and would usually fry a rider's mind, but Márquez showed remarkable maturity and control in remaining calm and focusing on getting a good start from last place on the grid. 'I concentrated a lot on the start and, at the end of the straight I was fourth or fifth,' he said. 'That boosted my morale and helped me manage the race. Once I was there, I was only thinking about winning, as 17-year-olds only think about the win!'[22]

Overtaking most of the pack to grab fourth into the first corner, Márquez was in third place by the end of the first lap. After passing Bradley Smith for second, he set about hunting down race leader Nico Terol – the only man who could take the championship from him. Márquez passed Terol into the first corner of the last lap and fended off an attack on the back straight to take the win by a minuscule 0.15 seconds. It was an extraordinary performance by anyone's standards, and pundits and fans alike realised they were watching a very special rider at work. Few riders have won races from last place on the gird, fewer still after such a panic-stricken drama immediately before the race began.

Márquez's mechanic, Jordi Castellà, was astonished. 'No one would have imagined that he would crash on the formation lap, then all the drama with fixing the bike in five seconds, and that he would go out there and win the race,' he said.

Even Carmelo Ezpeleta, CEO of Dorna Sports, which owns MotoGP, was impressed. 'To be honest, it was one of the most amazing sporting moments I've ever experienced – something that truly left me lost for words,' he said.[23]

That sensational victory gave Márquez a 17-point championship lead going into the final round at Valencia, but in motorcycle racing anything can happen, even when a rider has a big points advantage. Márquez felt the pressure. 'It was a difficult weekend – my first weekend with a world championship on the line, and I was certainly quite tense,' he reflected in 2015. 'I wanted to manage my position with regards to Nico; I didn't care at all about the other riders . . . but I knew exactly which position I needed to be in at any given time to be champion.'

Starting from pole position (his 12th in 15 races) and with the permutations rolling around in his head and constantly being recalculated, Márquez rode fast but carefully. With Bradley Smith out in front to take a start-to-finish win, Márquez sat behind Nico Terol in third place, knowing that if he followed his fellow Spaniard home, it would be enough to take the title. When Pol Espargaró started to threaten him, Márquez ran wide to let him through, afraid of getting involved in someone else's crash. His tactics worked, and he slowed his pace to secure fourth place and his first world championship.

As young as he was, Marc Márquez just missed out on being the youngest ever Grand Prix world champion – Loris Capirossi was also 17, but 98 days younger than Márquez when he won the 125cc world championship in 1991.

But Márquez didn't care. He had achieved his ambition of becoming a world champion and his performances had marked him out as a once-in-a-generation talent. In its list of top ten riders at the end of the 2010 season, bike racing bible *Motocourse* included Marc Márquez at number ten. He was the only rider on the list who was not in the MotoGP class. The words were prophetic: 'We may have been watching the start of something very special,' Michael Scott wrote. He was correct.

CHAPTER 3

DOUBLE VISION

'SOMETIMES I HAVE TO CHANNEL MY INNER ANGER TO WIN A RACE.'

Marc Márquez

His career might have been over at the age of 18. Retired, with just a single Moto3 world championship to his name. He would have largely been forgotten about by now; a mere footnote in the annals of motorcycle Grand Prix history. For almost five months, Marc Márquez didn't know if he would ever be able to ride again. His introduction to the Moto2 world championship was a tough one, and he still suffers from it to this day.

The Moto2 championship was only one year old when Marc Márquez entered the class in 2011. It had replaced the two-stroke 250cc class (which had run since 1949) the previous year, as part of Dorna's bid to have all Grand Prix classes run less toxic four-stroke machinery. In 2012, the last remaining two-stroke class – the 125cc world championship – would also go four-stroke, switching over to 250cc single-cylinder machines and being rebadged as Moto3.

The Moto2 class was not without its critics. The former 250cc championship had been for thoroughbred, prototype race bikes which, for many, were the most perfect race bikes ever built, with a near perfect balance of power, weight and agility. Moto2 could not have been more different. Honda supplied all the engines (detuned engines from its CBR600RR road bike), and a one-make tyre rule saw everyone running on Dunlops. There were many who argued that these specifications had no place in world championship Grand Prix racing – which had always been about prototypes – but those complaints fell on deaf ears and the championship carried on regardless.

What the regulations meant was that the only variables were the chassis and the riders. Although obliged to use a Honda CBR600RR engine, various firms sprang up to make prototype chassis for Moto2 bikes, including Suter, Kalex, FTR and Tech3. With the same engine and the same tyres, no rider could have a serious advantage, so it fell to each competitor to outride the others, and this, as was evidenced in the 2010 125cc world championship, was what Marc Márquez did best.

After his spectacular performances in that championship, Márquez naturally landed a plum seat for his debut in Moto2. With huge financial backing from Repsol, he was one of 13 riders who opted for a Suter chassis, but he was top of the pecking order when it came to new parts and factory support (he was, for example, the only Suter rider to receive a 2012 chassis at round 13). This came at a cost, though; according to visordown.com, the Repsol team reportedly paid Suter €200,000 for such a full support package.

Even though it only used detuned street bike engines, the Moto2 class was still a big step up in terms of power and weight for Márquez, who had never raced anything bigger than a 125cc machine. It would also be his first year on a four-stroke motorcycle, which has very different characteristics to a two-stroke.

Márquez's Suter made about 140bhp, as opposed to the 55bhp his 125cc Derbi had made. The top speed was quite a jump too, from around 140mph to 170mph. It's a big transition for any rider to make, and Márquez was no exception. He would need to learn to ride all over again if he was to conquer the intermediate Grand Prix class, but few doubted that he would, sooner or later, make a successful transition.

Repsol Suter chief mechanic Santiago 'Santi' Hernández was immediately impressed by the level of feedback his young rider could offer, especially on a bike that was completely new to him. 'It was very impressive for me, the first time he tried the Moto2 bike; how he explained the problems on the bike,' he said. 'It was like he already had a lot of experience on that bike. He was a young boy without any experience, he came from a 125cc two-stroke engine and went to a 600cc four-stroke engine and a heavy bike, and I was expecting it would be more difficult for him to explain what happened.'[24]

Márquez did at least have several points of reference to judge his performances by; he would be joined on the Moto2 grid by former 125cc rivals, Pol Espargaró, Bradley Smith and Tito Rabat.

Under the floodlights at Qatar for the season opener, Márquez drew first blood over his former rivals, qualifying second to reigning Moto2 world champion, Stefan Bradl. Bradley Smith in seventh was the best of the other class rookies.

But there was still lots to learn. Márquez fluffed the start and ended up mired in the pack in 29th place in a crowded field of 39 riders. He rode spectacularly and fought his way up to ninth place before crashing out on lap five. No points.

Jerez was next, and all Spanish eyes were on the new wonder boy, now 18 years old, but it would produce another no-score. After qualifying fourth and running fifth in the race as he clawed his way forward, he was taken out by an erratic Jules Cluzel on the tenth lap.

The Portuguese Grand Prix was another disaster. After qualifying fourth again, Márquez was in a group of riders battling for third place when he out-braked himself and tried to dive under Scott Redding but lost the front and took both himself and Redding out. He had lasted just eight laps.

With three rounds down and not a point on the board, Márquez must have been asking himself some serious questions. Two of the three crashes had been his own fault; the speed was there, but the crashing had to stop. 'It was naturally a bit difficult, and we needed time, but with the help of the team, that calmed me down, everything was easier,' he said of the first three races. 'We knew this was our first season; that we had to learn and note the mistakes to avoid them in the future. We did so, and that is why we started to get good results.'

He may have been crashing too often, but at least he had the pace when he was upright, and this provided a lot of encouragement, as Márquez acknowledged. 'The positive thing is that we suffered the crashes when fighting for the first positions. We knew that sooner or later the good results will arrive, because we were doing a good job, and we had a good level. We only needed a weekend where things went our way, without crashing, and we would get a good result . . . There are different ways to learn in this category and I learnt from crashing. This way you learn more, and faster.'

At Le Mans in France, his learning bore fruit. From sixth place on the grid, Márquez found himself in ninth at the end of lap one, but clawed his way through the pack and took the lead from Thomas Lüthi on lap 22 then broke away at the front to take his first win in Moto2 by over two seconds. 'Overtaking in this class is more difficult – you have to be sure before gaining a position – but when I saw they were battling, I was able to pass through them,' a jubilant Márquez explained after the race. 'Four laps before the end it started to rain a bit, and I decided to overtake (Yukio) Takahashi and Lüthi, because I thought that they could stop the race at any time due to the rain. I decided to push, and it went well, so I am very happy for this victory.'[25]

With all the pressures of his home round in Catalunya to deal with next, Márquez did well to stay out of trouble in a crash-happy race that saw 12 riders fail to finish. He brought his Suter home in second place behind Stefan Bradl and leapt up to seventh place in the title standings, just 45 points behind the German rider.

Conditions at Silverstone were typically diabolical, and Márquez struggled. He had taken his first Moto2 pole position in the dry qualifying session, but in the wet race he dropped to ninth on the opening lap, then slipped even further down the field before crashing out on lap seven. His wet weather riding skills still needed some polishing.

The Silverstone crash meant Márquez had only finished two of his first six races in the Moto2 class but, when he did finish, he was first and second. The Dutch Grand Prix saw him get back on track, and his win from second place on the grid saw him rocket up to second place in the championship standings, albeit 57 points behind the super-consistent Stefan Bradl.

At Mugello, Márquez took his second pole position of the year and converted it into a hard-fought race win. He had to battle throughout with Bradl, Bradley Smith, Alex de Angelis and Andrea

Iannone. Of Márquez's former rivals in Moto3, Bradley Smith was closest to him in terms of performance. Following the Mugello round, Smith was third in the points table to Márquez's second, but he had gained his position through consistency, while Márquez had been more erratic, either winning or crashing.

The crashes were becoming more infrequent by mid-season, however, and the German Grand Prix at Sachsenring saw Márquez deliver another perfect weekend with pole position and another win. It was doing wonders for his confidence, and he explained after the race that he knew he was faster than home hero Stefan Bradl, so simply sat behind him and made a move at his leisure on lap 21 of 29.

Setting pole for the third time in succession, Márquez displayed pure aggression and ruthlessness on his way to second place in the Czech Grand Prix, colliding with Stefan Bradl, Alex de Angelis and Andrea Iannone, and narrowly avoiding a penalty for irresponsible riding. Now comfortable and confident with his Moto2 mount, Márquez started showing the all-action, 'no prisoners' riding style that would become his trademark. His style and attitude divided race fans, with some thinking he was a liability and lacked respect for his rivals. Márquez didn't care; all he cared about was winning, and he was prepared to do anything to achieve victory. Over the coming years, he would develop a killer instinct like no other rider; it would land him in trouble on more than one occasion, but it would also make him the most feared rider on the grid, and that in itself was a powerful psychological weapon that Márquez used to great effect.

As the Grand Prix circus pitched camp at Indianapolis, Stefan Bradl and Marc Márquez had scored four wins each (the only other rider to win a race had been Andrea Iannone in the

Czech Republic), yet Bradl still had a 43-point lead due to his greater consistency. But as Márquez's confidence grew, the momentum started to swing his way. A crash during practice at Indianapolis affected Bradl's confidence and he could only qualify in a lowly 22nd place, while Márquez took his fourth successive pole position. There was no doubt now who the fastest rider on the grid was, but too many non-scores early in the season had hampered Márquez's title campaign.

In the Indianapolis race, he established a five-second lead by half race distance and never looked back, eventually taking the win from Pol Espargaró, while Bradl recovered well from his poor grid position to take sixth place. The points gap was down to 28: Márquez was closing.

Despite crashing during qualifying at Misano, Márquez still managed to post a time good enough for second on the grid behind Bradl, and the pair were involved in an eight-rider scrap for most of the race until Márquez decided to pull the pin. 'The first laps with a full tank were difficult, and I almost lost the front,' he said after the race. 'But, in the end, I could see from the TV (there were giant screens at various points around the track) that Bradl was close, so I pushed my best to get a small gap.'[26]

It was enough, but only just: Márquez won by 0.61 seconds to come within 23 points of Bradl, who brought his Kalex home in second place.

As Suter's favoured rider, Márquez received a raft of new parts for the next round at MotorLand Aragón, including a swinging arm and modified chassis and, boosted by this, he was unstoppable. Another perfect pole position and race win left no one in any doubt about the fastest Moto2 rider on the grid.

From a crash-happy start, Márquez had turned his season around, and was now a genuine contender for the title. 'What has changed is that I have more kilometres under my belt, I know the reactions of the bike better, I am much more comfortable on it, and I am starting to have fun,' he said after the Aragón race. 'In addition, we know each other better with the team, Santi (Hernández, chief mechanic) and I know each other a lot better, and we understand each other better. We have more experience together, and that helps us to now have a team that achieves the results we were looking for.'

With Stefan Bradl's rear tyre spinning on the rim and causing serious vibration, the best he could manage was an eighth-place finish at Aragón, and the German's misfortune meant Márquez was now just six points behind in the world championship standings.

Márquez set pole once again in Japan while Bradl was on the third row in eighth place, his confidence slowly ebbing away as the Márquez steamroller crushed all in its path. All but Andrea Iannone, at least: the Italian rode magnificently to steal the win from Márquez, but second place (with Bradl in fourth) was enough to give Márquez the championship lead for the first time – by a single point, with three rounds to go. He had clawed back an astonishing 82 points on Bradl, and the momentum was now with him. It was all to play for.

Despite his new-found maturity, Márquez made a serious error of judgement in Australia that could have had horrific consequences. He had crashed during the early part of the third free practice session and sat out most of the remainder before taking to the track in the dying minutes. As he crossed the line after his out lap, the chequered flag was thrown, meaning Márquez should have slowed and rolled back round to the pits. He didn't; he carried on at full race pace, desperate to salvage something from the session. As he came round the Southern Loop, he came across a gaggle of riders slowing to a halt, in order to practise their race starts. Unsighted, Márquez smashed into the back of Thai rider Ratthapark Wilairot, sending them both flying. Rear-end collisions can be particularly dangerous, and as the television images of the horrific impact were repeated, the paddock was badly shaken. It had been a close call, and a completely avoidable incident. Márquez was handed a one-minute penalty on his qualifying time, meaning he would start from the back row of the grid. Wilairot was badly battered in the crash and, although he didn't break any bones, he was out for the final two races of the season. It was the first time Márquez had fallen seriously foul of the race organisers. It would not be the last.

Starting from 38th place on the grid, Márquez – with a black eye and cuts to his face – barged his way up to 16th by the end of the first lap. By the end of the fourth lap, he was tenth and soon afterwards found himself involved in a nine-way scrap for third place; the incident in practice clearly forgotten about. At the flag, Márquez would sneak third place by a tenth of a second from Claudio Corti, his rear tyre in tatters from having to push so hard through the field. With Bradl finishing one place in front of him, the German retook the championship lead by three points as the paddock packed up and headed for Malaysia, and what would prove to be one of the most pivotal weekends in Marc Márquez's career.

The track was dry, apart from one section where a water pipe had burst, but the marshals made no effort to point this out to the riders with warning flags. For this dangerous oversight, the race organisers would later be fined the sum of €15,000. Jules Cluzel was first to hit the wet patch and crash, and Marc Márquez was next. He landed heavily and lay immobile in the gravel trap as Bradley Smith then crashed on the wet patch and his bike slammed into Márquez's Suter. Coughing up blood and suffering a damaged shoulder, Smith was unable to ride again that weekend. Márquez tried in morning warm-up, but then ruled himself out of the race. It would have been far too dangerous: his vision was completely blurred, and he was seeing double. He had diplopia. Specifically, he had suffered a paralysis of the fourth right nerve in his right eye.

Yet Márquez was lucky: he had a chance to recover; popular Italian rider Marco Simoncelli was not afforded that opportunity. He was killed in a crash in the MotoGP race that same weekend when he was struck by both his close friend Valentino Rossi, and American rider Colin Edwards. Neither rider had any chance of avoiding the crashing Italian and MotoGP lost one of its brightest stars and most fun-loving characters. It was a reminder that, despite vast improvements in safety measures over the years, MotoGP was still a highly dangerous, and sometimes fatal, sport. Not that anyone needed reminding.

Unable to ride for at least the rest of the season, Márquez was forced to concede the 2011 Moto2 world championship to Stefan Bradl, but that, for now, was the least of his worries. Although his eye gradually got better over winter, by mid-January of 2012 his vision was still not good enough to allow him to race a motorcycle and Márquez began to fear that his career was over just as it was really getting started.

After seeing double for two and a half months while waiting for his eyes to stabilise, Márquez submitted himself to surgery under the care of Doctor Sánchez Dalmau in Barcelona, who treated him for paralysis of the upper right oblique muscle, caused by trauma to the fourth right cranial nerve. It would require microsurgery to change the angle of the muscle slightly. Even Doctor Sánchez admitted it was a 'frightening injury'.

It was a dark time for Márquez. 'At the end of the 2011 season, and during the 2012 off-season, I was mentally destroyed with my injury,' he admitted. 'It was the most difficult moment of my entire career so far . . . I was mentally destroyed. I thought I'd never be able to ride again.'[27]

Doctors had told Márquez that his eyesight might never fully recover. 'We visited six or seven different doctors to try to understand the injury,' he explained. 'They also said maybe it will be okay for the future, maybe not – we cannot guarantee to you that you will ride a bike again.'[28]

Márquez had to sit out the first official test day at Valencia on 8 February 2012, handing a pre-season advantage to his rivals. But he knew this was no time for misplaced heroics. 'I am almost 100 per cent,' he said in January. 'I must admit that the first few weeks were difficult, I felt uncomfortable, but now I have returned to an almost normal life, although I still cannot ride a motorcycle. For this, my vision must be perfect, and I do not want to take risks.'[29]

It would not be until 6 March that he dared try to ride again, in a private test at the Alcarràs circuit. It had been almost five months since he had ridden a bike. After spinning some laps, Márquez decided his vision was good enough to at least try racing in the opening round of the 2012 season.

As qualifying began at the Losail circuit in Qatar on 7 April, Márquez was still not fully recovered, but was well enough to take part. He set the second fastest time behind Thomas Lüthi, then rode magnificently in the race itself, fighting off constant attacks from Andrea Iannone, Pol Espargaró, Tito Rabat, Simone Corsi and Thomas Lüthi. Márquez pushed Lüthi on to the kerb during the last lap, which dropped the Swiss rider down to fifth place, while Márquez beat Iannone over the line by just 0.06 seconds.

Lüthi was furious with Márquez's rash move, and Márquez was warned by the race organisers about his riding, but no official punishment was handed out. Despite missing some pre-season testing time, and still with less-than-perfect vision, Márquez the merciless was back, and his frightening experience with his eyesight obviously hadn't slowed him down or made him more cautious, despite being warned that another heavy blow to his head could affect his vision permanently.

At the following round in Jerez, Álex Márquez made his Grand Prix debut. He had been too young to race in the opening round but, having turned 16 four days before practice began in Jerez, he was now eligible to race. Riding a Moto3 Suter Honda, the younger Márquez impressed with 13th in qualifying and 12th in the race.

The Moto2 race was another hard-fought battle, further complicated when it started to rain and white flags were shown, meaning riders could come into the pits and change to their spare bikes, fitted with wet tyres. None of the leaders did, and Márquez – who had started from pole position – continued to battle with Pol Espargaró, Scott Redding and Thomas Lüthi. As soon as the race reached two-thirds distance, the red flags came out and a result was declared from the end of the previous lap. That gave the win to Espargaró with Márquez in second place.

After setting pole again in Portugal, Márquez was involved in another fierce fight with Espargaró, with the pair swapping the lead at least three times on the final lap. In the end, it proved too much for Espargaró, who crashed out while trying to dive up the inside of Márquez yet again. Márquez won the race by over two seconds to extend his championship lead over Espargaró to nine points. The pair had been racing against each other since they were little more than toddlers, but the stakes had never been this high.

Despite a crash during qualifying for the French Grand Prix, Márquez set pole again, but slipped off in the race and failed to add to his points tally. Pol Espargaró took the championship lead by a single point.

At his home race at the Circuit de Barcelona-Catalunya, Márquez courted much controversy. After making a desperate move on Andrea Iannone on the back straight (reminiscent of the rash move that saw him push Thomas Lüthi on to the kerbs at Qatar) and knocking him off, Márquez was involved in another chaotic struggle for the win, almost crashing out, but recovering to cross the line in third place. The result would not stand.

Race Director Mike Webb deemed Márquez's riding unacceptable and, this time, he handed out a penalty: the move on Espargaró had been a step too far. 'With any other rider, it would have been a warning,' Webb said, but given Márquez's repeated offences, the Race Director decided he needed a severe reprimand and docked him a full 60 seconds. That dropped Márquez to 23rd place, well out of the points. With Espargaró also not scoring, Andrea Iannone inherited the title lead, just two points ahead of Márquez.

Unusually, set-up difficulties plagued Márquez throughout the Silverstone weekend, and he could only salvage third place in the British Grand Prix, behind Espargaró and home hero Scott Redding, who fought desperately to steal second from Márquez. The 16 points he got for third place saw Márquez take a six-point lead in the championship.

Despite crashing twice during practice and qualifying at Assen, Márquez set pole for the fifth time in six races and played his cards well in the race itself. Andrea Iannone had established a 3.3 second lead by lap 14 and Márquez didn't seem to have an answer. But, when Iannone's pace slackened due to excessive tyre wear, Márquez the merciless smelt blood and, with four laps remaining, he caught his prey. After the pair swapped the lead several times, Iannone led on to the last lap, but Márquez out-braked him into the first corner and, when Iannone then missed a gear, his challenge was over, and Márquez took the win by four-tenths of a second and extended his championship lead over Iannone to a healthy 23 points.

The German Grand Prix saw another fast crash in practice, but it didn't stop Márquez from setting his sixth pole position of the year. His championship lead was boosted when Andrea Iannone crashed out of the race while battling with Márquez. After that, Márquez romped home to an unchallenged win, taking the chequered flag some two seconds ahead of former MotoGP rider Mika Kallio.

Heading into the summer break, Márquez was content with how things were playing out. 'The first half of the season has gone very well,' he reflected. 'At some circuits it has been harder for us and we have suffered a little, but overall I think we've done a great job. The first races – which were the ones that we were most concerned about because I had no pre-season (testing) – brought us good results. The later races proved trickier, but overall, I think we have to make a positive assessment.'[30]

Rating his performance in the first half of the 2012 season as an '8 or 8.5', Márquez realised that the most important thing he had learned was to be more consistent, and to settle for lower placings on a bad day rather than adopting a 'crash or win' approach. 'Basically, I have more experience and know the class better,' he said, by way of self-assessment. 'At this point last year, I had four DNFs, while this year I have just the one – and even that was in the wet. We should be happy, but not lower our guard. Other riders are also going very fast . . . When I can't feel completely comfortable with the bike, I have suffered a bit, and in a situation like that last year

I might have crashed, but this time I learned to settle for fifth and take points for the championship.'[31]

With this new-found consistency, Márquez was becoming ever more the complete racer. '125cc taught me to be quick on the bike,' he explained. 'Moto2, however, is the category of consistency. In Moto2, I have learnt to think on the bike: sometimes you cannot win and must pick up as many points as possible.'

It was at Mugello, during the Italian Grand Prix, that the big announcement was made. Repsol Honda rider, Casey Stoner, had announced at the French Grand Prix back in May that he would be retiring at the end of the season. As a double world champion (once for Ducati and once for Honda), Stoner was a hard act to follow, but he had simply had enough of the MotoGP circus. He hated the travelling, he hated the endless PR duties, the media interviews, and even the increasing role of electronics on MotoGP bikes. He wanted to spend more time at home in Australia with his family, and he wanted to go fishing, far from the razzamatazz of the GP world. Even a rumoured offer of £10 million from Honda to race for just one more year couldn't tempt him. He was just 27 years old when he turned his back on the championship, the money and the fame.

Stoner is considered one of the greatest, and one of the most naturally talented, MotoGP riders of all time, so replacing him was never going to be easy, but at Mugello, Repsol Honda announced it had signed the man it believed could emulate Stoner's success: Marc Márquez would be moving up to MotoGP in 2013.

Determined to move up to the premier class as the Moto2 world champion, Márquez played down his signing and concentrated on seeing out the second half of the season in the best way possible. 'To reach MotoGP next season with Repsol Honda is a dream come true, and I want to thank HRC (Honda Racing Corporation) for their confidence in me,' Márquez said at the press conference to announce his signing. 'I am very proud to be a part of the big Honda family for the future, and I don't want to forget all the people who have helped me since I began to ride motorbikes. Now my focus is on Moto2, where my team and I are working very hard and we are excited to achieve our goal, which is to win the world championship in 2012.'

It was clear that HRC bosses had had an eye on Márquez for some time, as they had campaigned since the start of the season to have the 'rookie rule' annulled in order to pave the way for Márquez's signing. The rule – which had been introduced in 2010 – banned rookie MotoGP riders from stepping straight into a factory team (instead, insisting that rookies spend at least one year learning the ropes in a satellite team), but that's exactly where HRC wanted Marc to be, alongside his one-time hero Dani Pedrosa. In the end, the prospect of Marc Márquez riding a full factory Repsol Honda RC213V in MotoGP was just too delicious to be ignored, and the rule was brushed under the carpet, to everyone's relief.

Livio Suppo was HRC's Communications and Marketing Director at the time and was present when Márquez signed for Honda. 'I remember we signed the contract in a hotel in Barcelona. He was super young, but it was clear that he was very special. If you look at his career in 125cc and then in Moto2, it was clear that he had something special – the race where he crashed on the sighting lap (Estoril, 2010) and they repaired the bike quickly, and he started from the back of the grid and won the race. He did something similar in 2012 (when Márquez stalled his bike on the line in Japan then overtook the entire field to win). He really had a special speed.'

Perhaps distracted by all the media attention surrounding the announcement in Mugello, but officially blaming set-up difficulties, Márquez could only manage fifth place in the Italian race, though he still had a 34-point lead over Espargaró as the championship moved on to Indianapolis in America.

From second on the grid, Márquez took the lead of the race on lap four and was never headed. He started the last lap with a seven-second advantage and cruised home to victory and an extended title lead of 39 points.

After Gino Rea's bike spilled oil all over the track, the Moto2 race at San Marino was restarted as a two-thirds-distance sprint. Starting from pole position, Márquez only took the lead halfway around the final lap and, after trading places with Pol Espargaró three times on the remainder of the lap, he held on to take his seventh win of the year.

Now 53 points clear at the top of the points table (more than two race wins' worth of points), Márquez was back on Spanish soil at Aragón for round 14. Starting from seventh on the grid, he was involved in a ferocious three-man battle for second place in the race with Scott Redding and Andrea Iannone. As they crossed the line, the trio was separated by just four-tenths of a second, with Márquez just stealing second spot.

The Japanese Grand Prix at Motegi was a showcase for Marc Márquez at his devastating best and proved that, when the chips were down, he was by far the fastest Moto2 rider on the planet.

Second on the grid to Espargaró, Márquez missed his gear selection and found his bike in neutral when the lights changed. There were tense moments as the rest of the field streaked past on either side of him; those from the back rows already travelling at high speed.

Márquez knew how fortunate he was to escape unscathed.

'At that particular moment I was very lucky,' he later said. 'Normally, when something happens to you at the start, or there's some kind of problem, you have 30 bikes coming at you from behind. So, the only thing I could do was put it in first (gear) and start as quick as I could. But I knew the other riders would be coming at me with their throttles pinned, which could have resulted in one of them ramming into me from behind and causing a crash.'[32]

What happened next was astonishing. After kicking his Suter into first gear, Márquez scythed his way through the pack, overtaking 22 riders in the first two corners to go from 32nd place up to ninth. By lap nine he was in second place behind Tito Rabat and, on lap ten, he took the lead; his rise through the pack after such an unsettling drama on the start line proving just how calm he could be under hugely stressful conditions. Nor did he overcompensate by taking wild risks and risking crashing; he looked controlled, focused and seriously fast throughout the 23-lap race. In fact, the setback on the start line might even have helped his charge through the field: 'Sometimes I have to channel my inner anger to win a race.'

Even on the last lap, while still being attacked by Rabat and Espargaró, he kept his cool to hang on and win by half a second. It was arguably Márquez's most impressive ride to date, and he certainly considered it to be his best race of the year. 'Japan, without a doubt,' he said when asked about his most outstanding performance of the 2012 season. 'After the start line error, I was able to remain calm and that was very important to me. Recovering from the first corner was difficult, but that gave meaning to the victory. When you win a race like that, it is a great personal reward.'

Monsoon conditions greeted the riders in Malaysia and Márquez rode cautiously, knowing he could secure the Moto2 world championship if he simply stayed on and scored some points. He didn't. After qualifying third he crashed out on lap 12 under braking 'while I was still in a straight line!' Unable to understand what had happened, all Márquez could do was head for Australia and hope he could wrap the title up there.

Ahead of the Phillip Island race, he knew the permutations: to keep the title fight alive, Pol Espargaró had to win but, even if he did, Márquez needed just two points to take the championship. Espargaró did all he could, setting pole position and winning by an incredible 16.8 seconds – more than twice the previous best win margin in the class. But it wasn't enough: Márquez took third place, and those 16 points put his title lead at an unassailable 39 points with just one round left to go.

At 18 years old, Marc Márquez was a double world champion in two different classes, and he had secured the most coveted seat in MotoGP for the following season. It was a far cry from the beginning of 2012, when he wondered if he would ever be able to ride again – or even to see properly again. He was as relieved as he was delighted. 'Getting this title has been very important,' he said shortly after the race. 'I owe it to my sponsors, my family and also to Emilio Alzamora. They have put so much effort into my success. And, above all, I thank them for their support during my recovery in the winter. It was very hard for me to overcome the disappointment (of) the injury. Every morning, I woke up distressed, waiting to finally stop seeing double. Besides that, withstanding the pressure and always being labelled as a favourite is hard. When you're not on top, you begin to be asked what is happening, and doubts arise. It was very important to win after enduring pressure all year.'

Although his Team CatalunyaCaixa Repsol Suter was as good a bike as anyone else's, it was no better, so beating the rest of the field so frequently and so comprehensively proved that Márquez's riding abilities were out of the ordinary. He took nine wins during the season and only finished off the rostrum once (fifth place in Italy), eventually winning the championship by 56 points from Pol Espargaró.

Reflecting on the key moments in his championship-winning season, Márquez said, 'There were many important moments, but most were in the races after the summer break, when I diced for the title with Pol. Indianapolis, Brno, Aragón and Japan were decisive races in which I battled him head-to-head, and I could not let him take points off me. I give a lot of value to a championship won on the closing laps. We have had many battles and perhaps not one in particular has been decisive, but when you win five on the final lap, each set of five points (race winners are awarded 25 points while second place is worth 20 points) makes the difference needed to take the championship.'

Repsol Suter team boss Aki Ajo had been seriously impressed by his rider all season long. 'I saw something special – that he never gave up,' the Finn said. 'He had some crashes, some accidents, injuries, but he always came back. Racing is everything for him, so I think he is ready to sacrifice big things to reach his targets. You need to be passionate – you can work on that. But I think being hungry has to come from within, almost automatically. You need to have high targets and be ready to do everything to achieve them.'[33]

In accordance with tradition, the last Grand Prix of the year was held at Valencia in southern Spain. There were no titles left to fight for – Jorge Lorenzo had secured the MotoGP crown, Márquez the Moto2 championship, and Sandro Cortese had won in Moto3 –

so there shouldn't have been any major drama in Australia, but MotoGP doesn't work like that.

Once again, Márquez had been sent to the back of the grid like an errant schoolboy, this time for an over-aggressive move on Simone Corsi which knocked the German rider off his bike. And that was just one example. 'It was aggressive contact, several times, with other riders during practice,' said Race Director Mike Webb. 'It was a recurrence of a number of things that happened during the year, and so that was like an accumulation of penalties to say, "Okay, you cannot ride like this," so he was sent to the back.'[34]

With the championship already in the bag, Márquez could have been forgiven for taking the final race of the season steady, but he clearly had no intention of doing so. Two crashes during practice and qualifying proved this, as did his phenomenal ride through the entire Moto2 field in the race itself.

When the lights turned to green, Márquez set off the line like a missile and overtook 22 riders on the opening lap to cross the line in 11th place, despite – or perhaps because of – the tricky damp conditions. Still, he pushed. With 12 laps to go he was in third place, five seconds adrift of Nico Terol. After hunting down and passing Terol, he had another five seconds to make up if he wanted to catch the race leader, Julián Simón. He caught him with three laps to go, breezed past on the start/finish straight, and claimed his ninth win of the season in the most dramatic of fashions.

Márquez was clearly too good for Moto2; it was time to move up and play with the big boys. It was time for MotoGP, and the anticipation to see what Marc Márquez could do in the world's fastest motorcycle championship was intense.

Speaking ahead of his move to the premier class, Márquez said, 'It's a dream come true. My dream was always to ride in MotoGP and make a space for myself amongst the best riders in history. Going up to MotoGP with the best team in my first year is a privilege. I thank everyone for giving me the opportunity. I am definitely not going to waste it.'

He didn't.

CHAPTER 4

THE ROOKIE

'I DON'T FALL OFF BECAUSE I WANT TO; I FALL OFF BECAUSE IT'S THE ONLY WAY I KNOW OF FINDING THE LIMITS.'

Marc Márquez

MotoGP motorcycles are not easy beasts to ride. Even experienced racers often catch themselves forgetting to breathe on occasion. To ride a MotoGP bike at its maximum is to skate right on the very edge of disaster. 'You have a lot of moments of breathlessness on a MotoGP bike without you realising it,' Marc Márquez has testified.

Not surprising, given the specifications of these multi-million-pound, thoroughbred, prototype racing machines. They're like nothing else in existence. In 2013, Honda's exquisite RC213V MotoGP bike weighed 157kg, made almost 300bhp, accelerated faster than a Formula 1 car, and had a top speed of over 220mph. It was a quantum leap from the 140bhp Marc Márquez had been used to in Moto2, but no one doubted the man from Cervera would be able to ride it – and ride it fast.

Casey Stoner had won the world title for Repsol Honda in 2011, and prior to that, the team had won five 500cc world championships with Mick Doohan between 1994 and 1998, one with Àlex Crivillé in 1999, one 500cc world title (2001) and two MotoGP world titles (2002 and 2003) with Valentino Rossi, and another MotoGP title with Nicky Hayden in 2006. Although he was on every MotoGP team's shopping list, Marc Márquez didn't even consider riding for anyone else. 'I didn't talk to any other manufacturer before moving into the premier class,' he said. 'Honda was the only option for me.'

After signing to ride for the team, Márquez revealed he had been offered a factory contract with HRC midway through 2011, but that he had declined for two reasons. One was that it would have meant riding for the satellite LCR Honda team, because of the still extant 'rookie law' banning MotoGP debutants from riding for factory teams. Márquez wanted a factory bike and wasn't prepared to compromise on that front. The other reason was that he only wanted to move up to MotoGP as the Moto2 world champion and, at that point in 2011, he was still some 60 points behind Stefan Bradl. There had also been no indication at the time that Casey Stoner would retire so early, so there didn't appear to be a factory seat available at Honda. Márquez decided to wait.

With Casey Stoner retiring ahead of the 2013 season, Dani Pedrosa became the most senior rider in the Repsol Honda team. A hero to Márquez just a few years before, Pedrosa was entering his eighth year with the team but, despite having won many races, he had never managed to deliver the championship. The team needed new blood, and Márquez appeared to be a once-in-a-generation talent; he was also Spanish, like Pedrosa, and, more importantly, like title sponsor Repsol. It was a match made in heaven.

While Márquez had wanted to take his entire Moto2 crew with him to Repsol Honda, HRC felt it was better to keep the existing

Repsol team (the same team that had worked with Stoner) because of their experience with the RC213V. Márquez did put his foot down on one point, however – he insisted on bringing his trusted Moto2 crew chief, Santiago 'Santi' Hernández with him. In fact, he delivered an ultimatum: 'No Santi, no me.'

Hernández had been a suspension technician for 1999 500cc world champion Àlex Crivillé, and Valentino Rossi in the Repsol Honda team, and had been a crew chief in both the 125cc and Moto2 championships before taking up the position as Márquez's crew chief in the two years that he competed in Moto2. Márquez rated him highly and, equally importantly, found him easy to work with and get along with: they bonded, and a strong relationship between a rider and his crew chief has always been one of the key factors in MotoGP success. A crew chief doesn't just look after the bike, he also looks after his rider and offers constant support through good times and bad. It's a crucial role.

Hernández had originally been chosen as Márquez's chief mechanic in Moto2 from a shortlist of three, and it was his attitude and eagerness that secured him the job. 'When we were trying to set up the perfect Moto2 team, we had got down to the final three candidates for the job as my chief mechanic,' Márquez explained in a 2020 interview. 'One of them (Hernández) didn't say a word about money at the interview; all he cared about was the job at hand. He wanted to work with me, and he didn't much care about all the rest. He laid the groundwork for an air of trust that holds good to this day.'

HRC capitulated and Hernández would become an indispensable weapon in Márquez's garage through all his years with Honda. 'With Santi, I know that I'm going to get what I need on the technical side to ride the way I want,' Márquez explained in his

2023 book *Being Marc Márquez*. 'We are inseparable now, after all these years together, but it was already clear how compatible we were, and how well we complemented each other back in Moto2.'[35]

His first ride on the fearsome RCV came at the Valencia test on 13 November, just after the final Grand Prix of the 2012 season. It was cold, wet and windy – not ideal conditions in which to have your first taste of a vicious MotoGP bike – but as the track dried out, allowing Márquez to fit slick tyres, he improved his pace and finished the test in seventh place, just 1.08 seconds off the best time set by his vastly experienced teammate, Dani Pedrosa.

Márquez, like every rider who tests a MotoGP bike for the first time, was seriously impressed. 'It was a different world,' he said of the experience. 'After the first few laps, I rolled back into the box with a huge grin on my face and told the technicians, "Wow! That's a *real* racing bike!"'[36]

Established MotoGP rider Cal Crutchlow was impressed too. 'He is probably the best rider in the world at the moment, although I don't think he will be challenging Pedrosa and (Jorge) Lorenzo for the title next year,' he said in late 2012. 'But he will give them a hard time. He is special, there is no doubt about that. He reminds me of Lorenzo in terms of speed, but they ride differently.'[37]

Jorge Lorenzo had won the MotoGP championship in 2010 and 2012 for Yamaha and was the man to beat again in 2013. Valentino Rossi had returned to the Yamaha fold after two disastrous years with Ducati (he failed to win a single race in that time), but there was a question mark over whether he could return to winning ways.

For his part, Márquez's ambitions at the start of his first season in MotoGP were relatively modest. 'Coming from the smaller classes, there was so much to learn,' he would later say. 'New electronics, brakes and tyres, and very experienced rivals. Above all, more than double the horsepower. I hoped to adapt to the bike, to learn to give my 100 per cent during the season, and try to perhaps win some races in time.'

That was the official line, at least, but privately, Márquez seemed to be aiming higher. After crashing three times in three days during testing in Sepang, he was taken aside by RC213V project leader Takeo Yokoyama and told he couldn't keep riding like that; he couldn't keep taking so many risks. Márquez held Yokoyama's gaze and, respectfully, told his boss, 'You need to understand that this is my style, and it will go on being my style. I don't fall off because I want to; I fall off because it's the only way I know of finding the limits.'[38]

Yokoyama could barely believe what he was hearing as Márquez continued. 'I told him, "You worry about fixing the bike. If I get hurt, the doctors will take care of it." And that was it. He went pale. The conversation was over.'[39]

It was a chilling statement of intent. Still just 20 years old, Márquez was basically saying he didn't mind crashing or hurting himself – he needed to know where the limits were, and taking huge risks was the only way he was going to find where the limit was. It was a policy that would become a trademark.

Most riders, even great ones, take a year or two to learn how to ride a MotoGP bike fast: Marc Márquez was an exception. He admitted that he found the transition from a 125cc to a Moto2 bike more difficult than the move from Moto2 to MotoGP. In the opening free practice session at the first round in Qatar in 2013, he topped the time sheets. As the others upped their pace, he got pushed down the order a little, but still qualified in a hugely impressive sixth place.

Crew chief Santi Hernández was impressed, if not surprised,

by how quickly Márquez had adapted to a MotoGP bike. 'As he demonstrated in Moto2, Marc is a hard worker who always knows what he needs to do in order to go faster,' he said after the pre-season tests. 'In turn, he also gives the technicians very clear information. This helps make the whole process somewhat faster.'[40]

In the Qatar race, Márquez was involved in a battle for second place with Cal Crutchlow and, crucially, his teammate Dani Pedrosa. There's an old adage in racing that says the first person you have to beat is your teammate (when you have the same bike, there can be no excuses) and Márquez was determined to beat Pedrosa in order to be considered the Repsol team's number one rider, even though he was competing in his very first MotoGP race. The number one rider in a team leads development of the bike, and Márquez wanted the next RC213V to be built around him. It was another key factor to success in MotoGP.

At mid-race distance, Márquez passed Pedrosa, but then had an even bigger fight on his hands as nine-time world champion Valentino Rossi began his attack. Clearly rejuvenated now that he was back on the Yamaha after two winless years with Ducati, Rossi was in no mood to be beaten by a rookie, but admitted it was only a matter of time. After beating Márquez over the line by just 0.21 seconds, Rossi admitted that 'I have to try to beat him as much as possible early in the season, because later it will be more difficult.'[41]

For his part, Márquez had been pinching himself in the race, almost unable to comprehend that he was racing against his heroes. 'I was right there with them, with Jorge and Dani – with Valentino, even!' he said incredulously. 'It was mind-blowing to me. I was very nervous, but I was also really enjoying it.'[42]

Valentino Rossi had been racing in the MotoGP class for 12

years when the 2013 season began and had won the title seven times, while double MotoGP world champion Jorge Lorenzo was entering his sixth year in the class. Márquez really had been thrown to the lions, but riding alongside such immense talents and genuine legends of the sport helped him enormously. 'It was very hard at the beginning,' he said, 'but I learned so much riding alongside Dani, Jorge and Valentino. I saw how they rode the bike and attacked tracks differently to how I did in Moto2 and learned from this.'[43]

During the race, Márquez broke the first of many records he would smash throughout the year; he set the fastest lap of the race as a rookie. The last man to do so had been Freddie Spencer in 1980, and he had been 112 days older.

Marc Márquez had finished third in his first ride on a MotoGP bike, with only legends and multiple world champions, Jorge Lorenzo and Valentino Rossi, ahead of him, and his Repsol teammate behind him in fourth. It was more than anyone could have hoped for, but what happened at the next round shocked everyone.

It was MotoGP's first visit to the all-new Circuit of the Americas (COTA) in Texas, meaning it was a level playing field for everyone. No rider had data or set-up information from previous races, only from the test that happened ahead of the Grand Prix itself, which Márquez had topped. It was a left-handed circuit, and those had always favoured Márquez due to his dirt-track background (on an oval dirt-track circuit, every corner is a left-hander), so the layout favoured him.

During the pre-season test at COTA, Repsol Honda Team Principal Livio Suppo knew he was watching a special talent. 'When we went to Austin to do a test before the race, Marc was immediately super-fast,' he said. 'Okay, that's a track that perfectly suits his style, but anyway, it was clear from the very beginning – from the Valencia test at the end of 2012 – that he had something special.'

Despite having a cold-tyre crash on the first day of practice in America, Márquez stole pole position from Dani Pedrosa and Jorge Lorenzo in only his second outing on a MotoGP bike.

In the race itself, he had to fend off a determined and sustained attack from Pedrosa, but the younger rider's consistency proved to be the elder rider's undoing and, after Pedrosa made a series of small errors on lap 19, the race was Márquez's to lose. He didn't lose it: he crossed the line 1.53 seconds clear of his teammate to become the youngest premier class winner in Grand Prix history. The previous youngest had been Freddie Spencer, way back in 1982, but it took him seven races to win, while Márquez won second time out. Spencer had been 21 at the time, but Márquez was just 20. He had also become the youngest pole setter in MotoGP history. Just two races into the 2013 season, and Márquez was rewriting the record books.

Even he was surprised. 'I didn't think I had the strength, the capacity or experience to lead the race,' he would later say of his first win. 'So, I decided to ride behind Dani, to learn, and I only put in a spurt at the end, to pass him and win.'[44]

Márquez admitted it took a little time for the magnitude of his first MotoGP victory to sink in. 'When I won the race, at first it felt like just another victory,' he said. 'But when I got home, I felt that a win in MotoGP is not just any victory, it is something special, and I was thrilled. I remembered all the people who had helped me achieve it.'[45]

It took just three races for Márquez to create controversy and make enemies in the premier class, and the first was Jorge Lorenzo.

On Spanish turf at Jerez, Lorenzo, Márquez and Pedrosa were all determined to be the fastest Spaniard, but while Pedrosa managed to clear off and win the race, the battle between Lorenzo and Márquez intensified in the last few laps before reaching a climax at the final corner of the last lap (which had been named after Lorenzo just the day before). In an extremely aggressive move, Márquez smashed into the side of Lorenzo's bike to force his way through to second spot, sending the hapless Lorenzo out wide and ruining any chance he had of taking second place.

When Márquez attempted to apologise to Lorenzo in *parc fermé* after the race, Lorenzo turned his back on him, refused to listen and refused to shake his hand. Afterwards, he marched straight up to Race Direction to protest the move. Race Director Mike Webb held back from issuing a penalty. 'If it was free practice, there would have been penalties,' he explained, 'but it was the last lap of the race.'

Márquez's second place stood, and he took the lead in the world championship; the youngest man ever to do so. Another of Freddie Spencer's records broken. But Jerez had been a sign of things to come; Márquez had made it clear that he would do anything to win, and if that meant shoving another rider out of his way, so be it. The other riders got the message: no quarter would be asked or given. If Márquez was prepared to put himself on a total war footing, the rest were going to have to do the same. He wasn't in MotoGP to make friends; he was there to win.

Most of the other riders believed it was a racing incident at Jerez, and that Race Direction had been correct in not issuing a penalty. Valentino Rossi was among them. 'It's a hard attack, and a hard overtake from Marc,' he said. 'He touched Jorge, but it's the last lap, the last corner, and sure, the guy behind tries something.'[46]

For now, the only disgruntled parties were Lorenzo and his Yamaha team, but other riders would soon feel the same way, once they themselves had been on the receiving end of the Márquez treatment, and Rossi would be chief amongst them.

The Jerez incident was largely put to bed during a flight from the circuit to Barcelona, after the Jerez test that followed the race weekend. Márquez found himself booked into a seat right next to Lorenzo and, while he swapped seats with his crew chief, Santi Hernández, for the flight, after leaving the aeroplane, Marc sought out Lorenzo, apologised, and once again offered to shake hands. This time Lorenzo accepted, but with the proviso 'I'll get my own back'.

Márquez has always defended his aggressive riding style, believing that there's simply no room for politeness if you want to win a MotoGP championship. 'I don't regret anything I have done on the track,' he said in 2023. 'I'm not there to make friends. It just can't be that way, because each of us on the grid wants to beat everyone else.'[47]

Being aggressive, Márquez believes, is the only way to beat the world's best riders. 'On a last lap, or the last two or three, fighting against Jorge Lorenzo, Dani Pedrosa and Valentino Rossi, there is no gap. There's no gap. They won't allow it. Sometimes you have to create that gap. You have to create it – throw yourself in.'[48]

The French Grand Prix presented another first for Márquez. He had never ridden a MotoGP bike in the rain before morning warm-up on the day of the race at Le Mans. It had drizzled during his first test on the bike at Valencia in 2012, but it wasn't fully wet. Once again, Márquez adapted instantly and posted the third fastest time. He had already set pole position in the dry but spun up off the line at the start of the race and survived a few scary slides before finding his feet. After that he rode superbly to make his way up from seventh place mid-race to third over the line, his 100 per cent podium record for 2013 still intact.

That run would be broken at Mugello, however, when Márquez suffered his first non-finish of the year. Now perhaps over-confident, he suffered four crashes over the weekend, the worst of which came in the race itself.

After breaking records all season, he broke another one when he suffered the fastest crash in Grand Prix history at Mugello. Data from Márquez's Alpinestars suit (race suits now monitor many aspects of a rider's position and speed, in order to deploy airbags in the event of a crash) showed he was travelling at 209.9mph when he jumped off his bike at the end of the start/finish straight. He had crested the notorious rise near the end of the straight, and his front wheel locked as it regained contact with the ground. Márquez was sent veering off to the left, on an oblique collision course with the circuit wall. Realising he was heading for a life-threatening collision, he threw himself from the bike. The force of the impact was so powerful it literally went off the scale on Márquez's smart suit: the suit could only register a maximum of 25g: Márquez reached and breached it. He was very lucky to walk away with his life, as Valentino Rossi pointed out – repeatedly. 'He was very lucky there,' he said. 'Very lucky. Very, very, very, very, very lucky, because it can be a lot worse.'

Márquez's spectacular crash gained a lot of coverage in the media and led some to claim that MotoGP riders were crazy for taking such risks. It was an attitude that he contested strongly, leaping to the defence of not only himself, but his fellow MotoGP riders. 'You can't be crazy and travel at 200mph,' he said. 'Quite the opposite, in fact: you have to be the sanest person on earth. We see things very clearly and we know when we can, and when we can't, try things.'[49]

Naturally, the crash didn't slow Márquez down any come race day, but after overtaking Dani Pedrosa for second place he pushed too hard and crashed out at Casanova-Savelli, his perfect run of podiums ended. The no-score saw him drop from second to third in the points standings, 26 behind Pedrosa and 14 behind Jorge Lorenzo.

Márquez's manager and mentor, Emilio Alzamora, sounded almost afraid when recalling those early races on a MotoGP bike. 'What Marc went through in the first five races, only he knows,' he said. 'Until he got to grips with the power, and had some experiences with the bike, he was taking enormous risks, every session. Every practice, every race, it was just "Let's see what happens."'[50]

Márquez himself admitted it was a scary, 'podium or hospital' approach. 'Every weekend I go out on Friday, for the first lap, at the limit, and I'd finish the last corner on Sunday at the limit. Every session was like "Let's see if I fall off, or if I can do it."'[51]

Back on home soil in Catalunya, Márquez became embroiled in another fierce fight with his teammate while Jorge Lorenzo maintained a comfortable lead. A last-lap lunge on Pedrosa almost saw Márquez crash out, but he somehow managed to stay upright and was still pushing hard as he crossed the line in third place, just half a second behind the elder Repsol rider. After his Mugello crash, Márquez had been determined to just finish the race in Catalunya. Already, people were saying his riding was too wild and too dangerous; a safe finish with no incidents had been important, and that's exactly what he achieved.

Jorge Lorenzo showed astonishing levels of commitment and bravery at Assen in the Netherlands. After crashing out on the fastest corner of the course and breaking his left collarbone during a wet Free Practice 2 session, he flew to Barcelona, underwent an operation to have ten screws and a titanium plate fitted, and immediately returned to Assen. After somehow being passed fit to ride, Lorenzo displayed tremendous courage to bring his Yamaha M1 home in fifth place, tears of pain streaming down his exhausted face as he removed his helmet. It had been just 34 hours since the operation. Lorenzo had forced himself to race through the agony as he knew he couldn't afford to lose too many points to Márquez. That was the kind of competitor Marc Márquez found himself up against.

Valentino Rossi won the race – his first victory in three years – with Márquez in second, nursing micro fractures in the little finger of his right hand and the big toe of his left foot from a morning warm-up crash. It was the best he could have hoped for on a bike which he claimed was not capable of fighting for the win at Assen.

The German Grand Prix at the Sachsenring would prove pivotal to Márquez's 2013 championship campaign. Not only did Jorge Lorenzo crash and land on his recently broken collarbone – bending the plate and ruling him out of the race – but Dani Pedrosa suffered a similar fate during practice, breaking his left collarbone after a fall in cold conditions. He was operated on and fully intended to race, but with worrying bouts of nausea and low blood pressure, he ultimately ruled himself out.

With both of his title rivals sidelined, Márquez started from pole position and had every intention of exploiting his unexpected advantage. On the fifth lap of the race, he overtook Valentino Rossi on the final corner, then made the same move on race leader Stefan Bradl, before clearing off to win comfortably on a track that suited him down to a tee; he would prove to be virtually unbeatable around the Sachsenring in years to come. Crucially, for his title chances, the German Grand Prix proved to be a turning point in mastering the Honda RC213V. 'By Sachsenring, I really felt good on the bike,' he said. 'It was the first time I felt the bike wasn't leading me.'

That win and, more importantly, the absence of his two main rivals, saw Márquez leapfrog his way back to the top of the points table, two points ahead of Pedrosa and 11 clear of Lorenzo.

Laguna Seca in California is a unique track and very difficult to learn; its undulating nature, blind crests and the infamous 'Corkscrew' section – where riders flip their bikes from left to right as they travel downhill from the height of a five-storey building – all combining to make it a unique challenge. Valentino Rossi had caused enormous controversy in 2008 when he took to the dirt halfway down the Corkscrew to force his way past Casey Stoner in a move that Stoner deemed highly dangerous.

Because the paddock area is so small at Laguna Seca, the Moto2 and Moto3 championships do not visit the circuit, meaning Márquez had never even seen the track before, let alone ridden it. Despite Rossi himself advising that Márquez spend this visit learning the course before fully attacking it the following year, it only took Márquez until the second free practice session before he was top of the time sheets; his ability to learn new bikes and tracks rapidly seemingly knowing no limits – although he did admit to having had some help from his PlayStation console. In the days leading up to the event, Márquez had completed endless laps of the circuit on his PlayStation. It may have been a far cry from the real thing, but in MotoGP, every little helps.

He also completed some laps on a scooter ahead of practice and paid particular attention to the Corkscrew section, carefully noting the manhole cover that Rossi had run over to facilitate his assault on Casey Stoner.

Despite a crash in practice, Márquez was fastest in qualifying until 30 seconds from the end when Stefan Bradl produced 'the lap of my life' to steal pole position.

Sitting in third place behind race leader Bradl and second-placed Valentino Rossi, Márquez made his move on lap three, and it was no surprise to anyone that it came at the Corkscrew in a near carbon copy of Rossi's move on Stoner, though he denied the move was premeditated, and that it was, instead, purely instinctive. Describing it afterwards, Márquez said, 'I held firm, tensed my legs, clasped the bike between my knees, gripped the handlebars, held my breath, closed my eyes and gave it the lot.'[52]

Rossi could hardly complain, since he had spent months defending his own move back in 2008. Realising he would appear hypocritical if he complained, he instead used humour to deflect his simmering anger. After being beaten by Márquez in Germany, Rossi had joked at the press conference that Márquez was 'a fucking bastard', and he used the Laguna Seca press conference to embellish his point. 'I told you last week he was a bastard,' he said, 'but he is more of a bastard than I thought!'[53]

The rivalry between Rossi and Márquez was, at that stage, still friendly, and Rossi seemed genuinely happy to see such a talented young rider bring a new lease of life to MotoGP. He almost considered him a protégé of sorts, saying, 'Marc's like a new and improved version of Valentino Rossi.' That situation wouldn't last forever, though: the clock was ticking, and moves like Márquez pulled at Laguna only added fuel to the slow-burning fire. Those flames would soon ignite and rage out of control.

After taking his time to size up and then pass Stefan Bradl,

Márquez pulled clear to win the American race by 2.3 seconds to put himself 16 points clear in the points table: Pedrosa had finished fifth and Lorenzo sixth, with their still painful collarbones. Márquez's second consecutive win also broke Freddie Spencer's long-standing record of being the youngest rider to accomplish that feat. He was on a roll, and his spectacular move on Valentino Rossi proved that he was no longer in awe of the MotoGP legends; in fact, he was fast becoming one himself.

Staying stateside, the MotoGP circus moved to Indianapolis where Márquez dominated. He was fastest in every practice session, fastest in qualifying, and fastest in morning warm-up on race day. He started from pole position, set a new lap record in the race, and won from Dani Pedrosa by 3.49 seconds. He simply could not have been any more dominant. And this from a rookie. His third win in a row also gave Márquez another record – he had amassed more points than a rookie ever had in the championship, and there were still eight rounds to go.

He added another 25 points at Brno after leading home Dani Pedrosa and Jorge Lorenzo again to carve out a 26-point advantage at the top of the points table, then dominated practice and qualifying at the British Grand Prix too, setting his fifth pole position of the year. But a crash in cool conditions during morning warm-up saw him dislocate his left shoulder, causing some concern that he might not be able to race.

Much to the annoyance of Dani Pedrosa and Jorge Lorenzo, he did race – just three hours after the dislocation – and he very nearly won, missing out to an in-form Lorenzo by just 0.08 seconds. It was another 20 points towards the championship and Márquez was delighted with his damage limitation exercise. 'After this morning's crash, I thought my weekend was finished,' he said afterwards. 'At the end I was struggling a little bit on the changes of direction . . . but I am so happy to have these 20 points. It is important for the championship.'[54]

It was the first time all season that Márquez had voluntarily mentioned the championship, proving he was now thinking of the bigger picture rather than just trying to win every race at all costs. His maturity was building, and he was becoming ever more the complete racer: Márquez 233 points, Pedrosa 203 points.

After dominating qualifying at Misano by setting a new unofficial lap record that put him in pole position, half a second clear of Jorge Lorenzo, Márquez once again settled for second place in the race rather than going all out to try to beat his rival. Again, he was focusing on the championship. 'Second was okay,' he said. 'The 20 points are important.'

At MotorLand Aragón, he found himself at the centre of more controversy over his aggressive riding. In what was a freak accident, he made very light contact with Dani Pedrosa's bike on the fifth lap and his clutch lever snagged and pulled out the (unprotected) cable leading to Pedrosa's rear wheel sensor. This, in turn, disabled the traction control system and, as Pedrosa tapped the throttle, he was spat off his RC213V while Márquez ran wide, lost some time, but carried on.

Again, the incident in itself was not deemed to merit a penalty, but Márquez had been racking up offences all year and some felt the cumulative effect merited punishment of some kind before things truly got out of hand. With more information about the crash emerging later in the day, any decision on a possible penalty was deferred until the next round in Malaysia.

Carrying on regardless in the race, Márquez took his seventh victory of the season, this time from Lorenzo. He also benefitted from the fact that Pedrosa scored nothing and dropped to third in the championship. Now Márquez led Lorenzo by 39 points with just four rounds to go. The impossible was starting to look possible – a rookie winning the MotoGP world championship. It had only ever happened once since the advent of the Grand Prix world championships in 1949, and it was a very special rider who achieved the feat.

Kenny Roberts had been quite content riding (and winning) in the AMA Grand National championship in the States – a series that combined road racing and dirt-track racing. He only agreed to try the world championship when Yamaha couldn't offer him a competitive dirt-tracker, but he made an instant impact.

When Roberts came to Europe in 1978, Barry Sheene was the undisputed king of Grands Prix, and the pair enjoyed a fierce but respectful rivalry. Sheene was a double world champion and was the defending champ when Roberts arrived on the scene, but he would never win another title. Roberts not only won the 1978 500cc world championship, but he repeated the feat in 1979 and 1980.

Adapting a rear-wheel-sliding, dirt-track style to a 500cc Grand Prix machine on tarmac, Roberts revolutionised the way Grand Prix bikes were ridden and blazed a trail for a host of other American dirt-trackers to dominate Grand Prix racing throughout the 1980s and early 1990s. He came, he saw, he conquered; he also had a dramatic impact on all aspects of Grand Prix racing, from improving safety measures to gaining better pay for riders and making the sport far more professional and scientific. He is still considered one of the all-time greats, and yet Marc Márquez was looking to equal Roberts's unique feat from 1978, winning the world championship as a rookie, some 35 years after the one and only time it had ever been done. Roberts had performed his miracle 15 years before Márquez was even born.

When the GP circus turned up in Malaysia in 2013, Marc Márquez learned of the punishment he was to face for riding into Dani Pedrosa at Aragón; one point was to be added to his licence.

In 2013, Dorna introduced a licence penalty system to punish riders who were deemed to be riding irresponsibly, and it was no coincidence that the system was adopted in the same season that Márquez made his debut in the premier class, as Race Director Mike Webb explained. 'Marc Márquez made us think about a points system, because he was very close to the limit so many times and we needed a way of accounting for that. Like, how many times have we told you to take it easy?'[55]

It was a cumulative system; score four points and a rider had to start the next race from the back of the grid; seven points, and he had to start from the pit lane; ten points meant a one-race ban. Márquez already had two points on his licence from Silverstone when he crashed under yellow flags and almost wiped out the marshals who were attending to the fallen Cal Crutchlow during morning warm-up; Crutchlow and the marshals had to literally run for their lives as Márquez's bike came smashing into Crutchlow's. Adding one more in Malaysia only made three in total, so Márquez was not issued with an actual penalty and started from pole, much to Jorge Lorenzo's chagrin. Lorenzo felt Márquez deserved a real penalty for just one too many incidents of dubious riding. Márquez, in turn, felt that any kind of penalty was unjustified. 'I'm most disappointed about that action because it was so unlucky for Dani,' he said on reflection. 'I think it was a race incident but, anyway, of course I completely disagree with that point of penalty because it was not meant. But anyway, we are here, we have the Race Direction, and we must respect the decision of them.'

Honda came off worse as their rear wheel sensor system was deemed to be dangerous. Race Direction ruled that it had not been routed as it should have been, and that Honda's software should have had a built-in safety mode, rather than just cutting out and sending Pedrosa over the bars. Honda was docked 25 points in the Constructors' Championship – an embarrassment to a company so obsessed with detail and engineering brilliance.

The licence penalty system was abandoned in 2017, with Dorna claiming it was no longer needed as long-lap penalties (where offending riders had to take in an additional loop added on to the track) and time penalties had become the standard way of dealing with unruly or dangerous riders. But, before it was abandoned, the system would play a crucial role in the outcome of the 2015 world championship.

But that was yet to come. In Malaysia, Lorenzo took a leaf out of Márquez's book and gave as good as he got in a furious tussle with Márquez in the opening laps of the race. Márquez finally got the upper hand but again showed his new-found maturity by refusing to hunt down race leader Dani Pedrosa. 'I thought of the championship,' he said, 'and the best decision was to keep 20 points. Jorge was my main target this weekend.' Beating Lorenzo into second place gave Márquez another four-point advantage over him. Márquez 298, Lorenzo 255. Three rounds to go.

Then came utter disaster in Australia. When sole tyre supplier Bridgestone realised its tyres could only last ten laps of the newly surfaced (and extremely grippy) Phillip Island circuit, a new race strategy had to be devised. Instead of the scheduled 27 laps, the race was cut to 19 laps and riders had to come into the pits at the end of ten laps to change tyres. While flag-to-flag races had been in existence since 2005, they were designed to counter rainfall during a race. Riders could come in and switch to their second bike, which would be fitted with wet tyres. But in Australia, for the first time, there was to be a dry flag-to-flag race. The regulations sounded clear enough – do ten laps, then come in and change tyres. Any rider failing to come in by the tenth lap would be disqualified for their own safety – the Bridgestones had been tearing themselves to pieces on longer runs during practice. But, as simple as it sounded, someone in the Repsol Honda garage clearly didn't understand the plan.

After two crashes in practice, Márquez qualified second to Lorenzo and was involved in a tight tussle with him and Dani Pedrosa during the early part of the race. At the end of lap eight – seeking to change bikes in a much quieter pit lane – Pedrosa was first in. Lorenzo, Márquez and Valentino Rossi opted to stay out on track but, while Lorenzo and Rossi dutifully entered the pits at the end of lap ten, Márquez didn't. His pit crew had not given him a signal board telling him to come into his box. Bucking, slithering and weaving on badly chunked tyres, he nevertheless pulled out a massive lead as every other rider had now pitted and lost time.

When Márquez flew down the start and finish straight to begin an 11th lap, his pit crew looked horrified and television commentators couldn't believe what they were seeing. With a world championship in the balance, a team as experienced as Repsol Honda making such a rookie mistake was unthinkable, and the team knew it. As Márquez flashed past his pit box, senior Honda technician Cristian Gabarrini looked into the garage and drew his finger across his throat: somebody was going to pay for this.

When Márquez did come in on the following lap, he rejoined the race with his blood fully up, coursing with adrenalin, and super keen to make up for lost time. As he exited the pit lane, he clashed with Jorge Lorenzo, who was travelling at high speed into the first corner and running a little wide. The pair collided, but neither fell. It would have been better for Márquez's points situation if they had.

As it was, Márquez was shown a black flag on lap 14, indicating that he was disqualified from the race and must enter the pits immediately. His race was run, and he wouldn't be taking home any points, while race winner Jorge Lorenzo took a full complement of 25. Coming into the Australian race, Márquez had enjoyed a 43-point advantage, but now it was down to just 18. One more no-score and Lorenzo could easily take over the lead.

It was ironic that a rookie rider had performed miracles all season long, only to be let down by one of the most experienced teams in the paddock. Márquez was furious when he returned to his pit box and quickly stormed out, but soon returned after clearly being advised that the team must present a united front to the world's media. In the end, he took it on the chin. It hadn't been any fault of his own and the team wasn't prepared to point the finger at any one individual; they were a team, after all. What was done was done; they had to regroup and take the fight to Lorenzo in Japan. Márquez presented a united front to the media. 'You know, sometimes I can make a mistake and crash, and sometimes the team can make a mistake,' he said. 'It was a team error, and the important thing is we moved on. We win together, and we make mistakes together, always as a team.'[56]

Repsol Honda team manager Livio Suppo would later claim that Márquez's ready forgiveness of his team was absolutely crucial in his championship campaign. Had he remained angry with them, the tension in the garage would have built, creating a toxic environment which was not conducive to fighting for a world championship.

Typhoon Francisco played havoc with the schedule for the Japanese Grand Prix and Márquez crashed during a steaming wet practice session and again in morning warm-up. He would be riding hurt and starting from second on the grid behind Lorenzo. That's the way the race would end too, with Lorenzo reducing Márquez's points lead to 13 with only the final round to go. Pedrosa's third place in Japan put him out of reach of the championship, so it was now a straight fight between two Spaniards on home turf at Valencia.

Márquez could at least take some joy from Motegi, where his brother Álex scored his first win in the Moto3 class. Álex had finished his debut season in 2011 in 20th place, with a best finish of sixth at home in Catalunya. He was a slower burner than his older brother, but he was now a race winner, and a rider clearly worth keeping an eye on.

With the world championship to be decided in just one race, Valencia was a complete sell-out, as expected. Some 104,000 fans had packed themselves into the compact circuit to watch the drama unfold, and to crown a new king of MotoGP. The permutations were simple: Lorenzo needed to win and, if he did, he needed Márquez to finish lower than fourth. Márquez approached the race as he had done every other throughout the year – he rode flat out, claiming it helped him to focus. He also claimed it was safer, saying, 'On a MotoGP bike, if you don't push, then the tyres and brakes don't work so well.'

That attitude saw him take pole position from Lorenzo, while Lorenzo had decided on a race strategy that relied heavily on others. His plan was to get to the front then to slow the pace, so more riders could bunch up and, hopefully get between him and Márquez (he was later reprimanded by Race Direction for these tactics, though was not given any sort of penalty). He tried valiantly, but the rest simply weren't fast enough to run at Lorenzo, Pedrosa and Márquez's pace.

Realising that winning the championship was far more important than winning the race, Márquez erred on the side of caution and allowed Pedrosa through into second place. With Lorenzo out front, the trio finished in that order, Márquez bringing up the rear in third place. It was enough to take the championship by a meagre four points.

It had been a difficult race, and one in which Márquez had to consciously curtail his usual 'everything or nothing' attitude. 'It was difficult, because something inside me says, "You need to fight," but I understand that it was much more important – the championship – than one race. It was maybe the longest race in my career. Last lap, I was *so* careful!'[57]

For Márquez, it was the greatest day of his life, and he struggled to believe it was actually happening. 'In your dreams, you always think about getting some kind of win, and to be fighting for the title – be among the top three. But fighting for the title, and then to win it, never entered my thoughts. I don't think I'll ever have the same feeling again.'[58]

At 20 years and 266 days old, Márquez had become the youngest ever champion in Grand Prix racing's premier class, taking the record from Freddie Spencer who had been 21 when he took the 1983 500cc world championship. He had won six races – two fewer than Lorenzo, but a record for a rookie – but Márquez's greater consistency had paid off. Although he crashed 15 times during the year (only Yonny Hernández crashed more), it was mostly during practice sessions when he was pushing past the limit to establish precisely where the limit was. In every race Márquez had finished, he had been on the podium. He also became the first rider to win the intermediate and premier class world titles back to back and only the fourth man to become champion in all three GP classes after Mike Hailwood, Phil Read and Valentino Rossi. Mighty company indeed.

Julià Márquez was bursting with pride at his eldest son's achievement. 'It's as big as it gets.' He beamed. 'There's nothing bigger. He's won the toughest championship in the world. He's the fastest rider in the world right now.'[59]

HRC Vice President Shuhei Nakamoto was staggered by his rider's performance. 'Our bike isn't easy to ride,' he admitted. 'All our riders have needed a year to adapt before they understand our machine,' he said. 'But Marc was able to read it from day one, and that's why he ended up as champion.'[60] Nakamoto also stated that Márquez has 'the best reflexes I've ever seen in my life', which is what allows him to make such instinctive and opportunistic moves when chance presents itself.

Despite losing so many records to Márquez, Freddie Spencer was also seriously impressed by the young Spaniard's skill and feel. 'Marc is able to feel the edge of the limit, even when there's a lot of movement from the bike – and he can control that,' he said at season's end. 'He has incredible feel and is able to anticipate what's going to happen next. He is extremely intuitive. He's able to feel things when he's on the edge of control, and that allows him to be more aggressive and still be in control. That gives him a real advantage.'[61]

It was Márquez's calmness under intense pressure that impressed HRC Team Principal, Livio Suppo. 'Even when he was given the black flag at Phillip Island and thought he had lost all hope of the championship, Marc was very calm,' he said. 'The day before the final round, he said, "Tomorrow, we finish third," because he knew that, even if Jorge Lorenzo won that race, if Marc finished third, he would win the title, and this is what he did. He had a very clever idea of what he had to do.'

With testing for the 2014 season being held in the days following the final race of 2013, Márquez's title-winning celebrations were somewhat muted. 'We had a bit of a party, but always in moderation, because the next day we had the testing plan to follow,' he said. 'I was lying in bed thinking about spending my first night as world champion, but in the end I'm still the same. Not much has changed. Obviously, seeing all the media coverage is impressive. I've also received many messages of congratulations via Twitter, from other athletes and celebrities, which really gives you goosebumps! Maybe I didn't realise how important it is to be MotoGP world champion!'

The real celebration would be held in Cervera, a few days after securing the title. Márquez was paraded through the crowded streets on the back of a truck, bands playing everywhere, locals hanging out of every balcony with '93' flags, bikes revving their engines, horns and claxons being sounded, people in fancy dress, marching drummers . . . organised chaos. Márquez then took to a specially built stage to address the townspeople. Fireworks illuminated the night sky, and the streets were thronged with well-wishers, all enjoying the party atmosphere, and all extremely proud of what one of their own had managed to achieve on a global stage.

Being MotoGP champion certainly didn't go to Márquez's head. Despite all the hype surrounding him, he took it in his stride. 'I think I'm the least affected by it all, because I've always been pretty good at managing this and kept my feet on the ground,' he explained. 'If I don't, then those around me have my permission to make sure I do!'

There were no vulgar displays of his new-found wealth either, no playboy mansions or flash cars. He didn't even own a car, and he still stayed at home with his mother, father and brother, who made sure he never lost contact with reality. 'I have to clean, make the bed . . . but only in my room!' Márquez laughed. 'I also lay the table for lunch, and my brother Álex clears up when we are finished. It's always been that way.'

Just as Valentino Rossi had used his home town of Tavullia and his friends and family to remain grounded, Márquez did the same with Cervera and his own family. To the rest of the world, he was a god, but in Cervera he was just the local boy who raced motorbikes and was very good at it. He was just Marc, and his mother Roser loved him for it. 'He's the same son as always,' she said proudly. 'He might be the champion, but he's the same. It's so great. That's the lovely thing – the essence of the family. At least he hasn't talked about leaving us yet!'[62]

The problem with winning a world championship is that you then have it defend it, and most champions will readily admit that's an even more difficult challenge. In 2013, Marc Márquez had proven that he was the fastest rider in the world. Now he had a target on his back; he was the man to beat, and every other rider wanted to beat him. His job in MotoGP had just begun.

CHAPTER 5

DOMINION

'HE HAS ALL THE POTENTIAL TO BECOME THE GREATEST OF ALL TIME – BETTER THAN ME!'
Valentino Rossi

Becoming the youngest rider in history to win a MotoGP world championship changed Marc Márquez's life, yet he seemed comfortable with his new-found fame. 'It is true that, after winning the MotoGP title, I noticed a significant increase in my profile, and not only on the track,' he admitted. 'Logically, going from Moto2 to MotoGP, there is a noticeable change throughout the entire season, but especially when I got the title everything exploded. People recognise you more, you feel appreciated by the fans, and this is very important. Feeling their affection makes you feel more confident in yourself, and in being yourself, because you see that you have been accepted. This, for a rider, is a dream. It is clear that sometimes you'd like to be a "normal" person and go unnoticed on the street, but when people stop you and ask you for a picture, both inside and outside the circuits, it makes you happy.'

Márquez's rivals now knew what they were dealing with, and

it was clear that he was both feared and respected. 'His strongest point is either his talent or his ambition,' Jorge Lorenzo said at the end of the 2013 season. 'He always wants to be in front, so you can't relax. He has not so many weak points – they are very small; you can't say they are weak points.'[63]

Valentino Rossi was also magnanimous in defeat, for the time being, anyway. 'All this year Marc did something unbelievable – something special,' he conceded after the final race of 2013. 'It's something people will remember for the history of MotoGP, because he won the championship as a rookie. He did a great, great job.'[64]

Rossi even went so far as to suggest that Márquez might one day take his 'greatest of all time' or 'GOAT' title, saying, 'He has all the potential to become the greatest of all time – better than me!'

Even his Repsol Honda teammate, Dani Pedrosa – who must have felt at least a little put out after being beaten on the same bike by a rookie – had to admit Márquez was something special. 'The will of Marc, together with his talent, is a good weapon for MotoGP,' he said. 'He showed well every race but, of course, he rides on the limit. He seems like he is crashing all the time, but he is controlling that.'[65]

Unlike most of his MotoGP rivals who came up through the two-stroke 250cc class, where precision is everything, Márquez was the first to come to the premier class via the Moto2 world championship, and it showed. He hadn't been used to lightweight, prototype racing machinery but, rather, to fairly cumbersome bikes that couldn't be set up so precisely and didn't handle nearly as well. Given a prototype race bike in MotoGP, there was no stopping Márquez, and he found he could boss it around at will, never caring if the wheels were out of line.

His hyper-aggressive riding style was also a product of the Moto2 championship, where every tenth of a second counts and elbows are as essential as horsepower. He wasn't afraid to fight; to him, it was normal. He was a new breed. He even brought more extreme lean angles to MotoGP. 'Leaning off the bike as much as I do comes from Moto2,' he explained. 'Because, in Moto2, you really need to use all the power of your body to push the bike to turn, so this also makes the bike turn better in MotoGP.'[66]

There was even more reason to fear Marc Márquez at the beginning of the 2014 season. The previous year, he had been a rookie and was still learning how the RC213V needed to be ridden. He also had to learn new race tactics, he had to learn the strengths and weaknesses of his rivals, he had to learn how to conserve the Bridgestone tyres; he had to learn *everything*.

That was no longer the case. Better still, the 2014 RCV had been built around him, not Casey Stoner or Dani Pedrosa. It felt much more like 'his' bike, and that meant he could focus more on his racing rather than having to think about the motorcycle. Márquez had also established himself as Honda's undisputed number one rider, meaning he would now lead the ongoing development of the bike.

But perhaps most importantly, as a reward for winning the title in his rookie year, Márquez was permitted to bring his entire crew from his Moto2 days with him to the Repsol box, meaning he was reunited with close and trusted friends who could provide a perfect, friendly and relaxed atmosphere to the pit box that would allow Márquez to perform at his absolute best, with nothing lost in translation. Some HRC team members – electronics engineer Carlo Luzzi and mechanics Andrea Brunetti and Roberto Clerici – were retained, but otherwise, Márquez was surrounded by his own people. It was a tactic that had worked well for Valentino Rossi, and it would stand Márquez in good stead too.

Being able to bring his own team with him into the HRC garage was a measure of Márquez's power in MotoGP, as Team Principal Livio Suppo explains. 'In the first season in 2013, Nakamoto-San (Shuhei Nakamoto, HRC Executive Vice President) and myself suggested we keep all the Casey Stoner team, but Marc didn't want this. We agreed to change only the chief mechanic, so we allowed Marc to bring Santi Hernández with him. But already by Misano that season, when he was already very strong, he started asking to change more people and, at the end of the day, we had to. Not many riders have this kind of power.'

Suppo witnessed first-hand just how strong the bond between Márquez and his team was. 'All the guys who were working with him now were friends, and every race meeting, from Wednesday to Sunday, he would have dinner with his mechanics, whether he had crashed or won. He refused to eat until the last mechanic had finished working on his bike. He always waited for them. I have never seen a rider spend so much time with his crew. When you have this attitude, the more you are friends with your team, the better it is.'

Add to all this the confidence he now had after winning the world championship in his debut year, and the 2014 version of Marc Márquez was an even more formidable weapon.

As if to prove it, he dominated the opening winter test in Sepang but then broke his right fibula in a dirt bike training accident at home in Spain and was forced to miss the second test in Malaysia and the following one in Australia. He was unable to ride a bike for six weeks.

Márquez wasn't the only rider starting from a stronger position in 2014 (broken fibula notwithstanding). After two utterly demoralising years on an uncompetitive Ducati in 2011 and 2012, Valentino Rossi had learned how to enjoy his racing again when he rejoined Yamaha in 2013. He finished the season in fourth place and took a win at Assen as he started to find his once phenomenal speed again. He now looked every bit as strong as his teammate Jorge Lorenzo. The man who had adorned Marc Márquez's bedroom wall had stepped out of the posters and into Marc's life as a very real and very genuine opponent.

Márquez was fully aware that defending a title can be more difficult than winning it in the first place. 'The pressure is there: to be champion, to defend the title,' he said before the season kicked off. 'I'll have to be careful, because right from the first session we will have the world watching us. For the first race we have the excuse of having missed pre-season, so also, we ourselves will have to see how it goes.'

Defending a title was a new experience for Márquez, but he seemed to relish the challenge. 'It will be interesting to have the experience of defending a title, as before I always won a class and moved on to the next one,' he explained. 'This year, even though I am staying in the same class, it is a new challenge for me. I've never had this experience before and think it will be nice. I'm not running the number 1 plate, because 93 has brought me luck and I did not want to change it, but I know I'm the current champion regardless, and we will try to defend the title.'

He needn't have worried about his leg not being fully healed for the first round of the 2014 championship. As was now traditional, the opening race was held under the floodlights of the Losail circuit in Qatar and Marc Márquez kicked his season off with pole position, despite his leg not being fully healed. Just as had happened the year before, the race came down to a straight fight between Márquez and Rossi. Last time out, Rossi got the upper hand, but this time it was different. With Jorge Lorenzo crashing out on lap one with cold tyres, the last few laps became a classic tussle between the MotoGP icon and the young pretender intent on dethroning him. On this occasion, he did, leading Rossi over the line by a quarter of a second.

Next time out at COTA in Texas, Márquez was fully in command, dominating the entire event, right from the first free practice session. On the left-handed circuit that suited his style so well, he was a full second ahead of his closest rivals throughout practice and qualifying and broke the lap record twice on his way to setting pole position.

His riding was extraordinary; he bounced over kerbs, he laid down huge lines of black rubber from his spinning rear tyre, he saved a crash on his elbow by digging it into the track to hoist himself and his bike upright again . . . It was other-worldly to behold, and every rider in MotoGP knew they would have to change their riding styles if they were going to have any hope of ever challenging the Cervera rider. The overall impression was one of sustained aggression, and a rider can only sustain aggression if he is perfectly at one with his bike, as Márquez clearly was with the 2014 Honda RC213V.

He was no less dominant in the race. After making a jump start, Jorge Lorenzo led the first lap, but as soon as he came into the pit lane for his ride-through penalty, he was out of the equation. Márquez took over, set a new lap record on lap three, and was never headed. His win over Rossi was ultimately a narrow one, however, forced as he was to perform yet another miracle in the final corner when he saved a near-certain crash as his usually laser-focused concentration wavered temporarily. Two races, two pole positions, two wins.

In Argentina, Lorenzo at least managed to finish the race, but only in third place; he simply didn't have the pace to match the two runaway Hondas of Márquez and Dani Pedrosa. Márquez had started from pole position yet again and led his teammate over the line by a healthy 1.83 seconds to rack up his third consecutive win. He was starting to look unbeatable, his points gap over Pedrosa already 19.

When Pedrosa and Lorenzo got uncomfortably close to Márquez during qualifying for the Argentine Grand Prix, he pulled his helmet back on, went back out on track, and lapped three-quarters of a second faster than them: he was beating the greatest riders in the world at will.

Once he caught initial race leader, Jorge Lorenzo, Márquez was content to sit behind him, conserving both his energy and his tyres, but always looking like he could pass whenever it suited him. On lap 12, when he realised Dani Pedrosa was catching up fast, Márquez slipped past Lorenzo and stormed off into an unassailable lead, while Pedrosa eventually took Lorenzo for second.

Although so dominant, Márquez proved at Jerez that he was still learning new tricks. In the final 15 minutes of qualifying, every other rider would stop once to fit a new set of tyres in a bid to set the fastest time. With the Jerez circuit being one of the shortest at just 2.74 miles/4.42km long, Márquez decided on a new tactic and changed tyres twice, giving him an extra run on fresh rubber. He was not only blisteringly fast; he was clearly smart too. To do three runs meant using both his main bike and his spare bike, something no other rider was confident enough to do. No matter that the bikes are identical and have been set up in exactly the same way, riders always say they prefer their 'main' bike and can feel differences on their second one. Tiny differences make a huge difference when pushing the limits, and only Marc Márquez seemed able to ride his spare bike just as hard as his main bike. It would prove to be a huge advantage in qualifying sessions. His tactics worked, and he took a fourth consecutive pole position at Jerez.

The race seemed effortless for Márquez. After getting the holeshot from the line, he was attacked and passed by Valentino Rossi, but re-passed the Italian later on the same lap and proceeded to pull away. With a lead of over four seconds, he even had time to lift his left leg off the bike – while at near-maximum lean – to 'wave' at the Spanish crowd on the final lap. He seemed utterly unstoppable.

Ahead of the French Grand Prix, the announcement was made that Márquez had signed to ride for the Repsol Honda team for another two years. How much money Honda had to pay to secure his services was not revealed, but it probably wasn't far short of the record £12 million Ducati had paid Rossi when he signed a two-year deal in 2011. There was no mention of discussions with other manufacturers either, even though the reigning world champion and runaway championship leader must have been at the very top of all their shopping lists. But why leave?

'I am 21 years old,' he said at the French Grand Prix press conference. 'I'm not thinking about the money.' If he wasn't chasing a bigger pay cheque, then there was absolutely no reason to leave what was then the best team in the paddock with the best bike in the paddock. In addition, Márquez had assembled his dream team of trusted and loyal technicians around him, and he was dominating the 2014 championship. Switching camps would have been foolish.

On paper, it appeared that he enjoyed another flawless weekend in France, with another perfect pole position and race win, but the results belie how hard Márquez had to ride to achieve that win. After getting tangled up in a group of riders in the first few corners, Márquez was then pushed wide by Jorge Lorenzo and dropped back to tenth place.

By lap nine, he had set a new lap record to push his way up to fourth place. After passing Stefan Bradl and Pol Espargaró, he had to hunt down Valentino Rossi, the rider who was then widely accepted as the GOAT – the greatest of all time. On lap 13, Márquez pounced when Rossi ran wide and took control of the race. By the start of the last lap, he had a 3.4 second lead then eased off to cruise home 1.49 seconds to the good. In the process, he had made the best riders in the world look distinctly average.

Mugello had not been kind to Marc Márquez in 2013. He had endured four crashes, including his record-breaking 209mph fall at the end of the start/finish straight. He approached the 2014 event with a little more caution, feeling his way in practice rather than pushing the limits and risking another crash. He still did enough to set pole position, then pulled a sly move regarding his bike set-up. Realising the slipstreaming potential down the start/finish straight and over the crest into the first corner (where he had set his fastest crash record the previous year), Márquez asked his mechanics to fit a taller sixth gear to give him a top speed advantage over his rivals on that part of the track.

After sitting behind Jorge Lorenzo for much of the race, Márquez decided to make his move on lap 18, slipstreaming the Yamaha rider on the start/finish straight, just as he had planned.

Lorenzo was not for quitting, though, and fought back time and time again, both riders taking turns leading over the next few laps. As the pair began the last lap, Márquez pulled his slipstreaming manoeuvre again and this time made it stick – just. He led Lorenzo over the line by 0.12 seconds.

Something incredible happened at the Catalan Grand Prix: Marc Márquez failed to set pole position for the first time in 2014. He had been on pole in all six races so far, but a crash during the second qualifying session (his first crash of the year) scuppered his chances in front of his home crowd and he had to settle for third spot on the grid behind Pedrosa and Lorenzo.

The race itself was a nail-biter between Pedrosa, Rossi and Márquez and it all came down to the last lap. Pedrosa overtook Márquez for the lead into turn one then, at turn four, Márquez regained control before Pedrosa immediately passed him again. The battle was ultimately decided at turn 11 when Márquez, back in front again, changed his line to a more defensive one. Pedrosa, expecting his rival to take his usual line, ran into the corner hot, trying to take advantage. The tyres of both RCVs touched, almost bringing both riders off, and Valentino Rossi took advantage by slipping past Pedrosa for second place. 'On the last lap, you always try to win, of course,' Márquez explained afterwards. 'You know the second rider will try to overtake you. On that corner (turn 11) in the other laps, I always went fast and wide, then came back, but on that lap, I braked and stayed a little bit in, stopped a little more, and then I feel the touch.'[67]

Pedrosa didn't complain; he was happy to be competitive again after a lean spell and had clearly enjoyed the fight. It was all smiles on the podium, even though Rossi and Pedrosa must have felt they were racing for second place in the championship: Márquez now had a commanding 58-point lead over Rossi and a further five over Pedrosa in third. Lorenzo, in fourth place in the points table, was 97 behind Márquez and all but out of the picture.

Marc Márquez had something else to celebrate at the Catalunya GP – his brother Álex won the Moto3 race. It was only his second victory, after taking his first in Japan in 2013, and it marked the first time in history that two brothers had won two solo races at the same Grand Prix. Álex was in good company too, winning the race from future MotoGP stars Jack Miller, Enea Bastianini, Brad Binder and Francesco 'Pecco' Bagnaia.

Rain affected qualifying at Assen, but Márquez still managed to post a time good enough for second place on the grid ahead of what was to be the first genuine flag-to-flag Grand Prix in real wet/dry conditions (the flag-to-flag race in Australia which Márquez's team had so badly bungled in 2013 was down to tyre life concerns, rather than weather).

The Dutch race was delayed by 20 minutes due to the heavy rain, then got under way in mixed conditions, Márquez taking the lead before the end of the first lap, with the rain becoming heavier all the time. Then it stopped after six laps and riders rushed into the pit lane to switch to their dry weather bikes.

Márquez had a huge slide on his out lap on slick tyres and lost four seconds, allowing Andrea Dovizioso to take the lead. It took until lap 16 to get back past but, when he did, Márquez pulled away to win by over six seconds, with Dovizioso second and Valentino Rossi third.

Julià Márquez had more painful fingers than usual for the second Grand Prix in a row. It had always been his habit to keep his fingers crossed when his son Marc was out on track, and now that he had two sons out there doing the winning, he was setting himself up for some arthritic problems in later life by keeping his middle and index fingers crossed on both hands. 'He spends the whole session with fingers crossed – the whole session!' said

HRC Communications Director, Rhys Edwards. 'Try holding your fingers crossed for longer than five minutes – and he does it for the whole race! It's actually quite scary to watch a race with him, because any little moment that Marc will have, he shouts, or makes some movement, and it scares me more. I can't stand next to him.'[68]

The brothers found their father's behaviour amusing. 'He hopes that will bring us luck,' Marc explained. 'My brother and I like to tease him that he'll end up with arthritis because of us, but Julià is undeterred.'[69]

For the second race in a row, weather conditions played a massive part in the outcome of a Grand Prix, but in Germany the circumstances were even more bizarre. Having completed their warm-up lap on wet tyres, most of the riders then pulled into the pit lane to change to their dry bikes. This was permissible but it meant those riders had to start from the pit lane, and their position at the end of the pit lane was on a first-come-first-served basis. Qualifying now counted for nothing as the riders squeezed together in the narrow pit lane in rows of five, jostling for position. Márquez, clearly as fast in the pits as he was out on track, managed to secure a front row pit lane position.

Local hero Stefan Bradl did not enter the pit lane and instead made a compromise by fitting slick tyres to his 'wet' bike on the grid (wet bikes are run on softer suspension settings than are used for dry races) rather than going into the pits to change to his wet bike.

Bradl's gamble gave him an early lead in the race, but Márquez got past on the sixth lap and rode steadily to carve out a one-second lead and take his ninth win in succession. It seemed that, whatever the conditions, and however bizarre the circumstances, he was able to adapt, remain calm, follow a race strategy, and be faster than anyone else.

After setting pole position for the eighth time in ten races, Márquez took an incredible tenth win in a row in the Indianapolis Grand Prix. It was a staggering statistic, especially as he was racing against all-time legends like Valentino Rossi, Jorge Lorenzo and Dani Pedrosa. Even Márquez struggled to understand how he had been able to do it. 'There's no one thing you can say is key to winning ten races in a row,' he said. 'It's a combination of the bike, the rider and the team and, if that all works well together, and everyone is on the same wavelength, you can end up with the same team dynamic, which helps you achieve those results a bit easier.'[70]

In the Indianapolis race, the crucial move came on lap 11 when Márquez managed to pass both Rossi and Lorenzo to take the lead. He would never relinquish it and led Lorenzo home by a comfortable 1.7 seconds. His perfect score over the first ten races had given Márquez an 89-point lead over Dani Pedrosa with Rossi a further four points back.

It looked like his incredible run was going to continue after Márquez set pole again at Brno in the Czech Republic, but things didn't quite go to plan. Márquez had been accused of 'playing' with his rivals at Indianapolis, such was his dominance and apparent ability to overtake and clear off at will. He denied this, and his defence rang true at Brno as, for the first time in 2014, he didn't win the race. Moreover, the Czech Grand Prix marked the first time Márquez had ever finished a race in the MotoGP class without standing on the podium.

He blamed set-up and traction control issues, as well as a lack of rear grip, for his fourth place behind Pedrosa, Lorenzo and

Rossi, but he found a fix during the post-race test at Brno and was ready to resume his dominance at the British Grand Prix on the last day of August.

As odd as it may seem, Márquez was somewhat relieved to finish off the podium in Brno. 'The more you win, the greater your advantage, so the pressure *should* be decreased, because each time you win, you are having to risk less on the following occasion in order to push for the championship,' he said afterwards. 'Instead, every time I won, I was having more and more pressure, because I felt like people were just waiting for me to make a mistake. I always felt that the day I failed would make big news. Finally, when I finished fourth at Brno, it actually came as a huge relief as I was able to say to myself, "Okay, now people will stop talking about whether I can win all of the races – they will move on, so things will go back to normal, and I will be able to concentrate more on myself."'[71]

With some of the pressure off his shoulders, Márquez was in magnificent form at Silverstone. He took pole position yet again and converted that into win number 11 of the season.

For the first 14 laps, Lorenzo led, with Márquez having to ride hard just to keep up. Lorenzo later admitted that he 'rode like an animal' to stay in front of his younger countryman but, once the tyres were past their best, Márquez was much more comfortable sliding the rear. He passed Lorenzo but the Yamaha rider fought back and retook the lead. The ultimate pass by Márquez was full contact – and earned further criticism from Lorenzo – but it was decisive and, after making it stick, he went on to claim the win.

Valentino Rossi was back to his magnificent best at Misano, taking his first home win in five years. He was, by now, a veteran, and MotoGP had changed massively since he first raced in the class in 2000. Back then, the premier class was for 500cc two-stroke machines, a world away from the current 1000cc four-stroke MotoGP bikes, with their sophisticated electronics and absurd amounts of power. Tyres had changed too, and two years spent riding an uncompetitive Ducati hadn't made things any easier for him either. But now in his second year back with Yamaha, Rossi had found his pace again and, on this occasion at least, Márquez couldn't stay with him.

Starting in fourth place – the first time he had been off the front row in 2014 – Márquez engaged a fierce early battle with Rossi and Lorenzo and, after disposing of Lorenzo, had decided to sit in behind race leader Rossi and await his chance to pounce. When he did decide to attack, he lost the front in a low-speed crash, his bike stalled, and he lost one minute and ten seconds getting it fired up again. By then, a decent result was out of the question, but he still tore through the backmarkers to grab a single point for 15th place – his hardest earned point of the season.

Márquez's first chance to lift the 2014 MotoGP title came at MotorLand Aragón, and he was desperate to accomplish this in front of a Spanish crowd: too desperate, as things turned out, given the treacherous wet conditions.

His title attempt got off to the perfect start with yet another pole position after he 'took some risks' on a cold tyre to better Dani Pedrosa. In the race, Márquez fought hard with Jorge Lorenzo on the opening laps before Pedrosa stormed past into the lead. As the rain became heavier, however, both he and Márquez crashed out, leaving Lorenzo to take the win. Márquez remounted and took three points for finishing 13th, Pedrosa one position behind him. It wasn't enough to take the title at home, but the next round offered the second-best option. If he couldn't win his second MotoGP world championship in Spain, he could at least do it in the backyard of his Honda bosses in Japan, and at a circuit (Motegi) owned by the company. There was nothing the top brass at HRC would have loved more.

In keeping with the Márquez tradition, it was a feat never before achieved: Honda had never won a MotoGP title at the circuit it had built 15 years previously. Márquez had a golden opportunity to impress his bosses and essentially secure a factory Honda seat for life if he could pull it off.

Things didn't start well. Márquez crashed out of the very first practice session, though he escaped injury. Qualifying didn't exactly go to plan either and the champion-in-waiting had to start off the front row for the second time that year, in fourth.

In the early stages of the race, he admitted to riding 'stiff', his nerves seeming to finally kick in the closer he got to the title. He dropped from fourth to seventh in the first corner, knowing he would have to do better, or the title battle would roll on to Australia. Picking up his pace and gathering his composure, Márquez began picking up places and started closing down Rossi in second place. Jorge Lorenzo was out in front, but he was so far down the points table that Márquez didn't need to overtake him. He did, however, have to pass Rossi if he wanted to lift the title in Japan. He did so on lap 15 and, although Rossi immediately repassed him, Márquez lunged again, and this time made it stick. As he crossed the line ahead of Rossi and 1.6 seconds behind Lorenzo, Marc Márquez became a two-time MotoGP world champion and tore up the record books once again. At 21 years of age, he was the youngest ever double world champion in the premier class, taking over from the great Mike Hailwood who had held the record since 1963.

Márquez's outrageous form in 2014 meant he lifted the title with a full three rounds to spare, which was probably just as well, given what happened in Australia. The Phillip Island circuit has always been hard on tyres, and the cold conditions in 2014 saw many riders crash out while still fully upright as the centre of their tyres cooled too much. One of them was Márquez. He had set pole position and was leading the race before losing the front under braking and leaving Australia with no additional points. Not that they now mattered, but there was one more record that Márquez looked set to break, so it was still a disappointment.

In the long history of Grand Prix racing, no rider had won more races in a single season than Mick Doohan. The five-time 500cc world champion scored an incredible 12 wins from 15 races in 1997. There were 18 races in 2014, so Márquez did have more opportunities to win, but it was still a record worth having. Márquez had 11 wins, with another two rounds to go. It was within reach.

At Sepang in Malaysia, he set another record before the race even began. Not only did he take his 50th career pole (across all classes), but it was also his 13th of the 2014 season, beating the previous record of 12 poles in one season, held jointly by Mick Doohan and Casey Stoner.

With Jorge Lorenzo seeming to be somewhat lost on the Yamaha M1, his teammate Valentino Rossi was re-establishing himself as the number one rider in the garage, and it was he, rather than Lorenzo, who was now really taking the fight to Marc Márquez: the seeds for the epic 2015 season were already being sown.

In the Sepang race, Lorenzo pushed Márquez wide and down to eighth position in the first corner, but the younger Spaniard soon clawed his way back through the field and up to the fight for the lead. By half race distance, it was just Márquez and Rossi, the veteran and the pretender, the icon and the upstart. Rossi was now in his 19th year of Grand Prix racing, and was 14 years older than Márquez, but he was riding better than he ever had before, and the years seemingly meant nothing.

Rossi attacked Márquez repeatedly, and Márquez rode the wheels off his RCV in counter-attack but, as both riders' tyres lost grip, it was Márquez who adapted best – as he so often did on worn tyres – and he slithered and skated his way to the chequered flag, some 2.4 seconds ahead of the rejuvenated Italian, equalling Mick Doohan's 12 wins.

That left only the final round at Valencia, where Rossi denied him a 14th pole position but was powerless to halt Márquez's progress in the race, which was affected by occasional rain showers, though not quite enough to convince riders to change bikes (all bar Jorge Lorenzo and Andrea Iannone who took the gamble but lost). By the time the light rain abated, Márquez had pulled clear of Rossi and won the race by 3.5 seconds.

It was his 13th win of the year – more than any other Grand Prix rider had managed since the world championship was established in 1949, and it gave Márquez the title over Rossi by 67 points.

But the Márquez family would have more to celebrate that night; brother Álex's third place in the Moto3 race gave him the championship by just two points from Australia's Jack Miller. It was the first time in history that two brothers had won Grand Prix world championships, let alone in the same year, and it raised the enticing prospect of one day seeing the two Márquezes battling head to head in the MotoGP class.

But that was a prospect for the future. For now, Marc Márquez was the new undisputed king of MotoGP after such a dominant, record-breaking season. But the old king, Valentino Rossi, was enjoying something of a renaissance and was looking more dangerous than he had since last winning the title in 2009. He was coming. Of that, there was no doubt, and it was clear that he would do whatever it took to wrestle the title back from Márquez. The scene was set for one of the most epic, and controversial, seasons in MotoGP history.

CHAPTER 6

THE GOOD, THE BAD AND THE UGLY

'I WARNED MARC THAT OPPOSING VALENTINO ROSSI WAS LIKE CHALLENGING THE POPE.'

Livio Suppo

Valentino Rossi had been Marc Márquez's hero since he was a child. He was hero to millions of others too; as the most famous and popular motorcycle racer of all time he had transcended the sport and taken it to the masses, becoming a household name along the way.

He won a race in his first season in the 125cc world championship in 1996, won the title in 1997, moved up to the 250cc class, took a year to learn, then won that championship in 1999. He won the last 500cc Grand Prix world championship in 2001 before the introduction of four-stroke MotoGP bikes in 2002. He then won the first MotoGP championship that year and went on to win it again in 2003, 2004, 2005, 2008 and 2009. Nine world titles in total. He was desperate for a tenth. At the start of the 2015 MotoGP season, Rossi was 36 years old and knew time was running out. After two winless years with Ducati in 2011 and 2012, he had found his feet again at Yamaha and had been Márquez's closest challenger in 2014. He was back to his brilliant best and, knowing that Márquez was only going to get faster with more experience, he knew that 2015 might be his last chance to secure an elusive tenth world title.

It was often said that every round of MotoGP was a home round for Valentino Rossi. Certainly, every venue the championship visited was awash with Rossi's trademark fluorescent yellow; proof of his overwhelming popularity all round the world. But there was now a notable increase in the amount of red merchandise and flags in support of Márquez. His popularity was increasing rapidly, and he was seen as Rossi's natural successor and the man who would inherit Rossi's millions of fans once the Italian finally retired. At least, that was the assumption ahead of the 2015 MotoGP season. It would prove to be a false one. The season would unfold to be one of the most dramatic, exciting and controversial in MotoGP history, and it would prove to be a watershed year for both Valentino Rossi and Marc Márquez.

At the start of the season, both riders were still on good terms. Rivals, certainly, but in a civilised way. Márquez looked up to his hero and Rossi in turn was full of praise for the young Spaniard's riding abilities and achievements. Indeed, on more than one occasion he suggested that Márquez was his natural successor. But then the racing started, and all civility went out of the window: this was going to be war.

If Rossi was the established icon of MotoGP and the king of motorcycle racing, Marc Márquez was the young pretender. He had already beaten so many of Rossi's records and had achieved greater success at a younger age. He had also changed the MotoGP riding style, forcing everyone else to mimic his style or risk being left behind.

Márquez's style was dramatic in the extreme when he first appeared in MotoGP. His braking technique was heart-stopping, his lean angles seemingly impossible, and he hung off the bike much more than any other rider. He had learned in Moto2 that, the more he could hang his body off the bike while trying to keep the bike as upright as possible, the better he could save tyres and, when he moved up to MotoGP, he found that style was still effective.

The only other rookie to win the premier class Grand Prix world title – Kenny Roberts – had changed the style of riding by dragging his knee on the tarmac much more pronouncedly than his rivals. His knees acted as gauges, allowing him to feel how far his bike was leaning over. Márquez took the next step and started using his elbows as well as his knees. He wasn't the first to scrape his elbows on the ground, but he did so more often and for longer periods than his rivals. This effectively gave him stabilisers, and he prevented many potential front-end crashes by digging his elbow into the tarmac after losing the front tyre and forcing the bike back upright again. He could save crashes that others couldn't, and his style clearly worked overall, so even Valentino Rossi was forced to adapt and learn from the new kid on the block. Photographs taken after Márquez's arrival in MotoGP in 2013 show Rossi leaning his tall frame off the bike much more than he did before: to beat Márquez, he had to imitate his riding style. It was working too. He beat him at Misano and Phillip Island in the second half of the 2014 season and started his 2015 campaign with a belly full of fire. If Rossi was still to be known as the GOAT, then he would have to prove himself against the young upstart – he had to beat Marc Márquez, as whispers grew louder that Márquez, not Rossi, was quite possibly the greatest Grand Prix rider in history.

Márquez himself was at a loss to describe why he rides the way he does. 'Basically, I don't know!' he said. 'Just, I try to ride the bike. I think that is the best riding style, but in the end, sometimes I try to be more smooth or try to copy the style of (Jorge) Lorenzo, Dani (Pedrosa) . . . but I can't. When I concentrate, when I try to push, I start to go with my elbow, my knee on the floor.'

In other words, it was pure instinct. Even his braking technique was more radical than the others. Márquez braked so hard that he locked the front wheel, which meant the rear of the bike lifted off the ground and then pivoted round and snapped back down on to the tarmac, helping Márquez to slide the rear end and turn through the corners even faster. He used all the kerbs too, slithering and sliding and scratching his way round racetracks like no one before him. He was on the absolute limit; every corner of every lap, and it was pure dynamite to watch – it just wasn't easy to replicate.

Another rider who had been influenced by Márquez's riding style was Jorge Lorenzo. Still smooth, he had learned to be more aggressive and to pull similar moves. Frustrated at being overshadowed by Yamaha teammate Rossi in 2014, Lorenzo too felt the need to re-establish himself. He also hadn't won a title since Marc Márquez appeared on the scene, and it appeared his star was on the wane, his status as Spain's greatest rider under serious threat. The scene was set for an epic three-way scrap, the outcome of which nobody could have predicted.

Honda's upgraded RC213V was something of a shock to Marc Márquez. It had a far more vicious power delivery than the previous year's model, making it much harder to ride and, with MotoGP regulations stating the engine must be sealed after pre-season testing – with no further development allowed – he was going to have to deal with it, vicious or not. 'We are not allowed to touch the engine,' Márquez said, 'so we will have to fix it with electronics.'

First blood went to a rejuvenated Rossi, who won the season opener in Qatar. Márquez rode heroically; after being pushed off the track at turn one and dropping to last place, he recovered to finish fifth. Lorenzo – whose helmet lining had worked loose and obscured his vision – came home one place ahead of Márquez in fourth. Advantage Rossi.

Márquez's performance during qualifying at the Circuit of the Americas underlined just how alien he was as a rider; a once-in-a-generation talent. He was lying seventh when he left the pits to complete his second run. During his out lap, his RCV flashed a red warning light, and he was under orders from his team to stop immediately should that happen; with only five engines being allowed for the full season, HRC couldn't afford to lose one to a blow-up.

Márquez parked the bike on the track at the far end of the pit wall, leapt over the wall, ran the length of the pits and mounted his second bike. Despite the fact it had a soft front tyre fitted (Márquez preferred the harder option that weekend) and was set up differently to his number one bike, there was no time to make changes: he had to go. There was barely time to complete an out lap before his one and only chance at setting a fast flying lap.

Despite all the panic, the exertion of running the length of the pit lane in his cumbersome riding gear, and having to ride a bike that felt so different to his number one machine, Márquez rode like a man possessed and stole pole position from Ducati's Andrea Dovizioso. It was a sublime performance that proved not only how fit Márquez was, but how calm and focused he could be in a pressure-cooker situation.

In the race, after a short but fierce battle with Dovizioso in the early stages, Márquez took control and cleared off to win the COTA Grand Prix for the third successive year, each time from pole position too. With Valentino Rossi finishing third, he held on to his points advantage, five ahead of Márquez.

The race in Argentina came down to tyre choice. Márquez chose the softer of the hard tyre options while Rossi opted for the extra hard, banking on it offering better late-race pace. It did, and he caught race leader Márquez on the second to last lap and should, against any other rider, have been able to pass him and win with relative ease. But that would be to underestimate Marc Márquez. Caught by his title rival, he fought like a cornered lion, biting back immediately every time Rossi passed him, despite his tyres being worn out.

Refusing to give up, despite Rossi's tyre advantage, Márquez eventually pushed too hard, made contact with the swinging arm on Rossi's Yamaha M1, and crashed out of the race. His no-score dropped Márquez to fifth in the championship, while Rossi's second win of the season saw him extend his lead over Andrea Dovizioso on the much-improved Ducati. Lorenzo's fifth place saw him edge one point ahead of Márquez in the standings.

Following a motocross training crash, Márquez arrived at Jerez with a broken finger which hampered him all weekend. Lorenzo, after a slow start to the season, finally found his form and dominated proceedings, setting pole and taking a convincing win, with Márquez exhausted in second place and Rossi third. The points gap was closing between the three main protagonists of the 2015 championship, the drive to win at all costs increasing.

Márquez struggled throughout the weekend of the French Grand Prix with an RC213V that was sliding dangerously into every corner. While that may sound normal for Márquez, he pointed out that with the previous year's Honda, he was creating the slides on purpose, whereas now, the bike was doing it all by itself and Márquez was constantly trying to counter it. As a result, he could only finish fourth, while Lorenzo won and Rossi finished second. The dominance Márquez showed in 2014 was a thing of the past; he was now having to fight hard for every point.

It was no easier at Mugello. Still struggling with the set-up of his RCV, Márquez was forced to go through Qualifying 1 (the bottom half of the field) for the first time in his MotoGP career. The top two fastest riders from Q1 go through to Q2, but Márquez failed to get through, meaning he started from a very unfamiliar 13th place on the grid.

It wasn't within Márquez to chip away and make slow progress throughout the race. Instead, he came out all guns blazing, forcing his way past six riders on the way into the first corner, and taking another scalp on the way out. By the end of lap three he was in second place, but despite setting a new lap record on his charge through the field, Márquez couldn't catch runaway leader Jorge Lorenzo and, on lap five, he crashed out while trying to. Everything or nothing.

It was much the same script at home in Catalunya. This time Márquez lasted only three laps before attempting to overtake Lorenzo, clipping his bike and crashing out once again. The Yamahas had been greatly improved for 2015, as had the Ducatis, but Márquez was struggling on his overly aggressive Honda and was having to dig deeper than ever before to stay in contention.

Lorenzo's win took him to within a single point of Valentino Rossi at the top of the points table (a position Rossi had held all year) and Márquez's third crash in six races had seen him drop to fifth place, 69 points behind Rossi. A third consecutive championship was looking increasingly unlikely, and Márquez was growing frustrated. After his utter dominance of the year before, it was all the harder to accept. But there was still a world of fight inside him, as he proved at Assen, in what was one of the most dramatic finishes ever seen in MotoGP. As the 2015–2016 edition of *Motocourse* stated, 'Every lap of the Dutch TT (for historical reasons, the Dutch round of MotoGP is still referred to as a "TT" or Tourist Trophy) was memorable. The last was an all-time classic, a moment to be replayed for years to come. With an outcome of the greatest possible significance.'

After the post-race test at Catalunya, Márquez was happier with his RC213V. He was now running a hybrid bike: a 2014 chassis fitted with the upgraded 2015 suspension units. That left him feeling more in control of the bike. 'The new bike was very precise, good for one fast lap,' he said. 'On this one, I can make mistakes and recover from them.'

The problem for Márquez was that Valentino Rossi had a new chassis and also found it to his liking. The changes made his M1 easier to ride and he found he had more grip too. Jorge Lorenzo also liked the new Yamaha chassis, but he didn't find the extra grip like Rossi did; it was clearly something that came down to riding style more than hardware.

By lap three of the Dutch race, it was Rossi from Márquez with Lorenzo in third, but it was clear he didn't have the pace to run with the legendary Italian and the precocious young Spaniard, and the battle for the lead was going to be a two-man fight.

And what a fight. For the first 19 laps, Márquez showed great restraint in following Rossi at close quarters (rarely more than two-tenths apart) without trying to pass. He had obviously addressed the earlier handling problem with his Honda and looked smooth and in control. As did Rossi. Something had to give.

After Márquez made his move on lap 20, Rossi pounced back four laps later and entered the last lap with a lead of four-tenths of a second. As they approached the final chicane, Márquez made a lunge but, as the pair turned into the corner, Rossi was ahead, so he maintained his line and full contact was made as the two collided, both aiming for the same piece of tarmac. Márquez managed to stay on track and completed the chicane, while Rossi had been punted into the gravel and accelerated his way towards the line without completing the final corner. He got there first, then all hell broke loose.

Márquez argued that Rossi had cut the corner; Rossi countered by saying Márquez had pushed him off-track and given him no choice. Márquez also argued that he had been on the inside line, so Rossi should have lifted to let him through, while Rossi claimed he had right of way because he had been in the lead. After repeatedly viewing all the many camera angles they had of the clash, Race Direction declared it a 'racing incident', and the result was allowed to stand – Rossi first, Márquez second. So fast had the pair been riding, Jorge Lorenzo was a full 15 seconds behind them in third place. Rossi's win gave him a 10-point lead over Lorenzo in the championship, while Márquez loitered down in fifth place, some 74 points behind Rossi.

But the season was a long way from over and, at the final round before the summer break, Márquez rode the perfect race from pole position to take his third consecutive win at the tight German circuit of Sachsenring. His teammate, Dani Pedrosa, took second place, depriving Rossi (third) and Lorenzo (fourth) of valuable points. Márquez now found himself 65 points off the championship lead as the MotoGP circus took its three-week summer break; the three main protagonists mulling over how best to approach the second half of the season.

When racing resumed at Indianapolis, Márquez picked up where he had left off, setting pole position and passing under the chequered flag first to give Honda its 700th Grand Prix win. It moved Márquez up into third in the championship and another nine points closer to Rossi. There were now just 56 points in it, with almost half a season to go. He hadn't given up on title number three just yet.

Lorenzo's dominant win in the Czech Republic meant that, after 11 rounds, both he and Rossi were tied at the top of the championship on 211 points. Márquez's second place in the Czech race moved him to within 52 points of the joint leaders, but then came the British Grand Prix at Silverstone.

It started well enough for Márquez with pole position in dry conditions, but in the wet race, he suffered his fourth crash of the season, while Rossi's victory saw him stretch his lead over fourth-place finisher, Jorge Lorenzo.

The ground war dragged on. Márquez's win in mixed conditions at Misano was as much down to strategy as skill. Starting on a 'dry' bike then switching to his 'wet' bike when the heavens opened on lap six, he later pitted again to switch back to his dry bike when conditions started improving. Some riders risked everything by staying out on slicks, others pitted only once to change bikes; Márquez's tactics proved best, and he not only won the race, but also benefitted from Lorenzo crashing out and Rossi finishing fifth. But he was still 63 points off the championship lead, and he was running out of time to close that gap.

Márquez's hopes of closing it were scuppered by a crash on just the second lap of the race at Aragón, and in Japan he never found his pace in the wet conditions and had to settle for fourth place, all hopes of successfully defending his title now gone.

He was still determined to win as many races as he could, however, and he laid on a masterclass in Australia after a prolonged four-way scrap that was considered one of the best MotoGP races of recent times. While Rossi, Lorenzo and Andrea Iannone battled it out all race long, Márquez took a breather mid-race in order to save his tyres for a late-race attack.

Despite Lorenzo having an advantage of six-tenths-of-a-second on the final lap, Márquez caught and passed him with apparent ease to win the race. Valentino Rossi could only manage a fourth place and, while he was no longer worried about Márquez in the championship chase, he *was* worried about his teammate. Jorge Lorenzo finished the Australian Grand Prix in second place to close to within 11 points of Rossi.

Whether the pressure was finally getting to him as a tenth world title seemed within grasp, or whether it was just more of his infamous mind games, Valentino Rossi made some odd remarks at the pre-race press conference in Malaysia. Given how swiftly Márquez had caught and passed Lorenzo on the last lap of the Australian Grand Prix, Rossi suspected that Márquez had had the pace to win all along and had just been 'playing' and trying to hold him and Andrea Iannone up to allow Lorenzo to take more points. 'I think that his target is not just to win the race, but also to help Lorenzo to go far and try to take more points on me,' Rossi told the world's press, as Márquez sat alongside him. 'So, I think that from Phillip Island, it's very clear that Jorge has a new supporter; that is Marc.'

Rossi's mind games had helped him defeat Max Biaggi, Sete

Gibernau and Casey Stoner in the past, but he had met his match in Marc Márquez, who seemed to be immune to the Italian's attempts to out-psyche him. He even admitted to playing his own mental games with his rivals – the difference being he preferred to play them on track. 'Sometimes in training I try to do a real belter of a lap to make sure everyone else doesn't sleep too easily,' he explained. 'I want them to be concerned about me. Sometimes you also have to play things up a bit at press conferences. You can't show any nerves. You can't let anyone else see your hand. In the main, however, I go by what Mick Doohan (five-time world champion) said in 2014: "Beat them on the track, not with talk."'[72]

According to Rossi, Márquez's motivation to hinder him went back to the Rossi/Márquez clashes in Argentina and Holland, both of which Rossi won. Now out of championship contention, Márquez was, according to Rossi, trying to help his fellow Spaniard to win the championship and deny Rossi a tenth world title. With Márquez's devastating form over the last two years, Rossi realised the Spaniard could eventually overtake his tally of nine world championships. If Márquez helped Lorenzo to the title (thereby depriving Rossi of a tenth title), Márquez would need one less championship to beat Rossi's overall tally. It was clearly playing on Rossi's mind. 'He wants to beat me on the number of wins,' he said. 'So, if I win another world championship, he knows he will have to win another world championship to catch up.'

Sitting next to Rossi at the press conference, Márquez at first laughed at this accusation but, when he realised Rossi was deadly serious, he looked genuinely shocked. Where had this come from? On what were Rossi's claims founded? Simply because Márquez had won in Australia by saving his tyres for a last lap attack, then executing his plan perfectly? Andrea Iannone agreed with

Rossi that Márquez had been 'playing with them' in Australia, but everyone was else was astonished that Rossi would make such an accusation.

Jorge Lorenzo, for example, thought Rossi's outburst was ridiculous. Márquez had overtaken Lorenzo for the win on the last lap in Australia – how was that helping Lorenzo to win the title? As laconic as the Spartan warriors he so admires, Lorenzo quipped, 'Sure he helped me – especially on the last lap.'

Showing more than a hint of paranoia, Rossi even produced a meticulously prepared lap-by-lap analysis of the Australian race to show all the times where Márquez had baulked him. It reeked of desperation.

As Jorge Lorenzo and Marc Márquez both pointed out later, riders who are genuinely at the top of their game don't need to resort to mind games; their sheer speed is enough to win races. Mind games only tend to come into play when a rider doubts himself. In 2023, Márquez offered an explanation as to why Valentino Rossi turned against him. 'In 2014, after the race at Misano, I went to his (Rossi's) ranch. We were there for a day. We were competing over who could beat the record on his track and, starting from that day, I think something changed – the relationship cooled off a bit. I don't know why. Maybe he was bothered that I beat his track record, I don't know. The word on the street is that was one of the reasons.'[73]

While Márquez may have been surprised, or even shocked, by Rossi's words at the Malaysian press conference, they were only words, and after they had provided some juicy quotes for the international motorcycling media, most people put the incident behind them and moved on. Marc Márquez didn't. To be accused of dirty and conspiratorial riding by his former hero was a hard pill to swallow, and if he hadn't been at war with Rossi at any point in the past, he certainly was now. After receiving such an insult, Márquez was determined to prove a point in the Malaysian Grand Prix, and he would prove it by showing Valentino Rossi what he could really ride like if he was trying to impede someone.

The race itself has already gone down in MotoGP history. Showing a return to form, Dani Pedrosa took the lead and never looked like being caught. With Jorge Lorenzo established in a safe second place, the main interest focused on Valentino Rossi and Marc Márquez in the battle for the final podium position.

The two passed and re-passed each other endlessly, and it was clear to the 320 million people watching around the world that it was more than just racing – it was personal. Márquez appeared to be deliberately hindering Rossi and preventing him from setting off in pursuit of Lorenzo. Then, on lap seven of 20, the unthinkable happened; the two clashed yet again, and this time Rossi pushed Márquez out to the very edge of the track then appeared to kick his left leg out, causing Márquez to crash out of the race.

No one could believe what they were seeing. Had the golden boy of MotoGP finally become the bad boy of the sport? Had he deliberately kicked Marc Márquez off his bike? It seemed unthinkable. MotoGP is dangerous enough – as Marco Simoncelli's death at the same circuit just four years earlier had once again proved – so, to be lashing out at riders on 225mph motorcycles was, by everyone's standards, completely unacceptable.

In the pit lane, members of Márquez's Repsol Honda team threw their arms in the air in disbelief, while team boss Livio Suppo headed straight for Race Direction to lodge a protest. Rossi's Yamaha team looked desperately sheepish, and every bit as shocked as everyone else. They sensed there would be a price to pay, if the incident had really played out as it first appeared on the television coverage. There was footage from multiple angles, and every piece of it was combed over, rewound and looked at again. And again. And again.

As the most popular rider in MotoGP history, Rossi had untold legions of fans, and they instantly sided with him, claiming Márquez had taunted their hero to a point that was insufferable. Márquez's reputation as a dangerous rider didn't help his case. Was he an innocent victim, or had he deliberately baited Rossi, making a clash almost inevitable?

Livio Suppo knew Márquez would come off worst in any controversial clash with Rossi. 'I always told Marc that going against Valentino is like going against the Pope!' he says. 'Valentino was in MotoGP for many years, and he was the most popular guy, and the guy who did most of the winning, so it was not easy being his rival.'

Márquez remounted, but his bike was too badly damaged to continue, so he pulled into his garage and the doors were brought down instantly and firmly, to shelter him from the media frenzy that had already begun.

Social media lit up across the globe, as even non-motorsport fans joined in the fierce debate over whether the previously saintly Rossi had turned villain. Mainstream news channels around the world carried the story too, bringing MotoGP into millions of new homes: this wasn't just a bike racing controversy, it was a sporting controversy, a moral controversy, and it seemed everyone had an opinion about it.

It had previously been supposed that, when Rossi eventually retired, Marc Márquez would inherit his legions of fans; he was young, he was spectacular to watch, and he was a born winner. It made sense, but it clearly wasn't going to happen now.

By the time of the Malaysian Grand Prix, Márquez was out of the championship fight. He was 74 points down on Rossi with only 50 points available in the final two rounds in Malaysia and Spain. The title fight was between Rossi and Lorenzo, and there were those who argued that Márquez should have stayed out of the way of the two main protagonists. Of course, he was entitled to try for the best position he could manage, but it's something of an unwritten rule in racing that you do not unnecessarily impede the title protagonists because of the risk of affecting the outcome of the championship. Márquez wasn't playing by those unwritten rules, but it had been Valentino Rossi's accusations against him that had riled the Spaniard to the point where he no longer cared for niceties.

Rossi had done a similar thing to his teammate Jorge Lorenzo at Motegi in 2010. Despite being out of the championship chase, Rossi repeatedly attacked Lorenzo, who already had one hand on the championship trophy, but could have lost it so easily if his teammate had caused him to crash. Lorenzo was furious, as were all the top Yamaha bosses, who sat Rossi down for some stern words. They fell on deaf ears. 'Yamaha asked me to race with more attention,' Rossi said afterwards. When asked what he would do in the event of a similar situation arising with his teammate again, he smiled and said, 'I will try to beat him again . . . with more attention.'

Rossi was now blaming Márquez for riding exactly as he himself had against Lorenzo in 2010. In fact, Rossi's 'crime' was made worse by the fact that he was Lorenzo's teammate, so his current argument was tainted by hypocrisy.

That said, Márquez did seem to go out of his way to harass Rossi and to prevent him from chasing down his real title rival,

Jorge Lorenzo. During the race in Sepang, Rossi had passed Márquez and was trying to break away from him in order to chase down Lorenzo, who was in second place, while Dani Pedrosa headed the field. Márquez clearly did not have the pace to go with either Pedrosa or Lorenzo but seemed happy to apply a gargantuan effort to pass and re-pass Rossi, to interrupt his rhythm, and to prevent him from closing in on Lorenzo. In the first seven laps of the race, the pair changed places no fewer than 17 times, with nine of those passes coming on lap five alone. That early in the race, it seemed like madness: two riders constantly disputing position allows other riders to break away (and those behind to catch up) and both Márquez and Rossi were keenly aware of this. So long as they tangled with each other at every corner, Pedrosa and Lorenzo would increase their advantage.

Frustrated to near breaking point, Rossi threw up a hand and gesticulated towards Márquez on more than one occasion, clearly bewildered and angered at the Spaniard's tactics. Then, on lap seven, he looked over at Márquez and deliberately, and dramatically, slowed his pace as he entered turn 14, running wide and forcing Márquez to take an even wider trajectory around the corner. Márquez eventually had to turn in or he would have been pushed on to the dirty and slippery outer limits of the track, or even off it altogether, and at that point, since Rossi was still drifting outwards, the two bikes collided. In the ensuing tangle, Rossi looked directly at Márquez again then appeared to lash out with his left foot and kick his rival, causing him to crash.

Márquez went down, thankfully unhurt, while Rossi carried on, though he immediately looked over both shoulders to see what had become of his rival. 'At turn 14 he passed me on the inside, I sat the bike up, he kept going straight ahead and I saw him looking at me,' Márquez explained once he had calmed down sufficiently. 'I didn't know what to do. Then he kicked out at me, knocking my brake lever, and I crashed. I've never seen anything like it – a rider kicking another rider . . . I hope, for the sake of the sport that this ends here.'

Rossi denied that he had deliberately kicked Márquez off his bike, but it seemed obvious to both Race Direction and millions of TV viewers around the world that he did. It was only when the helicopter footage was shown that things became a little clearer. The aerial shots showed the bikes becoming tangled and Márquez's right handlebar snagging Rossi's boot. Rossi appeared to free himself by flicking his left leg. It still wasn't clear cut by any means (there's not much difference between a flick and a kick after all), but it did at least give Rossi a chance of making a defence.

'It's very clear from the images, especially from the helicopter, that I don't want to make him crash,' he explained. 'I just want to make him lose time and go out of the line and slow down, because also in Australia he make his dirty game, you know? When I go wide, wide, wide, I slow down, and I look at him like saying, "Fuck! What the fuck are you doing?" His right handlebar touched my leg, and I lost my foot from the footpeg. If you look at the images from the helicopter it's clear that, when I lose my foot from the footpeg, Márquez has already crashed so I don't want to kick him. Also, if you give a kick to a MotoGP bike, it doesn't crash – it's very heavy.'

In the melee that followed the incident, security had to be called in to prevent Rossi's fan club management from storming Márquez's garage – an unprecedented situation in MotoGP, and not one that was welcomed. Never had the GP paddock been so divided and forced to take sides. Never had it threatened to erupt into violence.

The on-track clash divided not only the paddock and the racing world, but the world at large. Despite benefitting from Rossi's actions, Jorge Lorenzo gave him a thumbs down on the podium and exited stage left before the champagne was even sprayed. He, for one, blamed Rossi but, such was the unwavering devotion of Rossi's fans, Lorenzo was booed and jeered for his gesture.

Rossi's former rival, Casey Stoner, was one of millions to voice his opinion on Twitter. 'If anyone else had done what Valentino did, we would have been black-flagged immediately, no questions asked.' Britain's four-time World Superbike champion, Carl Fogarty, was of the same opinion, saying, 'I think if it was any other rider they would have been disqualified from the race, for sure.'

Andrea Dovizioso, who crashed out of the Sepang race on his Ducati, saw things differently and perhaps offered the most balanced view of the incident. 'Márquez was racing for the podium, but also to disturb Rossi,' he said. 'Valentino's reaction exceeded the limits and it is not what we want to see. I believe Marc was provoking him and Rossi fell into his trap. Rossi contributed to the rising tension on Thursday (the day of the inflammatory press conference), and we can say that their relationship is finally over. For sure, Marc was playing with Valentino, but he remained within the rules.'

HRC Team Principal Livio Suppo was outraged at the time but now takes a more fatalistic view of the incident. 'It was the old lion against the young lion, and only one could survive,' he says. 'At the end of the day, Vale had been very strong for so many years and he was so good at putting mental pressure – psychological pressure – on his rivals. He did it with Max Biaggi, he did it with Casey Stoner, but with Marc he found someone who was as mentally strong as himself in this kind of battle. So, it was just a kind of change of a generation.'

Vito Ippolito, the president of the FIM (Fédération Internationale de Motocyclisme – governing body of world motorcycling championships), was not so sanguine. He published an open letter condemning both riders for their behaviour, accusing them of bringing the sport into disrepute. In the end it was Rossi who was punished: he was issued with three penalty points which – when added to the one he had already accrued in Misano for obstructing Jorge Lorenzo during qualifying – meant he would be forced to start from the back of the grid in the final race of the season at Valencia. The decision, in effect, decided the outcome of the 2015 world championship.

'Our opinion was that there was some fault on both sides,' said MotoGP Race Director, Mike Webb. 'But, as far as the rulebook goes, Márquez did not make any contact, did not break any rules as such, but we feel that his behaviour was causing problems to Rossi, who reacted. Unfortunately, he reacted in a way that is against the rules. It looked like we were going to have a great race, but unfortunately it ended in an incident that's controversial.'

Rossi immediately appealed the decision on the grounds that the penalty was too harsh, but the FIM stewards overruled him. He then lodged an appeal with the Court of Arbitration in Sport (CAS) – the highest body any sportsman can appeal to – but the court ruled that the penalty should stand while further investigations took place. Rossi would not hear the final outcome until long after the racing season was over and, in the end, the CAS ruled against him, so it didn't matter.

Rossi fans began an online petition to have his penalty overturned and it quickly attracted over 750,000 signatures, but it was also to no avail: Rossi would have to start the final round of the season from 25th place on the grid, though still with a seven-point lead in the championship. With 25 points going to the winner of a MotoGP race and 20 points available for second place, he would have to either beat, or finish second to, Jorge Lorenzo, or hope that the Repsol Hondas of Dani Pedrosa and Marc Márquez could finish ahead of Lorenzo and deny him a maximum points haul. It was safe to assume Rossi could expect no help from Márquez.

The atmosphere at the final round of the championship at Valencia was unlike anything the sport had seen before. Spanish police declared the meeting a high alert event and extra officers were brought in to bolster the already heightened levels of security amidst fears that Rossi fans and Márquez fans would clash. Repsol Honda team boss Livio Suppo admitted in 2020 that he had even suggested to both Márquez and Pedrosa that they should pull out of the race after one lap to avoid becoming involved in the title fight between Rossi and Lorenzo. His advice was ignored.

Márquez was treated despicably, not only by Rossi fans, but by the Italian media. Fanatical Rossi followers had issued death threats to Márquez on social media, and it wasn't the first time they had threatened, or actually attacked, a rider who was beating their hero. At the British Grand Prix in 2008, Rossi's rival Casey Stoner was riding pillion on a scooter back to the paddock after crashing in practice. Rossi 'fans' blocked his way, hurled abuse at him and spat on him. 'A couple of them even jumped in front of us, trying to make the guy riding the scooter lose control or crash,' Stoner reported.

The actions against Márquez by an Italian television crew were even more vile. Both he and his family were physically threatened at home in Cervera when a crew from the show *La Lene* (*The Hyenas*) showed up on his doorstep to present him with a 'Cup of Shit' award. A post on the TV show's Facebook page later read:

'This afternoon we went to Spain to try to deliver to MotoGP rider Marc Márquez the "Cup of Shit": a special award created to celebrate the "deeds" of the Spanish champion. We arrived near the home of the parents of the rider where we met Marc Márquez, his father, his brother and their friend. When we tried to deliver our cup, we were attacked, and a scuffle broke the camera and removed the video cards. Probably they wanted a bigger cup.'

Márquez's management released the following statement after the ugly incident:

Yesterday there were some unfortunate events in Cervera. A group of people appeared at the home of [Marc Márquez] and uttered a series of insults, performed certain humiliating and ridiculous actions toward the rider himself, and even pushing and assaulting [his] closest relatives. Given the seriousness of the action, such acts have been reported and the normal course of criminal proceedings continue against such persons.

So high were emotions running at Valencia that the pre-race press conference was cancelled for fear of inflaming the situation, and Yamaha even cancelled its 60th birthday celebrations that had been planned for that weekend. It was a mess, but a mess draws crowds. According to official figures, 110,000 fans turned up and packed the racetrack to absolute capacity while thousands more materialised without tickets, just on the off chance they might somehow get in. A ticket for the Valencia GP was the most sought-after sporting ticket in the world that weekend.

In the race itself, Jorge Lorenzo distanced himself from the feud in the best way possible – by clearing off at the front of the field and staying there until the chequered flag. He was never headed and took not only the race win, but also his third MotoGP world title.

Rossi rode magnificently, passing 20 riders to take fourth spot at the flag, but it wasn't enough; the championship was gone. For his part, Marc Márquez circulated in a comfortable second place throughout and was then accused of riding shotgun for Lorenzo to protect his race lead and his championship hopes. There may have been some truth in this: despite sitting just half a second behind Lorenzo for most of the race, he never once attempted to pass him. Rossi, unsurprisingly, agreed with the conspiracy theorists.

In 2023, some eight years after the event, Márquez finally revealed his approach to the race. 'Could I have risked it on the last turn without knowing what would happen? Yes,' he said. 'But the thing is, this person (Rossi) had done all this to me just because I passed him. Was I going to help him win a title? No.'

Such was the global support for Valentino Rossi that Márquez found himself being jeered and booed when he took to the podium; and this at a home race, on his own Spanish soil.

As one of the most dramatic seasons in MotoGP history came to an ugly end, racing fans remained divided, and Marc Márquez and Valentino Rossi went into the off-season as the bitterest of enemies. It would take a tragedy during the 2016 MotoGP season to put things in perspective.

CHAPTER 7

INVINCIBLE

'I BEGAN TO REALISE THAT, PERHAPS, SOMETIMES THE "ON/OFF" STYLE CAN BE DANGEROUS.'

Marc Márquez

Luis Salom was just 24 years old when he was killed at the Catalunya Grand Prix on 3 June 2016. He lost control of his Moto2 machine during Friday practice and travelled at speed into the air fencing at Turn 12, his bike striking him heavily and causing immediate cardiac arrest. He was pronounced dead one hour later.

Motorcycle Grand Prix racing has always been dangerous, but constant safety improvements – particularly since the 1980s – have made it far less dangerous than it used to be. In the 1950s, 29 riders were killed, in the 1970s it was 27, and in the 1980s, 24 lost their lives. By the 2010s, the figure was down to three, but MotoGP remains a potentially lethal sport.

In the vast majority of crashes now, riders simply walk away or, if less fortunate, break bones and suffer other injuries. Fatal crashes are, thankfully, extremely rare in modern MotoGP racing, which made Salom's death all the more shocking.

Against this backdrop, Marc Márquez and Valentino Rossi's feud looked petty, and both riders realised it would be disrespectful to continue it. After Rossi won the race in Catalunya and Márquez finished second, the pair shook hands in *parc fermé* and, on the surface at least, buried the hatchet and drew a line under the 2015 season.

Márquez later explained that he didn't view Rossi differently to any other rival – he was just another rider to beat, and it was better not to hold personal grudges in such a dangerous sport. 'You know, for me, the rivalry is with all the riders,' he said. 'On the track, you want to beat your teammates, your friends and the guys from other teams. In the end, all the riders, we must have a professional relationship because we are taking a lot of risks on the track. I already said [to Rossi] after the Valencia race – my hand is here. It arrived late, but it arrived, and this is the most important. I don't have any problem.'[74]

But the Catalunya Grand Prix was round seven of the championship; when the season started, the gloves were still off, the tempers still hot.

The controversy and drama of the 2015 MotoGP season resulted in frenzied interest in the 2016 championship. And a shake-up of the regulations made things even more interesting. Michelin replaced Bridgestone as the sole tyre supplier, and all teams now had to run control Magneti Marelli electronics – a much more basic package compared to what had gone before when manufacturers were free to run whichever packages they chose, and much more sophisticated ones at that. Honda in particular struggled to get its new reverse-crank RC213V working with the new standard software. The Repsol team became so desperate they even tried fitting the 2015 RCV engine into the new bike, despite

Honda's strong aversion to falling back on old technology. Right up until the last day of pre-season testing, Márquez and his crew struggled to get the new bike working as it should, and there were serious concerns about the coming season. When asked to describe his 2016 RCV in three words, Márquez responded: 'Restless, aggressive, nervous.'

Márquez knew the opening few rounds were going to be especially tough, so he brought a new approach and new maturity to his title campaign. He realised that he had ultimately lost the 2015 world title through inconsistency, and an inability to settle for safe points when a win wasn't likely – he had crashed too often and lost too many points. In 2016, he had a new plan: settle for the best points he could get in the early part of the season until Honda's engineers figured out how to get the best from the new electronics, then go all out for victories as soon as he felt like the RCV was working for him.

'In the beginning we were behind, and the winter tests were complicated,' Márquez admitted. 'I had several meetings with Honda during which I promised them that I'd be more conservative, and I focused on getting as many points as possible in the first races, but they had to help me in the second half of the season. I asked them to show everyone how Honda is able to react to challenges, because we were so far from our top level.'

Despite his pre-season difficulties, Márquez continued to believe in both himself and his Repsol Honda team. 'It's very important to have confidence and faith,' he said. 'I remember during the winter test, many people in the paddock were saying that winning the title this season was almost impossible for us because we were struggling more than expected. I felt very motivated at that moment because my belief is that nothing is impossible, and you must always keep working. It's true that it was a difficult moment, but as I replied at the time, Honda is Honda – a great factory that's very capable of reacting and my team is . . . my team!'

In his first two years in MotoGP (2013 and 2014), Márquez's Honda had been the best bike on the grid. In 2015, that started to change as the Yamaha M1s became the most user-friendly and effective bikes on the grid. In 2016, with Honda's electronics issue, this gap was even more pronounced, and Márquez knew he would have a struggle on his hands to beat Jorge Lorenzo and Valentino Rossi. To make matters worse, the Honda was down on top speed too; in the opening round at Qatar, Márquez's bike was over 5mph down on the fastest Ducati. 'Honda is working on improving the acceleration, and I hope we can find a solution as soon as possible,' he said after the Qatar race. 'We are struggling also in the middle and exiting the corner. This is also an issue we are working on in order to be more competitive.'[75]

Starting from second on the grid at Qatar, behind eventual race winner Lorenzo, Márquez had to settle for third after a last corner lunge on Andrea Dovizioso saw him run wide, allowing the Italian to claim second place. Valentino Rossi finished fourth.

With tyres disintegrating alarmingly – and highly dangerously – on the Termas de Río Hondo circuit in Argentina, a two-part race was called for, much like the one in Australia in 2013 when Márquez had been disqualified for completing one too many laps before pitting to change tyres. He – or, rather, his team – would not make the same mistake again.

With Márquez qualifying on pole in Argentina, and Rossi in second spot, fans and media alike were salivating at the prospect of the first head-to-head clash of the two titans since the infamous Malaysian round in 2015. In the first half of the race before the compulsory tyre change, the two did battle closely but, aware that all eyes were on them, both riders kept it clean and fair.

Márquez won the race into the pits and, while both men enjoyed fast and efficient bike swaps, Rossi got baulked by Tito Rabat on the pit lane exit, allowing Márquez an advantage he would never relinquish. With Márquez winning, Rossi was lucky to inherit second place after Andrea Iannone wiped out his Ducati teammate Andrea Dovizioso in the penultimate corner of the race. Márquez took the championship lead, with Rossi in second.

Then came the American Grand Prix at COTA; a circuit where Márquez had never lost a race. He didn't this time round, either, setting pole position and winning by eight seconds from Jorge Lorenzo, while Rossi crashed out, failing to score points for the first time in 24 races. Lorenzo inherited second place in the championship. It was Márquez's tenth consecutive win on American soil.

Rossi made amends at Jerez, setting pole and taking a runaway victory at the age of 37. Márquez, although it pained him, forced himself to refrain from an all-out attack on second-placed Lorenzo, proving that he was sticking to his pre-season philosophy. 'You will see the old Marc again,' he promised after the race. 'It is a big fight inside myself, but the bike is not ready, so I must be quiet.'[76]

The race in Le Mans saw eight riders crashing out, with the finger of blame being pointed at Michelin's front tyres. The French company was still learning after its return to top-flight motorcycle racing, and the French Grand Prix highlighted this. Márquez was one of the fallers and, while he managed to remount and finish the race, he crossed the line in last place; the only consolation being that, with only 13 riders finishing, he managed to score three points. Championships have been won by less.

After the French race, Márquez explained how difficult it was to stick to his new conservative approach. 'It took me losing a championship (in 2015) to understand that we should not seek victory at all costs, and that is a high price to pay,' he said. 'When I lost my leading position at Le Mans, I swore to myself not to push any more if I didn't feel it. That's what I did, and it wasn't easy.'[77]

Somewhat predictably, Márquez came in for more abuse at Valentino Rossi's home round in Mugello, being booed by a certain element of the crowd whenever he appeared on the big screens around the circuit. He tried to remain philosophical about the unsporting behaviour. 'I don't know if [the boos] will stop,' he said. 'It is said that time cures all, but I try not to think a lot about this. I'm focused on my work, to do my best and make happy the people who cheer for me which, fortunately, are a lot.'[78]

Amongst other taunts, Rossi fans displayed Photoshopped banners depicting Márquez and Jorge Lorenzo both topless, arm in arm, like lovers. It was part of the ongoing conspiracy theory that the pair were working closely together to prevent Rossi from winning another world title. That was, of course, utter nonsense but, for a certain element in the crowd, facts were not important – only blind loyalty to their hero.

Those fans left in their droves after Rossi's engine blew up in the Mugello race, leaving Lorenzo and Márquez to engage in a furious battle for the victory. They passed and re-passed each other, making contact at least once, and causing Márquez to lose an elbow slider. Despite having a three-or-four-bike lead coming out of the final corner, Lorenzo's Yamaha M1 out-dragged Márquez's RCV to the finish line, backing up Márquez's claims that the Honda – with the new standard electronics not yet fully understood – simply wasn't making enough power. The Spaniard, famous for his last corner do-or-die attacks, was hobbled. 'Today, I lost the race in the last 50 metres,' he bemoaned. 'That has never happened before in my career.' It didn't matter too much, though; with Rossi scoring no points, Márquez extended his lead over him to 27 points, though he dropped five points to leader Lorenzo.

Then came the tragedy in Catalunya when Luis Salom lost his life following a crash in practice. The race was close to being abandoned but got a last-minute reprieve when the track was altered at Turn 12 (where Salom crashed) to provide a greater run-off area, and Salom's bereaved family nobly gave their blessing for the meeting to go ahead.

It's not easy for any rider to race after just losing one of their own, and the one-minute silence in tribute to Salom – held in front of a crowd of 100,000 – only served to emphasise the risks the riders were about to undertake.

A wayward Andrea Iannone took Jorge Lorenzo out of the race and that left a square fight between Márquez and Rossi, the Italian veteran riding as well as ever to take the win after an epic confrontation. Márquez took the lead with two laps to go, but later ran wide on the final circuit and finished 2.65 seconds adrift of Rossi.

Márquez left Catalunya with a new two-year HRC contract in his pocket and the championship lead. He now had ten points over Lorenzo and 22 over Rossi, despite all the problems he'd had with the 2016 RC213V. His new mature approach was working – by settling for solid points when winning would prove too risky, he had chipped away at his rivals and worked his way to the top of the points table. He was now the hunted, not the hunter, but he preferred things that way, as he explained after the Catalunya GP. 'Of course you like to be at the top, because then you have some margin, and some points between . . . now it's ten points. You prefer to lead the championship because, if you do a mistake – like in Le Mans this year where I crashed and took only three points – they reduce the advantage, maybe they overtake you, but you're there. But if you're second or third, you know that you cannot lose, you cannot do any mistake.'

Márquez had also learned that there was no point in risking anything against riders who weren't in championship contention, and he proved this by taking a safe second place behind Australia's Jack Miller, who won his first Grand Prix at Assen in atrocious conditions.

Márquez crashed twice during practice for the Dutch round, but that was part of his new strategy too; after losing so many points during the 2015 season, he realised he couldn't afford to crash out of races, so he now only pushed the limits in practice when he could afford to crash out. Once he had found the absolute limit, he could then pull back just a fraction for the race.

The 20 points he gained for second place at Assen were bolstered by Rossi crashing out and Jorge Lorenzo only being fast enough in the sketchy conditions for tenth place. That left Márquez with a 24-point lead, and perhaps a feeling – which he certainly didn't have throughout pre-season testing – that he might even be able to take title number three. The RC213V was finally coming good.

After taking three solid and safe second places, Márquez the gambler reappeared in Germany. The race had started wet, but as a dry line started to appear, he came into the pits and changed to his second bike which was fitted with slick tyres. He pitted on lap 17 and dropped from eighth place to 14th, some 38 seconds behind race leader Andrea Dovizioso. But his pace with slicks on a drying track was phenomenal. Within five laps he was up to sixth place, though still some 20 seconds behind the leader. He was seven seconds a lap faster than the lead riders, however, and none of the lead group had stopped to change bikes. Márquez took the lead on lap 25 and, by the start of the final lap he had a lead of over 20 seconds. It was pure Márquez magic; his brave gamble and exceptional riding in such treacherous conditions giving him another 25 points on a day when Valentino Rossi could only finish ninth (he failed to see his pit board instructing him to pit to change tyres) and Jorge Lorenzo an even more disappointing 15th, still struggling with bike set-up. It was the halfway point of the season and Márquez had a 48-point lead over Lorenzo and another 11 points over Rossi. He had taken control of the 2016 world championship.

When Grand Prix racing returned to Austria for the first time in 20 years, Marc Márquez became an early victim of the super-fast Red Bull Ring circuit. He crashed and dislocated his shoulder but, undeterred, had it popped back into place and managed to qualify in fifth place. Fighting through the pain, fifth place was the best he could manage in the race, but he was more than happy with the damage limitation exercise. 'After how yesterday went, I'm happy,' he said, adding that fifth was 'the best possible outcome, and we've only lost five points compared with Lorenzo (who finished third). With our difficulties, my objective was to think of the championship.'[79]

By the time of the Czech Grand Prix, Márquez had already made a habit of saving slides that would almost certainly have resulted in crashes for most other riders. He did so again during practice at Brno, somehow managing to right his bike with his elbow after it had registered an angle of 67.5 degrees and slid for an age. Even Valentino Rossi felt such saves were beyond him – although his compliment came with a sting in the tail. Rossi said Márquez saves the near crashes 'because of his position on the bike, and because of his talent. I don't know if I could do it. But I ride a bit slower, so I don't lose the front.'

With his Honda more upright, Márquez smashed the existing lap record to set pole position. But after opting for the softer rear tyre on a damp track during the race, he could only nurse his Honda to third place, while Cal Crutchlow and Valentino Rossi chose the harder rear tyre and finished first and second respectively.

Márquez also blamed a poor tyre choice for his fourth place in the British Grand Prix at Silverstone and, for the second race in succession, he lost points to Valentino Rossi, though he still held a commanding 50-point lead, thanks to his new, more measured approach to races – if you can't win, grab some big points rather than crashing out and scoring none. His consistency was paying off.

He played the same game in Misano – where he once more chose the wrong tyre for the race – and got the same result; another fourth place, while his teammate, Dani Pedrosa, made a welcome return to the top of the podium, his light weight putting less stress through his tyres. Márquez once again revealed he was thinking of the bigger picture, rather than of individual race-winning glory. 'When Dani passed, I tried to follow him,' he said, 'but I saw that it was more likely I would crash than finish on the podium.'

Pedrosa's win meant there had been eight different winners from eight races, so the strong finishes Márquez was picking up were crucial to his points tally. As wild as he still looked on the bike, he was now a calculating strategist and, in MotoGP, that's almost as great a weapon as raw speed.

That didn't mean Márquez had given up on winning; far from it. He was in devastating form at Aragón, setting pole and streaking away at the front of the pack come the race itself. Once again, his cat-like reactions saved him when he all but crashed on the third lap. This time, even he was at a loss to explain how he did it. 'I was on the ground!' he said. 'I don't know how I saved it.' Yet save it he did, and learned from it; after that, he forced himself to calm down and let his tyres come to him. Once they did, he was unstoppable, and he led Jorge Lorenzo and Valentino Rossi home to extend his points lead. He openly stated that he had to stop Rossi from gaining points on him, as he had done in the preceding rounds because, otherwise, the Italian's 'mentality would go up'. In other words, he couldn't allow Valentino to gain more confidence.

Having raced against them for almost three seasons, Marc Márquez was in a unique position to assess the strengths and weaknesses of his two main rivals, Jorge Lorenzo and Valentino Rossi. 'On the racetrack, when Lorenzo has the day, he is really, really fast,' he said. 'He is stronger than Valentino. For me, Lorenzo is faster around a lap, but on the other side, Valentino has a lot of experience; he knows how he can take the profit of any situation. He's very tough to beat when he's having a fast race. Even if he isn't the fastest guy of the weekend, he's able to get there. He is very consistent.'[80]

As the riders and teams set up their travelling circus at Motegi in Japan, there were still four races left in the 2016 world championship and, while Márquez had a healthy 52-point lead over Rossi, and a further 14 over Jorge Lorenzo, his lead was by no means unassailable, so no one was predicting the world championship to be won or lost in Japan. As things turned out, it was.

To take his third MotoGP world title, Márquez would have to win the Japanese Grand Prix, Rossi would have to finish no higher than 15th place, and Lorenzo would have to finish lower than fourth. It seemed highly unlikely.

The three title protagonists traded blows in the early laps of the race before Márquez pulled clear on lap four. Realising that they had to beat him to keep their title hopes alive, Rossi and Lorenzo pushed extra hard to stay in the fight; too hard, as it happened. Rossi crashed out on lap seven and Lorenzo on lap 20, handing the 2016 MotoGP world championship to a surprised Márquez, who led Andrea Dovizioso over the line by 2.99 seconds.

Including his Moto3 and Moto2 crowns, it was Márquez's fifth world title, and he was still only 23 years and 242 days old, making him the youngest rider to ever win three MotoGP titles. Mike Hailwood had previously held the record at 24 years and 108 days. With nine world championships and 14 Isle of Man TT wins to his name, Hailwood was considered by many to have been the greatest motorcycle racer of all time, so for Márquez to now be mentioned in the same sentence showed the giddy heights he had reached.

He also became the youngest rider to win five world championships, this time taking the record from his arch nemesis, Valentino Rossi. Márquez's bosses at Honda were ecstatic. It was his first race victory at Motegi – a circuit owned by Honda – and to lift the title with a race win in front of all the Japanese bosses of the company was something special.

Márquez himself seemed as surprised as he was delighted. 'It's incredible!' He beamed afterwards. 'Before the race I didn't expect to be champion, and I said that here it would be impossible. However, when I saw that Rossi was out of the race, I decided to push hard for the victory. I was riding my hardest, and when there were three laps to go, I read on my pit board that Lorenzo was also out. On that same lap, I made mistakes in four or five corners as it was difficult to stay focused! I'm very happy because this title is very special considering some of the crashes I had last year, and also because it came at Motegi – Honda's home. Honda has worked so hard this year, and you could see the fruits of that effort also at this track, where we've struggled in the past. I myself also improved during the season; for instance, I learned how to better use the front Michelin tyre. It has been a demanding year, but a fantastic one. It's great for my team, and of course I don't want to forget my grandmother, who passed away this year and would be very happy with this world championship. Now we can just enjoy it and go into the last three races with maybe a more "Marc Márquez" style.'[81]

There were still three rounds left of the 2016 season and, with the title in the bag, the old Marc Márquez showed up at the next round in Australia, ready to ride way over the limit because it no longer mattered if he crashed. And crash he did, in spectacular style. After dominating practice and setting pole position, he took off at the start of the race and never looked like being challenged. The only person who could beat him was himself, and this he managed to do on the tenth lap when he lost control at the hairpin on lap ten and completely destroyed the bike that he and his team had worked so hard to improve throughout the season.

Márquez was unscathed and flew to Malaysia for the penultimate round. Somewhere along the way he picked up a stomach bug and was forced to miss Friday practice. Having recovered by race day, he started from fourth on the grid, but his race lasted just 12 laps before he crashed out of fourth place. He remounted and fought back up to 11th, but must have been grateful that he'd wrapped the title up so early, given the disastrous results he'd had since the Japanese round.

There would be no fairy-tale win at the last race of the season in Valencia either, despite a hugely heroic effort on Márquez's part. Caught up in the pack after a bad start, overtaking was hazardous as there was only a very narrow dry line on the otherwise damp track but, throwing caution to the wind again – 'I had nothing to lose' – he carved his way up to second place and was lapping half a second faster than race leader Jorge Lorenzo when he simply ran out of laps.

It didn't matter. He had proven that the 2015 season had just been a blip in his otherwise perfect career trajectory. He had learned from it though and evolved a new style in 2016 because he had lost too many points being overambitious the previous season. 'I began to realise that, perhaps, sometimes the "on/off" style can be dangerous,' he explained at the end-of-year 2016 FIM conference. 'We tried to handle it a different way this year and we did it well.'

He was world champion again, he had renewed his contract with HRC for another two years, and he had everything he needed to challenge for another title in 2017. Marc Márquez was on top of the world.

CHAPTER 8

MAXIMUM RISK

'YOU NEED TO RELEASE THE BRAKES AND BELIEVE.'

Marc Márquez

When the racing stops, the hard work begins. After the last Grand Prix of the 2016 season, Marc Márquez said, 'Now, the part of the job I find the hardest starts, even though it may be the least physically demanding aspect, but for me it's the busiest: interviews, events, press . . .'[82]

There would be some time to relax before his title defence began, but precious little. 'We'll rest up for at least two weeks, a bit of relaxation and rest so my body can recuperate. Then, we'll start with the pre-season work properly, training like normal and how we have done for the past year, all in preparation for the first test in Malaysia.'[83]

After spending months dialling in his 2016 bike with the new one-make electronics package, Márquez faced another struggle in 2017 with Honda's latest version of the RC213V. With a lighter crank and a new 'big bang' firing order (where all four cylinders fire in one revolution), the Honda's power delivery was hyper-aggressive once again, and it would take four months for the team to fine-tune it to Márquez's liking. 'It has changed a lot, and in different ways,' he said of the new bike. 'Above all, we have worked a lot on electronics because the engine is different this year and we have had to adapt many things. We have also worked hard to have a solid base for all circuits, because on a race weekend we do not have much time to test things out.'[84]

Márquez remained optimistic, however, and felt ready to mount his defence. 'We come into this season better than last season, but this does not mean that the result will be better,' he said. 'What is true is that we have prepared well. Physically I am at 100 per cent and mentally I am also very motivated, as always, to try to fight for the title for another year.'[85]

There were two major rider changes for the 2017 season. Jorge Lorenzo, tired of being Valentino Rossi's teammate, had jumped ship to Ducati, and Maverick Viñales moved over from Suzuki to replace him. While Lorenzo initially struggled to adapt his riding style to the Ducati, Viñales was fast from the off, setting pole in Qatar then converting it into a race win.

With the race being shortened due to weather conditions, both Márquez and Dani Pedrosa had no choice but to run the softer rear tyre (both riders preferred the harder rear, but it was built for a longer race) and both suffered accordingly. The new Honda was already struggling with acceleration out of corners, and the slippery conditions and unfavoured softer tyres only made matters worse. Márquez finished off the podium in fourth place with Pedrosa right behind him. The tyre choice had been the 'biggest mistake of the weekend', Márquez said. 'I couldn't brake hard, and after a few laps the tyre was already wearing off. Braking is my strongest point.'

After qualifying in pole position in Argentina, Márquez was planning to make up lost ground, but the second round of the championship was even worse for him. Despite race day being cool and dry – ideal conditions for Márquez and the Honda – he would crash out and score no points. He had made a blistering start and, by the end of lap three, had a 2.2-second lead over Maverick Viñales but lost control of the bike at Turn 2 on the fourth lap – the same spot where he had crashed during practice. In his five years in MotoGP, it was the first time Márquez hadn't taken a podium in the first two rounds. He had never been as low as eighth place in the points standings either. He needed a result.

He got one in America. Again. There would be another two crashes during practice, but Márquez seemed to be completely invincible on US soil. Since he first raced stateside in Moto2 in 2011, he had won every race at every American circuit the MotoGP championship visited – Circuit of the Americas (COTA), Indianapolis and Laguna Seca. The sheriff's badge logo he wore on his helmet at COTA had been well earned.

With Viñales crashing out of the race and Márquez clearing off to win after brief tussles with Valentino Rossi and Dani Pedrosa, he leapfrogged up to third place in the championship as the circus moved on to Jerez in southern Spain.

It was to be Pedrosa's weekend and, while Márquez closed to within a second of him late in the race, he almost crashed in the attempt to catch him and decided that caution was the better part of valour. Second place would do.

The real surprise of the weekend was Jorge Lorenzo taking a podium on the Ducati, after having finished 11th in Qatar, ninth in America and crashing out in Argentina. It looked like the Spaniard had finally figured out how the Desmosedici needed to be ridden.

The paddock in Le Mans was a sombre one as news filtered through that 2006 MotoGP champion, Nicky Hayden, was fighting for his life following a road cycling accident in Italy. The former Repsol Honda rider was a hugely popular character, and the news came as a huge shock not only to the Repsol team, but to the wider racing world.

The weekend proved to be another crash-fest for Marc Márquez. Not only did he fall twice in practice, but he also crashed out of the race on the 18th lap, very lucky to escape injury at the frighteningly fast Turn 1. Crashing in practice was one thing, doing it in the race was another. Márquez knew better than to take massive risks and, potentially, take no points, but he blamed the front Michelin tyre, or rather, his lack of confidence in it. Other riders were experiencing the same issue, and Michelin admitted the firm was still learning the fine art of producing MotoGP tyres, despite now being in its second year as sole supplier.

With no points scored in France, Márquez dropped to fourth in the championship standings while race winner Maverick Viñales took over the lead from Valentino Rossi. More worryingly, Márquez's own teammate, Dani Pedrosa, was now in front of him. His title defence was not going to plan.

Huge tributes to Nicky Hayden dominated the paddock at Mugello and 69 seconds of silence (reflecting his race number) were observed on the grid in his honour before racing got under way. The American had lost his fight for life shortly after the paddock had decamped from the French Grand Prix.

Márquez once again struggled with the Michelin tyres – as did every Honda rider – and decided to settle for a safe sixth place rather than risk crashing. Andrea Dovizioso won the race and was becoming an ever-increasing threat as he got the Ducati working for him. Márquez no longer had just Valentino Rossi and Jorge Lorenzo to worry about; he now had Dovizioso and Maverick Viñales joining the party as regular race winners.

Even for a rider so used to pushing beyond the limits, five crashes during practice and qualifying in Catalunya was rather extreme, but at least Márquez didn't add a sixth in the race. Instead, he was again hampered by tyre problems and knew that if he pushed any harder, he would crash out. Once again, he chose the safer option and settled for second place, while Andrea Dovizioso took a second consecutive win. Viñales now led the standings on 111 points while Dovizioso had 104 and Márquez 88. It was still all to play for.

But the fight, and the stress, were taking their toll on Márquez. After the Catalunya Grand Prix, he went for a haircut and was told by his barber that he was losing hair from the back of his head. Concerned, he then visited a doctor. Márquez later revealed what the doctor told him. 'He said, "You need to change the mentality – you need to absorb the problems in a different way, because you are creating inside of you a kind of stress; a nervous mix of things, so that you are losing the hair." Since that point I changed a bit the mentality. I was able to be better on the bike, but also to understand, and absorb in a different way, the problem.'[86]

Valentino Rossi's win at Assen saw him leapfrog Márquez in the points table after the latter had just pipped fellow Honda rider Cal Crutchlow for the final podium spot. Despite only finishing fifth, Andrea Dovizioso took the lead in the championship points for the first time all year. The top four were now covered by just 11 points – a new record, this deep into a season (eight rounds down).

In those eight races, Marc Márquez had only taken a single victory (in America) and looked like he'd lost the glorious dominance he had enjoyed in previous years. He badly needed a win if he was to have any hope of battling for a fourth MotoGP title.

It came at his beloved Sachsenring; the tight, twisty, anti-clockwise German circuit that had always been a happy hunting ground for Márquez. He ruffled new feathers during qualifying; this time those of Maverick Viñales. It looked like a racing incident to neutral observers, but Viñales insisted Márquez cut across him on purpose, trying to assert his dominance. Even after Márquez apologised, Viñales was simmering. 'It's hard not to do that on purpose – it was timed,' he said of Márquez's move. 'I'll remember it, and when I have to use it, I will. If Márquez is trying to wind me up, he won't find anything.'[87]

Starting from pole position at the Sachsenring, Márquez had a surprise challenger in the form of home hero Jonas Folger, but put the hammer down in the last three laps to beat the German rider by 3.3 seconds. It was Márquez's eighth straight win at the Sachsenring and it elevated him to the top of the points table, but the margins were tiny: he had a five-point lead over Viñales, who in turn had a one-point lead over Andrea Dovizioso, with Rossi just four points behind his fellow Italian. MotoGP had never been tighter after nine rounds.

The paddock was once again in mourning at Brno in the Czech Republic, this time over the death of Spanish racing legend Ángel Nieto. The 13-time world champion of the 50cc and 125cc classes had been riding a quad bike in Ibiza when he was hit by a car. The news especially affected the large Spanish contingent in the paddock, amongst them Marc Márquez. In light of the loss, Márquez decided to throw caution to the wind, to try to win the race in Nieto's honour. It was, he said 'a day to take risks', and risks he certainly took.

He began taking them in practice, almost crashing on two

separate occasions, but both times avoiding going down by digging his elbow into the tarmac and lifting his RCV upright again. As paradoxical as it seems, Márquez took this as a great sign; it meant that he finally had the RCV dialled into the way he liked to ride it and could now perform minor miracles on the machine. He could ride like Marc Márquez again, trusting his instinct and feel, and getting enough feedback from his bike to push it to the outer limits relatively safely. It was an ominous sign for his rivals.

Márquez's performance in the Czech Grand Prix was a near-perfect combination of race strategy, risk and sublime feel for the conditions, as well as total mastery of his 300bhp motorcycle. He led off the line from pole position, but by the second lap was dropping down the order at an alarming rate. He pitted at the end of the lap to change from wet tyres to slicks as a dry racing line began to appear on the damp track. The leaders continued racing on their wet tyres, unwilling to take the gamble of changing to slicks on a track that was still more wet than dry, and unwilling to lose track position to their rivals.

By the time he rejoined the race on lap three, Márquez was in 19th place and 22 seconds down on race leader Jorge Lorenzo, but such was his pace on slick tyres, even in treacherous conditions, he was soon up to 12th place and lapping ten seconds faster than new race leader Valentino Rossi: the game was on.

As more and more riders entered the pit lane to change bikes, they lost time, handing the advantage to Márquez who worked his way back up to the lead and then carved out an advantage of almost 20 seconds over the fastest riders on the planet. He eventually beat Dani Pedrosa over the line by 12.44 seconds and increased his championship lead. Márquez 154, Viñales 140, Dovizioso 133, Rossi 132.

The tide was turning. Márquez now had his Honda set-up exactly to his liking, and he had now won three races; it looked like momentum was back on his side. 'The improvements that we've made to the set-up during the season helped me to feel so much more comfortable on the bike,' he would later say. 'And when you have good feelings, you have more confidence, and this allows you to push to the limit.'[88]

Bike racing annual *Motocourse* stated that the Austrian Grand Prix served up 'the most exciting finish of the year, perhaps the century, with Márquez in full-on maniacal attack mode'. It was a big claim, but it was most justified; Márquez's last-lap battle with Andrea Dovizioso on the factory Ducati was indeed an all-time classic.

As a rider, Dovizioso was the polar opposite of Marc Márquez; smooth, steady, wheels in line, but still blindingly fast. A very calm, measured and strategic racer, Dovizioso would soon earn the nickname 'The Professor', suggesting that he thought even more deeply about his racing than 'The Doctor', Valentino Rossi. With good reason too: Dovi often displayed an almost ethereal calm when all around him was chaos. And at the Red Bull Ring in Austria, that chaos came in the form of Marc Márquez.

After battling with other riders for the first 22 laps, Márquez and Dovizioso had broken clear with six laps to go and a battle royale commenced between two riders with radically different styles. Márquez later admitted that Dovizioso was stronger on the day, but that didn't stop him giving everything he had to try to beat him. Under different circumstances, he might have settled for 20 points but, with the championship being so close, that wasn't an option on this occasion.

The race perfectly illustrated the difference between the two riders: Márquez, sliding, spinning, bucking and weaving his way around the track and over the kerbs, while Dovizioso rode so smoothly and consistently, he almost looked slow. He wasn't.

It all came down to the last lap. 'Marc always in the last lap will try something,' Dovizioso said after the race, 'but I didn't expect in the last corner because there is no braking. But I heard him open the throttle early, so I left the door open so I could exit faster. Otherwise, he would hit me.'

Márquez just got in front of Dovizioso, diving up the inside of him as they rounded the final corner, but he then ran wide and had his RCV absolutely sideways on the kerb while his Italian rival remained impeccably smooth and nosed back in front on the run to the finish line. He took the victory by just 0.12 seconds.

The result saw Dovizioso leapfrog Maverick Viñales into second place in the championship, just 16 points behind Márquez.

It was becoming clear that Ducati now had a seriously competitive bike in the Desmosedici. The Italian firm had only ever won a single MotoGP title, back in 2007 with Casey Stoner, and it had been in the doldrums for years with a bike so troublesome that even Valentino Rossi failed to take a win on it when he rode for Ducati in 2011 and 2012. The bike had always been fast, and could take advantage on circuits with long straights, but it now worked at most circuits and Andrea Dovizioso had clearly figured out how to get the most from it. 'We all knew that Ducati had a very good bike for certain circuits,' Márquez said. 'But what has impressed us this year is that they took a big step in those circuits where they used to struggle more. This shows that they have been working hard to be in front. Lately, when you follow a Ducati, it's hard to see weak points.'[89]

Dovizioso's competitiveness during the 2017 season caught

Márquez unawares. 'This year, when the people were asking me which opponent is the most dangerous, I was saying always Maverick, Dani, Valentino, maybe Lorenzo . . . but I never said Dovi. It's something that I learned this year – that you need to be careful with everybody, and try to pay attention to everybody because, in the beginning of the season, (it) looks like Maverick was the fastest one, but in the end the most constant, the most complete guy to fight for the title was Dovi.'[90]

Márquez wasn't the only one surprised by Dovizioso's pace in 2017. The Italian had only ever won a single MotoGP race and that was at a wet British Grand Prix way back in 2009.

This time around, the British race was held in scorching weather conditions and Dovizioso would win again, this time from Maverick Viñales and Valentino Rossi. Márquez, having set pole position, would only last for 14 laps before the unthinkable happened – his factory Honda RC213V blew up. It was his first ever mechanical failure in MotoGP, and it was all the more shocking because Honda had a reputation for building bulletproof engines. His no-score saw Andrea Dovizioso take the championship lead for the first time, and he went to San Marino with a nine-point advantage.

The pressure was on for Márquez. 'It's difficult to explain, but it's something that makes you insecure, that gives you doubts, makes you tense,' he said of dealing with pressure. 'It's something that wears you out mentally and physically, and you finish the weekend completely destroyed. Since all this tension just sucks so much energy out of you, you have to manage it. I'm very lucky to have a big family in the paddock; my team that helps me to disconnect when we're not just thinking about racing, and this helps me to stay relaxed.'

While he clawed back vital points with a wet weather win at San Marino (while Dovizioso was third behind his Ducati teammate Danilo Petrucci), Márquez didn't exactly lessen the pressure on himself – he and Dovizioso were now dead level on 199 points. At MotorLand Aragón the season would effectively start anew.

Ignoring the fact that his Repsol Honda was handling terribly around the Spanish circuit, Márquez rode like a man possessed from the first lap to the last, taking, as he himself admitted, 'maximum risk' throughout. There was, he knew, a championship on the line. Starting from fifth on the grid, he forced his way past Valentino Rossi (who rode heroically after breaking his tibia in two places just 22 days previously), Maverick Viñales, Jorge Lorenzo, Andrea Dovizioso and Dani Pedrosa to take the win while his main title rival, Dovizioso, could only finish seventh. Advantage Márquez, by 16 points. For now, at least.

That margin was significantly reduced at a sodden Motegi after another last lap, last corner duel between Márquez and Dovizioso. Dovizioso had come out the winner under similar circumstances in Austria, and he did so again in Japan. Márquez had always been the most dangerous man when it came to last corner lunges, but it seemed he had met his match in Dovizioso, the Italian rider's ultra-calm approach seemingly rendering him impervious to pressure.

Always fast in the wet, Danilo Petrucci led the first 12 laps of the race, but once Márquez, and then Dovizioso, came past in rapid succession, it was a two-horse race. The pair fought frantically for the remaining 12 laps and there was still nothing to choose between them as they approached the final corner of the last lap. Márquez made a desperate lunge to briefly take the lead, but Dovizioso had predicted just such a move (it was Márquez's trademark, after all) and allowed Márquez through to run wide, while tightening his own line to retake the lead and hold it to the flag. He had now outfoxed Márquez with the same cool, calculated, last corner tactic on two occasions and his sublime performance in Japan saw him close to within 11 points of him in the standings. The pressure was still on, and Márquez was having to ride harder than ever against the new breed of super-fast Ducatis. Speaking of his wet-weather duel with Dovizioso in Japan, he said, 'I was going into corners faster, not because I wanted to go in faster, but because I couldn't stop the bike! I was locking the front, releasing the brake, going in, and seeing what happens. You need to release the brakes and believe.'[91]

Unlike the bitter battle between Marc Márquez and Valentino Rossi in 2015, the one between Márquez and Dovizioso was good-natured; they were friends, at least for the time being, and hugged warmly in *parc fermé* after their Japanese duel.

The Australian Grand Prix was a real dogfight, and no one is better in a dogfight than an in-form Marc Márquez. In a race that saw no fewer than 70 overtakes, Márquez was part of an eight-man battle for the lead. Even as deep into the race as lap 14, the top eight riders were covered by just over a second: Valentino Rossi, Johann Zarco, Marc Márquez, Jack Miller, Andrea Iannone, Cal Crutchlow and Álex Rins all swapping paintwork and, as often as not, the lead. There were numerous collisions and just as many lucky escapes as the rabid pack fought tooth and claw amongst itself. The notable absence was title fighter Andrea Dovizioso, who made a poor tyre choice and suffered the consequences. He could finish no higher than 11th place, seriously denting his championship hopes.

In a race which even the riders themselves admitted was 'crazy',

Márquez reigned supreme, his willingness to take risks paying dividends yet again. He now had a 33-point lead over Andrea Dovizioso with just two rounds remaining.

Márquez loved every minute of the Australian clash. 'For me the fun is when things get wild!' he said at the end of the season. 'That race was Australia when the title was at stake – there were all kinds of collisions, incidents, broken fairings and more, but I did not stop thinking about the championship. It was me against five riders (seven, at the peak of the battle) who weren't competing for the title, only for that race, and I did not hesitate for a moment to get into the battle. This is motorcycle racing; I had a lot of fun, and, in the end, I won the race, but it was what racing is all about. There was overtaking – it did not matter who was competing for the title and who wasn't; it was a race, and we all ended up happy. Nobody complained and it was the most beautiful race.'[92]

It was a different Marc Márquez who stepped off the aeroplane into the sweltering heat and humidity of Malaysia. The swashbuckling, gladiatorial rider of Australia was replaced by a much more cautious one, his eyes firmly on the title and his mindset one that wished to avoid any unnecessary risks. Restraint was foremost in his battle plan.

The permutations were simple enough: if Dovizioso won the race and Márquez finished second, the latter would take his fourth MotoGP world title. Any lower than second and the fight would spill over to the final round in Valencia. Dovizioso, determined to battle until the bitter end, did win the wet race, but the new, super-cautious Márquez failed to take second place, instead coming home in fourth place, putting his championship celebrations on ice.

Márquez summed up his cautious approach after the race, saying, 'Today was the most difficult possible for the championship.

I thought about passing Zarco, but the risk was too big to have a 24-point advantage rather than 21. This wasn't a race to win the title, but to get closer to it.'[93]

With 25 points available for a race win in Valencia, a 21-point lead may sound a lot, but in MotoGP, anything can happen. Riders can crash of their own accord, they can be knocked off by other riders, they can have handling or set-up problems, suffer from poor tyre choices, or even suffer mechanical breakdowns, as Márquez had experienced in the British Grand Prix earlier in the season. In short, there's still an awful lot that can go wrong, and nothing can be taken for granted.

Dovizioso needed Márquez to crash in Valencia if he were to have any chance of winning the title. He also needed to win the race. Neither of those things happened. Although he crashed twice during practice, Márquez pulled off the save of his career during the race when it looked to all other eyes but his that he must surely crash out.

He started the final race of the season from pole position with wild-riding Frenchman Johann Zarco next to him. Not shy of making contact with other riders, Zarco's position on the grid reportedly worried Márquez's mother so much she had a word with him the night before the race – not to let her son past, but just not to knock him off and ruin his championship hopes. The Frenchman revealed: 'She said, "Zarco, please take it easy tomorrow," and I said, "Yes, Mother, I will listen to you."'

As things turned out, Márquez did find himself stuck behind Zarco in the race and desperately needed to get past to keep his concentration levels up – Zarco's pace wasn't fast enough for Márquez to concentrate fully. After overtaking the Frenchman, he put the hammer down in a bid to escape him and suffered the mother of all front-wheel slides entering the first corner. 'The front had gone,' he said afterwards, 'but the rear was still gripping, so I knew I could save it with my elbow.'

He was living dangerously. Running off the track and into the gravel trap after he had picked the bike up on his elbow, he dropped to fifth place. Márquez's miraculous save was referred to as 'the most breathtaking ever captured on film' by Julian Ryder in the official *MotoGP Season Review 2017* book.

The Ducati camp appeared to be in disarray and Dovizioso's challenge never came to fruition. After repeated coded messages were sent to Jorge Lorenzo's dashboard, telling him to let his teammate through, the Spaniard still refused to oblige. Lorenzo's team then hung up a pit board that read, 'Suggested Mapping: Mapping 8'. It was clear to all experienced eyes what it meant (move over and let your teammate through), but Lorenzo refused to budge, later claiming that he was trying to tow Dovizioso up to the leaders. In the end, it didn't matter as both Ducati riders crashed out; Lorenzo on lap 24 and Dovizioso a lap later.

As he remounted and rode back to his pit box, Andrea Dovizioso was given a standing ovation by the crowd. He had put together an incredible season and had beaten Márquez fair and square on more than one occasion. But his final round fall handed the 2017 MotoGP world championship to Marc Márquez, who – after his terrifying slide – rode a steady race to third place behind Johann Zarco and race winner Dani Pedrosa.

'I'm living a dream,' he said after the race. 'The truth is that I'm incredibly happy because we worked so much this year, and today the race was incredibly tense and exciting – a bit "Márquez-style". I made a mistake, but I also made my best save of the year. From that moment on, I just tried to finish the race in a good position.

I'm sorry that Andrea didn't finish the race, as he deserved to do so. He had an incredible season, and I would have liked to have him on the podium with me today.'[94]

It was Márquez's fourth MotoGP title (his fourth in five years) and his sixth in total across all three Grand Prix classes. Still just 24, he was the youngest man to win four premier class crowns (taking the record by over a year from Mike Hailwood) and the youngest to win six all told (taking that record from Valentino Rossi, also by more than a year). He also became the first rider in the 69-year history of Grand Prix motorcycle racing to win at least five races per season, across three or more classes.

It hadn't been easy. After six rounds, Márquez had been 37 points adrift in fourth place, with only a single win to his credit. He also set the record for most crashes during the year, with a total of 27 (and he estimated he had another 50 near misses). He was patient with his Honda and his team when his bike wasn't performing as he wanted it to early in the season, then attacked magnificently when his set-up allowed him to and turned his season around. He also applauded his team for never giving up on him, no matter how many times he crashed. 'This year I crash 27 times, but they never, never, never complained,' he said. 'They never said, "What are you doing? You need to be careful." They never complained. It was the opposite way: "Push, push, push! We will repair the bike, but you need to find the limit." This is something that gives me so good confidence and such a good relationship inside the box.'[95]

Márquez conquered all his old foes (Rossi finished the season in fifth place, Lorenzo in seventh, and Pedrosa in fourth) and beat off the new challengers in the shape of Andrea Dovizioso and Maverick Viñales. It had been a vintage season. Marc Márquez had established himself as one of the greatest riders in MotoGP history but, just two rounds into the 2018 season, he appeared to fall apart completely, and his feud with Valentino Rossi was rekindled. He would once more be labelled the bad boy of MotoGP.

CHAPTER 9

MONSTER

'WHEN YOU BEAT MARC, IT IS ALWAYS SPECIAL . . . WHEN YOU HAVE TO FIGHT WITH A MONSTER LIKE HIM TO THE LAST LAP.'

Jorge Lorenzo

Marc Márquez and the Repsol Honda team had struggled for two years to get the RC213V to work with MotoGP's control electronics and Michelin tyres, but in 2018 the six-time world champion finally had a bike that would do exactly what he wanted. A new carbon fibre swinging arm also helped with tyre life and HRC had found more power too, giving Márquez a near-perfect package with which to battle for another world title against the ever-improving and super-fast Ducatis.

Yet, while the bike worked for Márquez, that didn't mean it was an easy machine to ride. The RCV had to be ridden extremely aggressively for it to be at its most effective, and Márquez could do that better than anyone. In 2018 he accumulated almost as many points on his own (321) as the other five Honda riders combined (348). It was a statistic that spoke volumes.

While he signed another two-year extension on his Honda

contract before the season began, HRC began to realise that Márquez was flattering its bike, and that other riders struggled to get the most out of it. It wasn't a problem yet, but it was a problem on the horizon: if they didn't build a user-friendly motorcycle that suited riders with varying styles, they'd be in trouble should Márquez ever get seriously injured, retire or jump ship to another manufacturer. At the same time, it would have taken a very brave – or very foolish – company to radically redesign a bike that had taken four out of the last five MotoGP world titles. It was a dilemma, and it would play out fully in the years to come. For now, though, Márquez had the tools he needed.

The only major change to the Repsol Honda team for the 2018 season was the replacement of Livio Suppo with Alberto Puig as team manager. Out with the genial Italian and in with the stern-faced, no-nonsense Spaniard. A former 500cc Grand Prix winner himself, Puig wasn't in the paddock to have fun – he was there to do a job, and he was ruthlessly efficient. He was not, however, good friends with Márquez's manager, Emilio Alzamora; the two would have to dance warily around one another during the season.

Suppo had worked with Márquez for five years, between 2013 and 2017, and had seen his fame and power grow, but testifies that it never went to Márquez's head. 'The fact that Marc never changed is what impressed me most about him,' he says. 'He remained the young, and very happy, boy I met in 2011; even if he became super famous and super rich, he remained a simple, honest guy.'

When the championship got under way at Qatar, Andrea Dovizioso outfoxed Marc Márquez in the final corner of the race for a third time. In a carbon copy of what had happened in Austria and Japan the previous year, Márquez made a desperate lunge on the Italian and passed up the inside of the blood-red Ducati.

But, once again, Dovizioso kept his calm, waited for Márquez to run wide (which he duly did), cut inside of him, and gunned his Desmosedici to the line, just 0.02 seconds ahead of Márquez. All clean, all fair, all good fun. That would not be the case in Argentina.

Márquez appeared to comprehensively lose the plot at the Termas de Río Hondo circuit, riding with complete abandon and picking up penalty after penalty. The bad boy of racing was back.

It all started because of the weather. There had been intermittent rain throughout the weekend and the race was declared a wet one, despite a dry line beginning to appear. Pole position man Jack Miller assumed his place on the grid, his bike fitted with slick tyres, while all other riders came into the pit lane to change their wet tyres for slicks. The race was delayed for 15 minutes while the organisers hastily drew up new rules. By rights, all riders who entered the pit lane should have started the race from there, while Miller would start alone from the grid. But that was deemed to be too dangerous, so it was decided that everyone except Miller should start from the back of the grid. It clearly wasn't possible to have everyone starting from the back row, so a bizarre compromise was reached: Miller would start from pole, while all the others would start from five rows back, in their qualifying order.

Then, Márquez's RCV had an electrical problem and stalled on the grid. Correct procedure would have been to raise his hand and await assistance to guide him into the pit lane where he would have to start from. Márquez did raise his hand, but then lost patience, pushed his bike in the wrong direction to bump-start it, then made a U-turn and headed back to his grid slot. He was handed a ride-through penalty for breaching protocol by riding the wrong way on the track. Penalty number one.

Once the already bizarre race was under way, Márquez was

handed another penalty, this time for making a dangerous move on Aleix Espargaró. His punishment this time was to drop one place. He dropped two, just to be sure.

Then he made another desperate move, this time on Valentino Rossi, and this time with more severe consequences – he knocked his old enemy off. It was just like 2015 all over again, and the hatred between the two – which had remained simmering rather than boiling over the previous two seasons – was reignited. Márquez was now handed a third penalty; this time 30 seconds was to be added to his race time after the chequered flag. That dropped him from fifth to 18th place and out of the points.

But that wasn't the worst of it. Márquez, his manager Emilio Alzamora and team boss Alberto Puig all headed straight to the Yamaha box to apologise but were brusquely rebuffed by Rossi's right-hand man, Uccio Salucci, and refused entry. Rossi and Yamaha team boss Lin Jarvis wasted no time in visiting Race Direction to complain, and Rossi repeated the charge he had made to the press that Márquez was ruining MotoGP. 'This is a very bad situation, because he destroyed our sport,' he said. 'He don't have any respect for his rivals. Never.'

Rossi even claimed he was 'scared' to share a track with Márquez and said that 'he goes between your leg and the bike. He does it purposely, because he knows he won't crash, but he hopes you will. I don't have fun when I race with him, because he don't play clean. So, if you start to play like this, you raise the level to a very dangerous point. Because if all the riders race like this, without any respect for the rivals, this is a very dangerous sport and (it will) finish in a bad way.'

While Márquez admitted liability for the clash, he denied it was due to over-aggressive riding, instead blaming the sketchy weather conditions. 'Today, what happened to Valentino was a mistake – a consequence of the track conditions, because I locked the front,' he said. 'You needed to understand how the track condition was. Of course, in that line, it was dry, but I [hit the] wet patch, locked the front, released the brakes. Okay, I had the contact – I tried to turn and then, when I see that he crashed, I just try to say sorry.'[96]

The outcome for both riders was that neither scored any points in the Argentine Grand Prix, but the penalties weren't over: Márquez would be handed another before the race even began at the Circuit of the Americas in Texas.

This time he was forced to drop three places on the grid after dawdling on the racing line during qualifying and obstructing other riders. This happened the day after a very lively Riders Safety Commission meeting in which Márquez's riding during the Argentine Grand Prix came under scrutiny. He was not penalised further, but race officials declared that, in future, they would be keeping an even closer eye on anyone deemed to be riding dangerously, or intentionally obstructing others, and would punish them appropriately. Everyone knew who the comments were aimed at.

But this was America, and Marc Márquez remained undefeated on US soil. He'd taken 11 wins stateside and was in no mood to see his incredible run come to an end. Wishing to avoid close-quarter battle because of the scrutiny he was under, his tactics were simple – get to the front and break away into an unassailable lead on an empty track. They worked: once Márquez had seen off the close attentions of Ducati rider Andrea Iannone, he was in a class – and a race – of his own, leading Maverick Viñales home by three seconds.

Márquez's first win of the year put him second in the

championship behind Andrea Dovizioso and his second win, in Aragón, put him top. Despite two crashes in practice and another during race day morning warm-up, Márquez dominated the Aragón Grand Prix, though only after Jorge Lorenzo's rear tyre went off. After a difficult year in 2017, Lorenzo was finally getting to grips with the Ducati; until the Spaniard started losing grip, Márquez had said he was 'almost impossible to pass'.

A win at Le Mans meant Márquez had won three in a row for the first time since his dominant 2014 season, and it moved him 36 points clear of Maverick Viñales in the title chase.

On the Thursday before the Italian Grand Prix at Mugello, Lorenzo revealed he would be leaving Ducati at the end of the year. The Italian manufacturer had failed to renew his contract. Few were surprised. Ducati had reputedly paid €24 million for Lorenzo's services and had expected a championship contender. They didn't get one; five races into his second season on the bike and Lorenzo hadn't won a single race. Three days after announcing he was leaving, he finally did.

After everything he had tried to get his Ducati to work for him, in the end it came down to a piece of foam padding added to the rear of the fuel tank to help support Lorenzo's upper body under heavy braking. With that low-tech solution in place, he was unbeatable at Mugello (where his Ducati teammate Andrea Dovizioso set a new MotoGP top speed record of 221.45mph), leading from start to finish, apart from Márquez's brief lead into the first corner. Mugello had never been a great circuit for Márquez and nor would it prove to be this time around; he crashed out, remounted and finished in 16th place, scoring no points.

If Lorenzo's win had come as a shock to Marc Márquez, he was in for an even bigger one at Catalunya when it was announced that

Lorenzo had signed for Repsol Honda as Márquez's teammate. His move came at the expense of Dani Pedrosa, who had ridden for Repsol Honda for 13 years and taken 31 MotoGP wins but never the title. His future, he eventually announced, would be as a test rider for KTM.

Despite the fact he had been so comprehensively outperformed by Márquez, the relationship between the two riders had always been a good one, as former HRC Team Principal Livio Suppo explains. 'Marc and Dani made good teammates. There was a bit of tension after the Aragón race in 2013 (when the pair collided and Pedrosa crashed), but that's just racing. Dani has a very good character. He's a very clever guy, and there was no problem between him and Marc at all. Marc speaks very well about Dani and vice versa.'

There *had* been some tension between the two in 2013 and 2014. How could there not be? Márquez came into the Repsol Honda team as a MotoGP rookie and comprehensively outperformed the team's number one rider. The relationship became strained as Márquez's success meant he started to lead development of the RC213V and received first choice on any new parts. He even admitted he tried to stop Pedrosa getting new parts because he, Márquez, was the one leading the championship, not Pedrosa. But by 2015, things had settled down, everyone knew their place in the garage, and Márquez and Pedrosa worked largely in harmony as teammates for the remainder of their time together. 'I've never been a nice teammate,' Márquez has admitted. 'You've got to make your teammate's life impossible, if you can. It's true that after 2015–16 everything calmed down and we had a good, normal teammates' relationship. After a while, I think you learn to accept the situation, right?'[97]

Pedrosa agreed, admitting that, 'We ended up getting along great.' The two remain friends to this day.

How things would work out with Márquez and Lorenzo – never the best of friends up to that point – in the same garage remained to be seen, but fireworks were predicted. When Lorenzo shared a garage with Valentino Rossi at Yamaha during the 2010 season, they built a dividing wall down the middle of it. There was every chance that things would get equally bitter between Lorenzo and Márquez.

But that was in the future; for now, Márquez had to focus on his home Grand Prix at Catalunya. It proved to be another Ducati rout, with Lorenzo leading Márquez home by over four seconds. But with Lorenzo only seventh in the points standings, he wasn't an immediate threat, and Márquez extended his lead over Rossi by another four points. Márquez 115, Rossi 88.

The Assen race was a classic and saw Marc Márquez deliver one of his greatest performances to date. He started by taking his 47th premier class pole position, but with the top 11 fastest men being within half a second of each other, there could be no predicting the outcome of the race.

It was more like Moto3 than MotoGP, with an eight-rider pack disputing the lead for most of the race. Five different riders took turns leading over the line and there was no shortage of contact either; Márquez almost coming to grief twice, in separate collisions with Álex Rins and Maverick Viñales, while Valentino Rossi and Jorge Lorenzo were both incredibly lucky to escape unhurt after a full-on collision, when Lorenzo lost the front and slowed so drastically that Rossi rammed into the back of him.

With the race being so fraught, Márquez – one of just a few riders to have opted for the softer rear tyre – tried to make a break and get free of the chaos. With four laps to go, he pulled the pin. 'During practice, I was comfortable, with a good rhythm, but I suspected it would be difficult to open a gap,' he said. 'So, I decided to wait, but in that transition, there was a big fight. I tried to manage the tyre, and in the last four laps, I gave it everything . . . The most difficult thing was to defend and attack at the same time.'[98]

By the flag, Márquez had somehow managed to pull two seconds clear of Suzuki's Álex Rins to take a 41-point lead from Valentino Rossi in the championship. Even better for Márquez, the Sachsenring was up next, and he had yet to be beaten there.

After setting pole again (as he had done every year in Germany since 2010), Márquez spent the first 12 laps of the race nursing his soft rear tyre before slipping past Jorge Lorenzo and making the race his own, eventually beating Rossi over the line by over two seconds. Márquez's advantage over the veteran Italian as he headed into the summer break was a very fitting 46 points.

After a fierce fight with the Ducatis of Jorge Lorenzo and Andrea Dovizioso at Brno, Márquez settled for a safe third place while Dovizioso took the win. The short two-week summer break was over, but Márquez had clearly decided during that break to alter his approach to the second half of the season. 'Maybe before I would have tried to fight to win,' he said of the Brno race, 'but my main target this weekend was to increase my championship lead.' He did, but only by three points – Rossi had finished just one place behind him in fourth.

The sheer brute speed and new-found agility of the Ducatis meant they were always going to be a threat at the super-fast Red Bull Ring in Austria, but Márquez dominated every session of practice and qualifying and more than held his own against the Italian bikes in the race. It came down to a dogfight with Lorenzo, who would take the win by just 0.13 seconds. Afterwards, he admitted what it meant to beat his future teammate. 'When you beat Marc, it is always special . . . when you have to fight with a monster like him to the last lap.'

The British Grand Prix at Silverstone was a 'disaster' according to not only Marc Márquez, but everyone else. Silverstone was no stranger to rain, but the newly laid surface wasn't allowing water to drain away and the result was lethal pools of standing water that made racing just too dangerous. The new track surface was hideously bumpy too, causing Andrea Dovizioso to bemoan, 'It's bad for everybody when you have to fight the bumps at the best track in Europe.'

The situation was so bad, and so dangerous, that, for the first time in the modern Grand Prix era, the entire meeting was abandoned. That hadn't happened since snow caused the cancellation of the Austrian Grand Prix way back in 1980.

If Silverstone was cursed, Marc Márquez was blessed ahead of the Grand Prix at Misano. In a pre-event publicity stunt, he, Dani Pedrosa, Andrea Iannone, Danilo Petrucci and Jack Miller were invited to a private reception at the Vatican to meet Pope Francis.

The pontiff spoke of the importance of sport and its many positive attributes, saying, 'Sport, respecting the rules, is an important way to learn – especially for young generations. Or rather, it's irreplaceable. Sport promotes a healthy way to overcome the self and selfishness, train the spirit and promote loyalty in personal relationships; friendship, respect for the rules.'[99]

It was perhaps just as well that Valentino Rossi wasn't present, given the lack of friendship and respect between him and Marc Márquez. Márquez was clearly moved by the unique opportunity. 'It was a great experience in a different kind of suit!' he said afterwards, referring to the formal dress code of the meeting. 'I think once in your life it's good to meet him if you have the opportunity. It was so nice; we spoke, and we were able to meet him, but also talk to him. It was a pleasure to be here. What he said was great, in terms of understanding and motivation – he said you need passion in life and a goal and, if you follow that passion, you can achieve a lot.'[100]

Each rider presented Pope Francis with one of their race helmets as part of the reception before heading to Misano for the next round of the championship, perhaps all feeling just that bit more invincible following their encounter with the pontiff.

But all talk of friendship and personal relationships took a sour turn at the pre-race press conference, when the ongoing feud between Márquez and Rossi flared up again. Rossi had the support of his legions of fans but, yet again, it was he who refused to show a sense of sportsmanship and to bury the hatchet. After Márquez stated he'd be happy to 'make peace' with Rossi, an interviewer asked if the two would be prepared to shake hands. Márquez smiled and reached across the podium, offering his hand to Rossi. Rossi kept his arms firmly folded. 'It sounds to me a bit strange because, in reality, we don't have any problems between me and Marc,' he then said. 'So, I don't know why we have to "make peace". For me it's okay.'

It had been the perfect opportunity to draw a line under the ugly 2015 season and the ongoing needle between the two, but Rossi firmly refused to take it. There may have been a deeper reason for this than met the eye. Instead of letting bygones be bygones, Rossi's hatred of Márquez seemed to grow rather than dissipate. The reason may have been that Márquez was still winning, and Rossi wasn't. He had only taken one win in 2017 and none so far in 2018 (in fact, his 2017 Assen victory would prove to be his last).

His hopes of clinching a tenth world title were dissolving; time was running out, and it was Marc Márquez who had deprived him of that elusive title. Márquez was the man who dethroned the once invincible Valentino Rossi, and neither Rossi nor his millions of fans could ever forgive him for it. They still don't.

It was no different in Rossi's backyard at Misano. During Qualifying 2, Márquez performed another minor miracle, so soon after meeting the Pope. After crashing out, he was on his feet and running before his RCV had even stopped barrelling through the gravel trap. He was back in the pits and on his second bike precisely 2 minutes and 15 seconds after crashing. Grit in his eye hampered his charge for pole position, however, and he started the race from fifth place. Unable to live with the pace of the Ducatis, Márquez was gifted second place when Jorge Lorenzo crashed out of the race, but he was unable to catch Andrea Dovizioso. Rossi could only manage seventh in front of his home fans, the glory days seemingly over. Dovizioso's win saw him replace Rossi to go second in the championship, 67 points behind Márquez.

A corner was named after Márquez at Aragón (Turn 10), but once again he came under fire for over-aggressive riding at the event. This time it was Jorge Lorenzo's turn to complain after Márquez pushed him wide in the first corner and made him crash out. That was Lorenzo's take on the incident anyway. But he also admitted that he didn't want to waste his pole position, so accelerated hard despite being pushed out on to the dirty part of the track. Unbiased observers might have said the crash was as much Lorenzo's fault as it was Márquez's.

After gambling on switching to a soft tyre on the grid as he 'thought it would be the only way I could fight with the Ducatis' around Aragón, Márquez had another epic tussle with Andrea Dovizioso.

Top: American idol. Marc Márquez is virtually unbeatable at left-handed circuits like the Circuit of the Americas, thanks to his dirt-track background. © Hoss McBain/ZUMA Wire/Alamy

Below left: The first podium. At just 15 years old, Marc Márquez took his first ever podium in the 125cc race at the British Grand Prix. © Andrew Yates/AFP/Getty

Below right: Sweet 16. Márquez was fast in his second season of Grand Prix racing in 2009, but still had to iron out the crashes. © Jean Francois Monier/AFP/Getty

The ant from Cervera wins the Japanese 125cc Grand Prix, en route to taking his first world title.

Stepping up. Márquez moved up to the Moto2 class in 2011 and kept on winning, but his season was cut short when he suffered diplopia after a crash in Sepang.

Right: Valencia, 2013. Marc Márquez crosses the line to become the youngest MotoGP world champion in history.

The sky's the limit. There was no stopping Márquez in 2013. A study in style at MotorLand Aragón in Spain.

Elbow down, knee down. Márquez changed the riding style in MotoGP forever. © Gaetano Piazzolla/Alamy

Mugello, 2014. Márquez beat Jorge Lorenzo to take a sixth consecutive victory. He would ultimately win ten in a row. Unheard of.

© Antonio Calanni/AP Photo/Alamy

Adulation. The youngest champion in Grand Prix history gets hoisted aloft after winning the 2013 title.

© Alberto Saiz/AP Photo/Alamy

Left: Feel the joy! Márquez celebrates his third MotoGP title in four years at Valencia, 2016. *© Xavier Bonilla/NurPhoto/Getty*

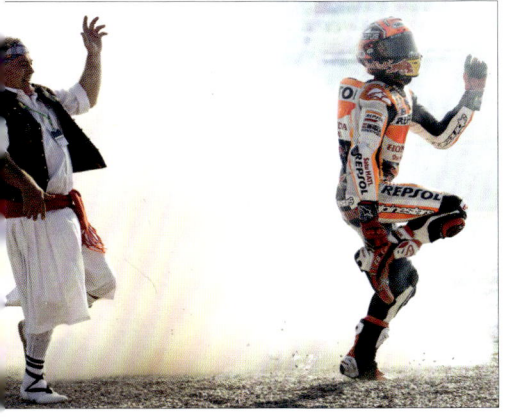

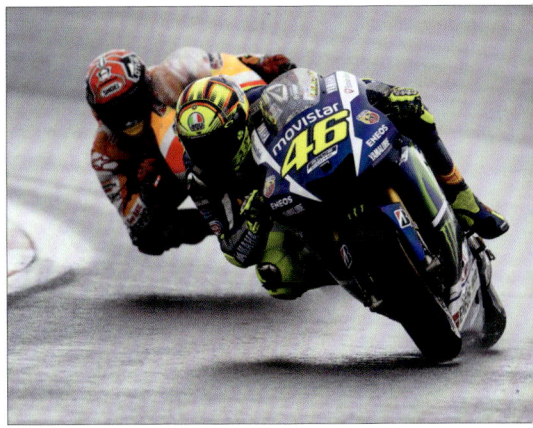

Right: Nemesis. The bitter rivalry between Valentino Rossi and Marc Márquez would become the stuff of legend. *© Mirco Lazzari gp/Getty*

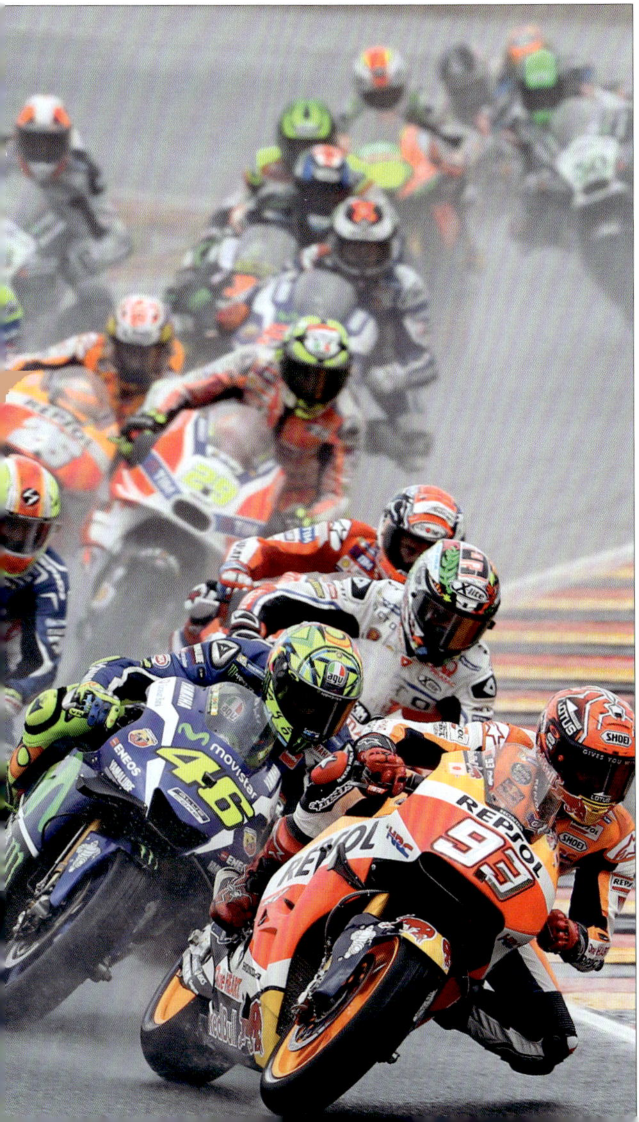

Leader of the pack. Márquez acts as pathfinder in hideous conditions at the Sachsenring, Germany, in 2016. He won the race.

© Jan Woitas/dpa/Alamy

If looks could kill. Valentino Rossi has never forgiven Marc Márquez for the 2015 season. This is four years later, and the hatred is still clear to see.

Severely injured, and riding an uncompetitive Honda RCV, Márquez tries too hard and oversteps the mark in Portugal in 2023.

A study in speed at Silverstone, 2019.

Marc and Álex Márquez share the podium in Germany, 2024. Marc was second, Álex third. It was the first time two brothers had stood on a MotoGP podium together.

© Mark Wieland/Getty

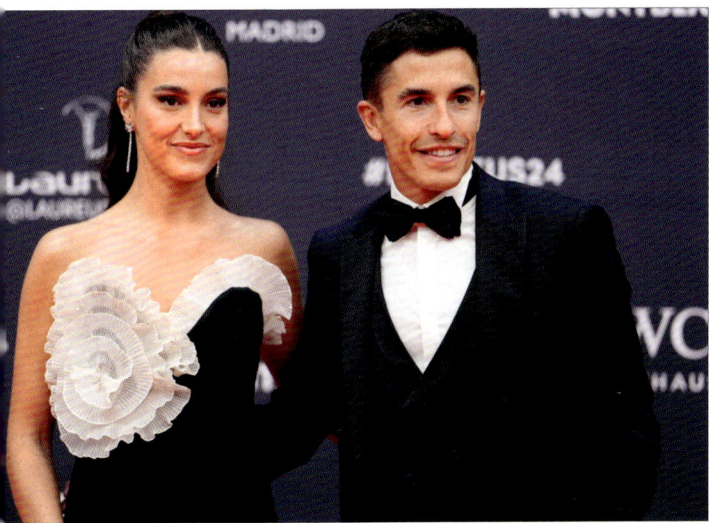

Márquez has found happiness in his personal life with Spanish model and influencer Gemma Pinto.

© Manu Fernandez/AP Photo/Alamy

The beginning of something special. As soon as he tested the Gresini Ducati Desmosedici, Márquez knew he could return to winning ways.

© Cesar March/Alamy

Right: Seeing red. After four years of agony, Márquez gets his reward – a seat on the best bike in MotoGP. Testing the factory Ducati, Buriram, February, 2025.

© Manan Vatsyayana/AFP/Getty

Below: Everything or nothing. Marc Márquez is the red-hot favourite to lift the 2025 MotoGP world championship on the factory Ducati.

© Hazrin Yeob Men Shah/Icon Sportswire/AP Images/Getty

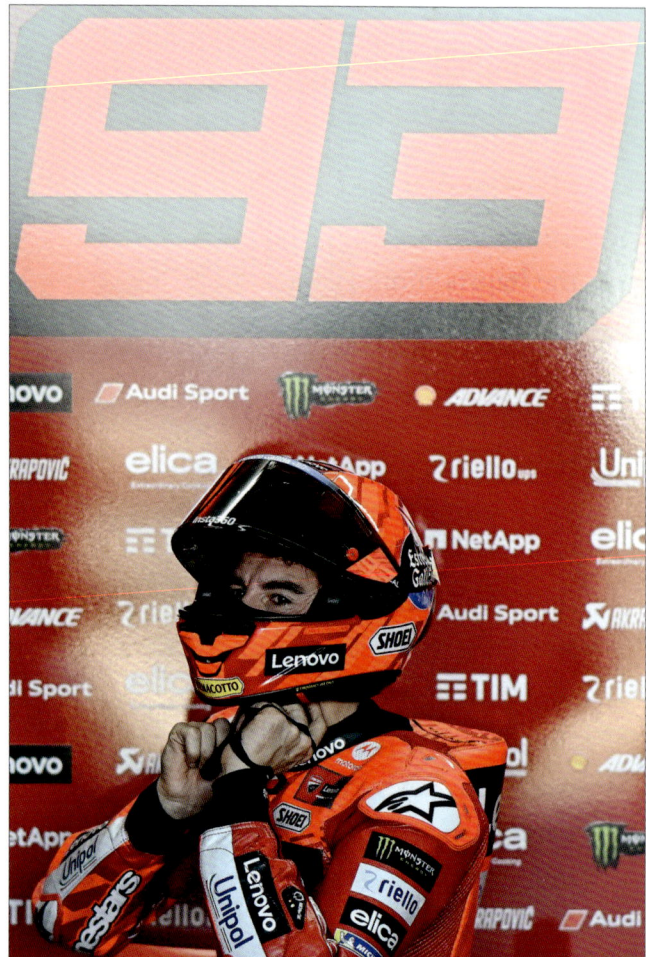

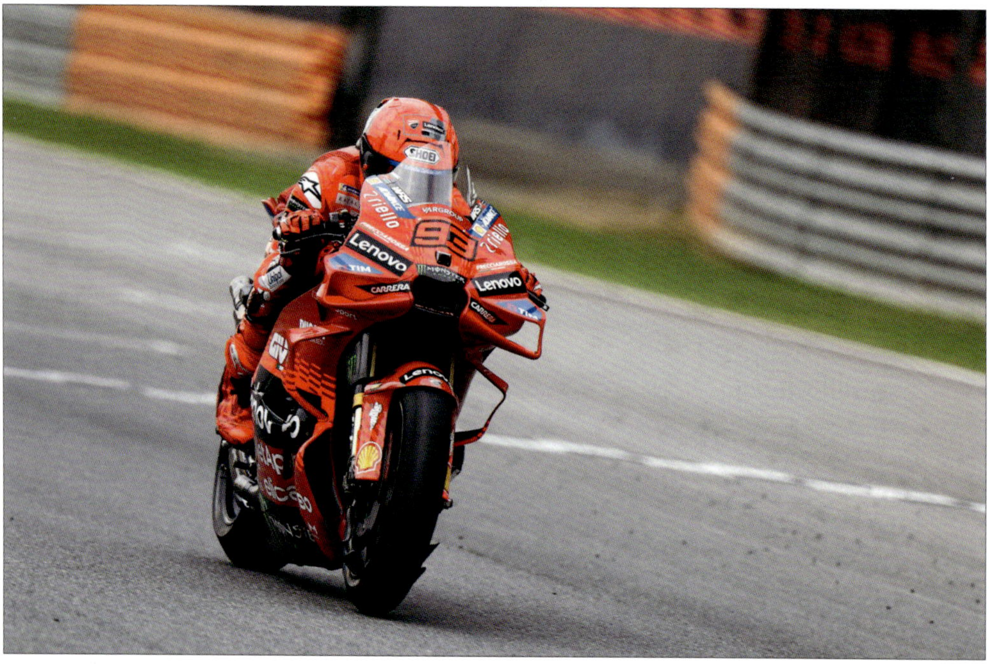

He eventually eked out a win by just six-tenths of a second, having learned his lesson when it came to last lap, last corner clashes with the Italian. 'I didn't want the race to go to the last corner as we did a few times last year,' Márquez admitted afterwards.

It was an important result for Márquez's confidence, and it would prove to be pivotal in his championship campaign. 'At the start of the second part of the season, in Brno, Ducati riders were very, very strong, very fast and winning all the races,' he said. 'They were catching me step by step, and it was important in Aragón to stop that. That was nice, because I was able to win, increase my advantage and get the confidence again.'[101]

MotoGP has a two-tier qualifying system. The top ten fastest riders during practice automatically go through to Qualifying 2 while the slower riders have to take part in Qualifying 1, which is a last chance saloon; only the fastest two riders in Q1 go through to Q2 to then fight for position on the first four rows of the grid.

At the inaugural Thai Grand Prix at the Chang circuit, Marc Márquez found himself in Q1 – for the second time that year and the fourth time in his career – due to a crash in Free Practice 3 which had prevented him from setting a fast lap time. Not only did he make it through to Q2 as expected, he was then also the fastest rider in Q2 and took pole position. It was the first time any rider had ever gone through Q1 and then worked his way up to pole position. Yet another record, not that Márquez cared much. 'Honestly speaking, I never thought about the records, and I never will think about them,' he said at the end of the season. 'It comes naturally if you work in a good way. You just need to enjoy the moment and then everything will arrive. Records are, of course, important, but the most important things are the titles and fighting every season for a new one.'[102]

The pole position was Márquez's 50th and the race itself was a hectic tussle between himself, Andrea Dovizioso, Valentino Rossi and Maverick Viñales. In the last five laps alone, Márquez took the lead five times, only for Dovi to take it back. It all came down to the final corner, but this time the roles were reversed. Dovizioso made a lunge and passed Márquez but then ran wide, allowing Márquez to nip back up the inside and take the win. 'This time, it was the opposite.' Márquez beamed after the hard-fought race. 'I was Dovi, and he was Márquez!'

With a 77-point lead and just four races to go, Marc Márquez headed to Japan with a strong chance of lifting the 2018 world title. Only Dovizioso could stop him. As expected, Dovizioso's Ducati was strong at Motegi and he and Márquez staged a dogged battle for the win until the Italian ran wide at Turn 10 on the penultimate lap and crashed out, his title challenge over. Márquez was MotoGP world champion for the fifth time in six years. For the third time he had achieved this goal in front of his Honda bosses at the circuit Honda owned. It was his seventh world title in total, and his third consecutive MotoGP crown. Márquez was now the youngest rider to win seven world titles (taking the record from Mike Hailwood) and the youngest to win five premier class crowns (satisfyingly deposing Valentino Rossi). Only Rossi, with nine world titles, Ángel Nieto with 13, and Giacomo Agostini with 15, now stood ahead of Márquez in the all-time winners' list.

It was all a bit much to take in. 'I don't want to think about names like Agostini, Hailwood and Nieto, because they are legends of MotoGP,' Márquez said. 'When I equalled Mick Doohan, it was very strange because he was the first guy I saw when I started to understand motorbikes on TV – Doohan fighting with Àlex

Crivillé are some of my first memories, not just of motorbikes, but in my whole life. And to now equal him is very special. But where I am among the greats, I have no idea.'[103]

It was a spectacular achievement, even if it came with a little discomfort. Aprilia rider Scott Redding had stopped alongside Márquez on the slow-down lap to congratulate him. A little over-enthusiastically, as it turned out; his man-hug was so fierce it dislocated Márquez's left shoulder. It was becoming a common occurrence and brother Álex was adroit at popping the shoulder back into place, but Marc would have corrective surgery on it at season's end.

It was a small price to pay for such an achievement, however, and the battle with Dovizioso had been a good-natured one with none of the bitterness that had defined the 2015 battle with Rossi. Such was the respect between the two, Márquez even bemoaned the fact that his rival did not get to enjoy the podium in Japan. 'When I saw the pit board "DOVI OUT" at the start of the last lap, my first reaction was to be pleased because I knew I had won the championship,' he said. 'But now I am disappointed, because Andrea rode a great race, and he deserves to be on the podium with us.'[104]

It was perhaps just as well that Márquez wrapped up the title early, because things didn't go well in the last three rounds of the championship and he would only take 25 points from the 75 on offer.

In Australia, Johann Zarco survived a horrifying crash when he ran into the back of Márquez at 174mph. The Frenchman's bike reared up the back of Márquez's RCV and he was sent flying, landing very heavily, but miraculously unhurt. Márquez's bike was too badly damaged to continue. It was just another example of what can go wrong if a title fight goes down to the last round. With the championship already in the bag, the Zarco incident didn't matter, but it so easily could have.

The Malaysian paddock rumours all centred around Valentino Rossi. Increasingly frustrated by the poor performance of his Yamaha M1 – once the best bike on the grid, but now completely eclipsed by its rivals – Rossi was said to be considering early retirement. His performance in the race seemed to offer evidence that the M1 wasn't quite over the hill yet, however. Rossi led for the first 16 laps, with Márquez seemingly powerless to do anything about it. The race was Rossi's to lose, but lose it he did. As Márquez started taking tenths out of the Italian's lead with each lap from lap 13 onwards, Rossi began to feel the pressure and, on lap 16, he crashed out. Márquez inherited the win but was disappointed not to get a chance to battle with his nemesis. 'It was a pity,' he said afterwards. 'I was looking forward to the last lap.'

Conditions for the final round at Valencia were so bad they led to a record number of crashes over the weekend – 155 in total. Márquez would be one of the many victims, crashing out of the first attempt to run the race and unable to take the restart after the red flags were thrown.

It was an ignominious end to what had been an incredible season in which Márquez won half of the 18 races, but also crashed 23 times. That, however, was all part of the plan. 'My style is all about my ambition,' he explained to *Australian Motor Cycle News*. 'If I need to crash 18 times to be world champion, then I'll crash 18 times. That's my style – my ambition means that I give everything on track . . . Among the top riders I am the one that falls the most, but it's not because I am a worse rider. A moment may come when you're afraid of hurting yourself, but if you think about this, you will never be fast. I need that little bit of unconsciousness, to approach the limit. I like to play with this tiny border.'[105]

That said, Márquez was only human, and he has admitted to feeling afraid at times; pushing a 220mph motorcycle past its limits tends to instil a certain amount of fear into everyone, even Marc Márquez. 'You're scared shitless on the first few laps, but you've got to break that habit pretty fast. You can't have any respect for the tools of the trade – you have to master them. My bike has to do what I want it to do, and nothing else.'[106]

The biggest surprise of the season to Márquez was how fast Jorge Lorenzo was on the Ducati once he had figured out how it needed to be ridden. 'I already expect a really strong rival that was Dovizioso, and yes, he was very, very fast, but maybe the one that surprised more, in one part of the season, was Jorge Lorenzo, because he was very, very strong since the Mugello race. It surprised me, because last year he struggled a lot with Ducati and this year he was very fast.'

He was now also Marc Márquez's new teammate at Repsol Honda. Two Spanish bulls in one garage; something would have to give.

CHAPTER 10

FAME

'IT'S THE THING THAT I MISS MOST – STILL TRYING TO BE NORMAL AND LIVING IN MY HOME TOWN. BUT I CANNOT BE A NORMAL BOY.'

Marc Márquez

During the 2018 season, Marc Márquez had finally decided to move out of the family home, but he didn't move far from the embrace of his mother, father and brother, and he knew what his priorities were. 'I am in the process of building a house in Cervera,' he explained in a Repsol promotional video in which a montage allowed him to interview himself. 'The first thing I told the architect was that I need a large garage. I need it for my training bikes. As for the house itself, the most important thing is a good sofa because the living room is the sacred room. Sitting on a Sunday with a blanket watching a movie is something that happens at my house too!'

Sofa and garage aside, there were other reasons why Márquez needed a place of his own – he had become incredibly famous, particularly in Spain, and he needed his own space away from prying eyes and photographers. 'It's interesting, because five years ago I thought that I would always keep the same style of living,' he explained. 'I thought that I didn't need a big house, I don't need VIP in the disco, I don't need a private jet, and I didn't want any of it. But the life moves you in that direction. I'm building a new house, a big one, because I need my privacy inside it.'[107]

Now a seven-time world champion, Márquez also decided to splash out on his travel arrangements because he was mobbed at every airport in Spain. 'Now, sometimes I travel with a private jet, especially in the summertime in Europe, because I can't move. I like to travel normally but imagine how busy the airport in Barcelona is in summer – I nearly missed a flight last year because it took so long to get through there!'[108]

The pressures of fame were taking their toll on Márquez, and severely affecting the kind of life he could lead. The VIP lifestyle was almost forced on him because of the level of his celebrity. As much as he would have preferred to live just as he had always done, it was simply no longer possible. 'I don't like to go to nightclubs and sit with my table in the VIP area, because I'd rather be on the dance floor with my friends, but I can't,' he bemoaned. 'Life moves you in that way, and I don't like it or want it. It's the thing that I miss most – still trying to be normal and living in my home town. But I cannot be a normal boy. I am very social – I would like to be more in the middle of the people, but I have realised it is impossible.'[109]

At least his new house in Cervera was acceptable to the Spanish public, unlike his proposed move to Andorra back in 2014. After he had found a house there, the Andorran government reportedly leaked the news and Márquez found himself facing a backlash from fellow Spaniards who felt he should be paying his taxes in Spain rather than taking advantage of the tax breaks that Andorra famously offers.

It was an accusation that hurt Márquez deeply, to the point where he even spoke publicly about it to try to explain his motives. Never one to discuss his private life in public, a clearly emotional Márquez addressed the media ahead of the 2014 Superprestigio dirt track event in Barcelona. 'I never speak about my private life, but I think that this is an important moment,' he said. 'Those who know me know that I have always been very straightforward and very honest. I am 21 years old, I live with my family, and I have always had a very close relationship with them, but like any young person I decided to get my own space, my own house and (I chose) to live in Andorra because I've been there many winters, many times of the year and, above all, because I'll also be there for many winters and many times of the year. It is an ideal and favourable environment to prepare myself physically.'

Many top-level motorcycle racers live in Andorra for the year-round training opportunities and favourable tax rates, and it's easy to understand why. Márquez was paying a 50 per cent tax rate in Spain while in Andorra he would only pay around 10 per cent. But he denied this was the reason for his planned move. 'Taxes have not been the motivation,' he insisted. 'Moreover, I do not know what is going to happen in the future, but I want to make it clear that I pay – and I'll continue to pay – my taxes in Spain.

'I know that there have been all kinds of opinions, and all of them are respectable. I don't want to justify myself to anyone here, but I think that there has been some very tough criticism aimed at me. In the end, you never know when the career of a rider will end and, when I was 19 years old, I was about to leave racing after damaging my eyesight. Thanks to Dr Bernat Sánchez, I could return (at this point Márquez paused to wipe away tears). This past week has been bad, and I just want to thank all the people that have been supporting me and my family. The only thing I want is to continue enjoying riding my bike.'

While the move would have been perfectly legal, the furore it caused (unfairly, it could be said) decided Márquez against it and he remained in Spain, eventually building a house in his home town instead. He didn't need the constant distraction of bad press, nor did he want to be viewed as a tax dodger amongst his own people; he just wanted to concentrate on his riding, and there was a lot to concentrate on in 2019 with a new teammate in Repsol colours.

The combination of Marc Márquez and Jorge Lorenzo was hailed as a dream team by the media – one of the strongest teams in the history of Grand Prix racing, on paper, at least. They had eight MotoGP world titles between them (12 world titles including the smaller classes) and they had won every MotoGP title since 2011. They had taken 150 wins and over 250 podiums and, with both riders mounted on the bike that had won four out of the last five world championships, the scene was set for an epic intra-team battle for the title between two of the greatest riders of all time. Both men put brave faces on the set-up that would be a nightmare for most team managers. Márquez and Lorenzo were fiercely competitive, and both were desperate to be the best Spanish rider; one of them was going to be brutally disappointed. 'With this kind of story, having two roosters in the same backyard, people usually see only the negatives,' Lorenzo said pre-season. 'But having two excellent riders will help us both to grow . . . It's natural for Marc and me to compete. It's a love-hate relationship that makes us better.'[110]

Márquez was not enjoying the angle the press was taking. 'I don't like this idea of a "dream team",' he said. 'It is only a dream team if, at the end of the season, we're still in the running.'

It certainly wasn't a financial dream for Lorenzo. With Márquez already demanding an astronomical wage, Lorenzo was forced to take a drastic pay cut, rumoured to be down £4 million rather than the £12 million Ducati had paid him; a condition he agreed to because he desperately wanted a competitive bike and, at the time he signed for Honda, he had been struggling badly on the Ducati.

Both riders began the new season with injury problems. Márquez had crashed in practice at the final round of the 2018 season and dislocated his shoulder yet again so had complex corrective surgery over the winter and wouldn't feel completely comfortable on the bike until the fourth round in Jerez. 'Complicated situations are what make you strong, and this winter was one of the toughest in my career because I couldn't do what I like most in the world – ride my motorcycle,' Márquez explained. 'I couldn't train because I needed the operation, but I overcame it with the help of all the people who pushed me. I arrived at the first race, maybe not 100 per cent, but in the best way I could be. You always think that all that work has to have a reward. Once you start and you see the results coming, it gives you even more strength.'[111]

Lorenzo's Honda career got off to a bad start when he broke his left scaphoid in a dirt bike training accident, meaning he missed the crucial three-day pre-season test in Sepang. Not what he needed, with a bike that he struggled to ride from the start.

Jorge Lorenzo's riding style was as smooth as silk. He was not the last of the late brakers, nor was he one for spinning and sliding a bike in the way that Marc Márquez had always done. His greatest strength lay in his mid-corner speed and for this he needed complete trust in the front end of the Honda. He didn't have it, and the more he pushed, the more he crashed.

To be fast on a Honda, riders needed to brake so hard that they squeezed the tyre into the tarmac, thereby expanding its contact patch. That just wasn't Lorenzo's style, and it soon became clear that he just wasn't suited to the Honda, nor it to him. It suited Márquez and, increasingly, only Márquez.

Because of their radically different riding styles, Márquez and Lorenzo set their RCVs up very differently. Lorenzo opted for a revised seat unit, fairing and fuel tank, as well as running a different ride height to Márquez but, no matter what he tried, he never found the confidence in the front that he needed to be his usual fast and smooth self. The dream team was showing chinks in its armour before the racing had even begun.

When it did begin, under the floodlights of Qatar, as was now tradition, Lorenzo treated the first few races as tests, trying to find a base setting that he could then gradually refine. Márquez had no such problems. The RCV had a new chassis and swingarm for 2019 and he was happy with it from the outset and was competitive throughout the Qatar weekend while Lorenzo crashed and broke a rib in practice. He bravely chose to race but could only finish in 13th place while Márquez spent the race battling with Andrea Dovizioso for the win. He didn't get it. Yet again it came down to a last lap, last corner move, and yet again, Dovizioso proved the better man, getting a faster exit out of the last corner and blasting the Ducati over the line just 0.02 seconds ahead of Márquez's Honda.

The Argentine Grand Prix was a very different affair. Márquez had never particularly liked Qatar but at the Termas de Río Hondo circuit he was imperious, setting pole position, posting the fastest lap of the race, and taking the win by the biggest margin he'd ever achieved in MotoGP – an incredible 9.82 seconds. He led the race from lights to flag and could have won by an even greater margin had he not slackened his pace over the last few laps.

On occasions like that, Marc Márquez made the greatest riders on the planet look decidedly average, such was his advantage. He may have been almost ten seconds behind, but in his 23rd season of Grand Prix racing, Valentino Rossi proved there was still life in the old dog by taking second place. After accidentally pressing his pit-lane limiter on the start line, Jorge Lorenzo had another tough race to 12th place.

The track surface at the Circuit of the Americas was so bumpy that Márquez couldn't even hold full throttle on the back straight, and the constant vibration and jarring from all the bumps played havoc with his shoulder. It didn't prevent him from setting pole position – as he had done at COTA every year since 2013 – and it didn't stop him from carving out a 3.6-second lead after just eight laps of the race. It looked like being another rout but, on lap nine, the front of his RCV folded and sent him sliding out. Márquez was at a loss to explain what had happened and it was only when his team returned to Europe that they discovered the crash had been caused by a glitch in the bike's engine braking software.

Jorge Lorenzo only lasted one more lap than Márquez: he had just scraped into the top ten before his Honda cruised to a halt with another electronics failure. His chain had already jumped off during practice. For him, the 'dream team' was turning into a nightmare.

After setting so many records over the years, Marc Márquez lost one at Jerez when 20-year-old rookie Fabio Quartararo became the youngest ever rider to set pole position. The Frenchman had been signed by the new satellite Petronas Yamaha SRT team to ride alongside Franco Morbidelli and he had already fired a warning shot during his MotoGP debut at Qatar when he set the fastest lap of the race after having to start from the pit lane.

Quartararo's pace and potential were all the more surprising given that he had only ever won a single Grand Prix in the Moto2 class and hadn't exactly been on every MotoGP team's shopping list. But he took to the Yamaha M1 instinctively and became yet another rider Marc Márquez would have to deal with. New blood. A new threat. And with a pace that reminded everyone of Márquez when he first burst on to the MotoGP scene in 2013.

Quartararo had been lying second to Márquez at Jerez before the young Frenchman's gear lever jammed on lap 14 and forced him out of the race, in tears. But he was clearly a coming force.

After Quartararo's demise, Márquez was untroubled and won the Jerez race as well as retaking the championship lead by a single point from Suzuki rider Álex Rins, who had taken his first MotoGP win in America the previous month. The Suzuki was now a proven race-winning package and yet another threat to the reigning champion. The threats were mounting.

Nobody could touch Márquez at Le Mans, however. Despite suffering several falls during practice, he saved another massive slide in the most spectacular fashion: his left leg was entirely off the bike, the front wheel on complete opposite lock, and only his right elbow and knee saved him when he dug them into the tarmac to push his RCV back upright. Even he was impressed. 'This was a good one, because I was on the kerb,' he said. 'I had to push a lot from the knee.'

It was all part of the master plan, though; he found the limits in practice, then pulled back slightly for the race, while still being by far the fastest rider out there.

After starting from pole position for the 55th time (which equalled Valentino Rossi's tally), Márquez had to fight in the early stages of the Le Mans race but had extra pace when it mattered. His 47th class win equalled Jorge Lorenzo's overall haul and handed

Honda its 300th premier class win since it first started competing in Grands Prix in 1966.

Nothing was going to stop Danilo Petrucci winning the Italian Grand Prix – not even Marc Márquez, although he came very close. Petrucci was in his eighth year in MotoGP but had never won a race. Now on a factory Ducati, he had the means to end that barren spell, and he took full advantage. An Italian, on an Italian bike, in an Italian team, winning the Italian Grand Prix? It was as good as it gets for the hugely popular Petrucci, and no one in the paddock begrudged him a win at last, after trying so hard for so many years. He wasn't a championship threat, however, so Márquez was content with a very close second place (0.04 seconds behind), having passed his main title rival, Andrea Dovizioso, on the final lap. Márquez feared that if he attacked Petrucci, he risked them both running wide and allowing Dovizioso through. He played it safe, again thinking of the bigger picture.

Jorge Lorenzo's Honda misery continued at Catalunya when he crashed out on lap two, taking out Andrea Dovizioso, Maverick Viñales and Valentino Rossi at the same time. Lorenzo's admission that it was 'very difficult to go all race without making a mistake' on the RCV served to make Márquez's performances on the bike all the more astonishing. With Dovizioso out, Márquez romped to a comfortable win and extended his championship lead over the Italian to 37 points.

Things went from bad to worse for Lorenzo at Assen. After crashing out of the Catalan Grand Prix, he crashed again in the test held there after the race, then again during Free Practice 1 at Assen. This time there were more serious consequences: he fractured the T6 and T8 vertebrae in his back and would have to wear a body brace for a month.

In the Assen race, Márquez settled for a safe second behind runaway winner Maverick Viñales, saying, 'I knew I couldn't win today, because we always struggle here with the direction changes, and because the Yamahas were very, very fast.' With Dovizioso only finishing fourth, it was another few points in the championship bag, and Germany was up next; Márquez had still never been beaten at the Sachsenring.

His record would continue in 2019, with a tenth pole position and race win and a new outright lap record to boot. He also set a new record for lean angle; his data showing he had hauled the RCV over to an astonishing 66 degrees. It was, he felt, too much. 'One reason is not turning a lot, so I need to lean more to compensate,' he said. 'But 66 degrees is too much – I must find another way.'[112]

After another dominant performance, Márquez went into the summer break with a lead of 58 points – more than two race wins' worth of points. Better still, brother Álex also won at the Sachsenring and retook the Moto2 title lead. It would be a happy three-week break for the family Márquez.

When action resumed at a very wet Brno, the other riders could only look on with wonder and envy as Márquez was clearly now at the peak of his powers and almost able to walk on water. He could certainly ride on water; in wet conditions he took pole by an outrageous 2.5 seconds. It was his 58th pole position and it equalled Mick Doohan's record. There had been no need to take such risks in treacherous conditions, but Márquez later admitted he just couldn't help himself. 'I realise now it was too much risk, especially with the situation in the championship,' he said. 'But it is my ambition – my mentality. When I was younger, it was always my weakest point.'[113]

In other words, he slithered, slid, bucked and weaved his way to a lap 2.5 seconds faster than any of his rivals just for the sheer fun and hell of it: he was a natural born racer.

Márquez was never troubled in the race and took his sixth win of the season while his brother won in Moto2 again, and also extended his title lead.

By this point in his career, Márquez's rivals had changed. Dani Pedrosa had retired, Jorge Lorenzo was still out with his broken back and lying in a lowly 16th in the championship, and Valentino Rossi was no longer the force he had once been – he took sixth place at Brno to consolidate his sixth place in the championship. In their stead were riders like Andrea Dovizioso, Maverick Viñales, Álex Rins, Fabio Quartararo and Danilo Petrucci but none of them, as yet, had any answer to Marc Márquez: he was utterly dominant and in a class of one. If he was beaten, it was usually because he had opted not to take any extra risks, especially to beat a rider who wasn't a championship threat.

There were, however, rare occasions when he was beaten fair and square, and the Austrian Grand Prix was one such example. Starting from pole position (he had now set more pole positions than any rider in history), Márquez battled so fiercely and so closely with Andrea Dovizioso on the last lap that their bikes became entangled, and only separated when the front brake lever guard snapped off Márquez's Honda RCV. Dovizioso then used the Ducati's raw speed to outgun his rival to the finish line by 0.21 seconds. Márquez was magnanimous in defeat and had clearly enjoyed the battle. 'To win the war,' he said, 'sometimes you have to lose some battles.'

He would lose another battle at Silverstone, now fully resurfaced after the previous year's debacle, and with improved drainage too. Álex Rins's winning margin over Márquez was the fourth closest in Grand Prix history – just 0.02 seconds. The Suzuki rider mugged

Márquez on the line to take a brilliant win, fair and square, from the fastest rider on the planet. It was an impressive performance.

Jorge Lorenzo was back in the Repsol box at Silverstone but was a shadow of his former self, qualifying in last position, some 3.6 seconds off the pace. Still hurting from his back injury, Lorenzo could only manage 14th place in the race, prompting further rumours that he would not see out his two-year contract with Honda.

Marc Márquez had crashed out of Free Practice 1 at Silverstone. Nothing new there. Except, there was: he hadn't crashed for three months – his last fall had been during round five at Le Mans, back in May. Silverstone was round 12, so Márquez's crash posed a question: was he no longer having to push as hard as before? With Rossi, Lorenzo and Dani Pedrosa no longer hounding him, was he finding it easier to win against his new rivals, or had he just had a lucky streak?

Fully accepting that crashing is part of racing, Márquez had a strategy worked out to deal with the inevitable falls. 'Whenever I crash, I always go straight back out on to the track, even if only for a single lap,' he explained. 'It doesn't matter if I'm in pain, it's always got to be clear out there that I'm in charge. It would be totally inappropriate to be in awe of quick turns and tricky areas. You can never let it come to that. If you do, you might as well give up right away, because you're going to be a second slower than you used to be.'[114]

It seems the real reason for the lack of crashes was the 2019-spec Honda RC213V. With more torque, Márquez found it an easier bike to ride, meaning he wasn't having to force it do what it didn't want to do. The bike clearly didn't suit Lorenzo, but then, it had been built around Márquez for the last seven years, and it suited his particular, and unique, style. With the ongoing refinements to the RCV, by 2019 Márquez had a bike that he felt truly comfortable on, and that meant fewer crashes.

He was lucky to avoid crashing out of Qualifying 2 at Misano when he clashed with his old nemesis, Valentino Rossi, who dive-bombed Márquez and forced him to pick his bike up and run offline. It seemed an unnecessarily risky attack during qualifying and many suspected it was a hangover from the long-standing rivalry and hatred between the two men. Both were called to appear in front of the race stewards, though no further action was taken. 'I saw his bike arriving very late on the inside, with a speed that was impossible to turn the corner,' Márquez said of the incident. 'I don't understand such a move in qualifying.'

Misano was practically in Rossi's backyard (in fact the eight miles of roads between his house and the circuit were closed off to allow him to ride the route on his race bike as a promotional stunt) so he was unlikely to be punished for dirty riding there, unless it was an extreme case. Had Márquez made the same move, things might have been different.

The race turned into a frantic battle between Márquez and Fabio Quartararo, with the fast Frenchman only being beaten on the last lap. He was exultant. 'It was not only the best moment in my career, but the best in my life!' he said afterwards. 'When a seven-time champion is behind you all race, then he overtakes you in Turn 1 and you overtake back . . . This time we finished second, but really close.'[115]

With Andrea Dovizioso only managing a sixth-place finish, Márquez had a massive lead after Misano – a very fitting 93 points. The omens were good. He didn't have a serious challenger for the championship; it was his to lose. The only person who could beat Márquez now was Márquez himself, through an unforced error that led to injury. Winning a MotoGP world title is never easy, but Márquez was in about as comfortable a position as any rider could be in. He was fully fit, had a huge points lead, a bike he was comfortable with, and he was riding better – and more consistently – than any other rider in the field. He was at the very peak of his powers, and at MotorLand Aragón, he showed it.

Dominant throughout practice, he then set pole position for what was his 200th Grand Prix start, then decimated the opposition, building up a five-second lead before last lap celebrations saw him slow up to cross the line some three seconds ahead of Andrea Dovizioso. He now needed to score just two points more than the Italian at the next round and the title was his. He hadn't finished lower than second all season. It was a remarkable show of dominance in what Márquez said was his 'best ever season.'

It almost came apart at the Buriram circuit in Thailand, however. A terrifying crash in Free Practice saw him being stretchered off to hospital. He was highsided from his bike at Turn 7 and landed heavily on his left-hand side, his Honda destroyed, and the rear tyre completely ripped off. Márquez had been extremely lucky to avoid being hit by the flying RCV. He was whisked off for an MRI scan, his lower back and left leg causing him a great deal of pain.

But Márquez had a championship to win and couldn't let pain get in the way. He had crashed on the Friday morning but was back out on track in the afternoon, hurting, but able to ride once adrenalin had done its job. He set the sixth fastest time, despite his condition, and went on to take third place on the grid, having crashed again during qualifying.

For much of the race it looked like Márquez simply couldn't match the pace of impressive rookie Fabio Quartararo, or had perhaps settled for second place and the championship. The young Frenchman had a one-second lead over Márquez after ten laps, but Márquez badly wanted to take the title with a win, so he decided to push hard and see if he could close the gap.

He did, and by the final corner of the last lap he was ready to attack, slipping past Quartararo to deprive him of what had looked like a sure-fire win. The Frenchman was visibly deflated while Márquez was jubilant. 'On Thursday before starting the Grand Prix, I already said that my intention was to win this weekend, or at least try,' he said afterwards. 'Then your rivals tell you if you can or can't; they give you the answer immediately on track. That's why I tried until the last corner, because it's more beautiful to achieve the championship with a race win.'

Márquez had finished first or second in every race of the 2019 season, apart from the American Grand Prix where he crashed out due to an electrical fault. It was his sixth MotoGP title and his eighth across all classes. One more and he would match Valentino Rossi's overall tally of nine world championships. And Márquez was still only 26; he had years left in him.

There were still four rounds to go, and he couldn't afford to take it easy at the next race in Japan. Under orders from on high, he was expected to gain enough points to secure Honda's 25th Constructors' Championship in the company's own backyard. Márquez obliged by taking his first ever pole position at Motegi and his tenth of the year. In doing so, he completed the set – he had now set pole position at every circuit on the calendar. There seemed to be no stopping him.

There was no stopping him in the race either; he dominated yet again, though his bike ran out of fuel just a few corners into the slow-down lap. It had been close.

Yamaha's Maverick Viñales set pole position in Australia and looked odds-on to win, given that his time was half a second faster than anyone else's. Even Márquez admitted that Viñales was the man to beat, saying, 'He was faster than me, but sometimes the faster rider does not win the race.'

Yet again, Márquez kept his powder dry for a last lap lunge. He had shadowed Viñales for much of the race before taking the lead on the last lap. Desperate to regain it, Viñales lost control at Lukey Heights and crashed out, his bike almost taking out Márquez as it slid down the hill. Márquez crossed the line to take his 11th win of the season.

Viñales would have his revenge, taking the win in Malaysia while Márquez took second place and set yet another record: his haul of 395 points over 18 races bettered Jorge Lorenzo's previous best of 383 – and there was still a round to go.

While Marc Márquez didn't win in Malaysia, he celebrated every bit as hard when his brother Álex lifted the Moto2 world championship after finishing second to Brad Binder. 'It was beautiful,' Marc said of his brother's victory. 'It was amazing. I enjoyed celebrating his win in Malaysia more than my victory in Thailand.'

The brothers had done a title double in 2014 when Marc won the MotoGP title and Álex the Moto3 crown. Now it was a MotoGP/Moto2 double, and Marc was genuinely as excited to see his brother win as he was about his own championship victory. The whole Márquez family was ecstatic: things just couldn't get any better.

It was party time, and there was nowhere better to celebrate a sixth MotoGP title in seven years than Bangkok. 'We celebrated the title as it deserves to be celebrated, because it's a world championship and you never know when this dream is going to end, so you have to celebrate it to the fullest,' Márquez said on his return to Spain. 'We spent the night in Bangkok and had a good time with the whole team. I will not reveal the details, but there was dancing, shouting, partying – a little bit of everything.'[116]

Despite being so dominant in 2019, Márquez acknowledged that he still had more to learn; that there was more to come. 'When you have an excess of confidence that's when mistakes can happen,' he said, looking back on his season. 'It happened in the race we least expected, which was Austin (the Circuit of the Americas is located just outside Austin, Texas), where I fell when I was leading with a four-second advantage. It was a seemingly done victory and, because of how relaxed I was, I fell. That's why you always have to be completely focused, you can't get confused, and you have to learn from mistakes. It's been a very good year, but that doesn't mean that we can stop working.'[117]

While Álex Márquez crashed out of the final round at Valencia, his brother rounded out his best ever season with yet another win and secured the Teams' Championship title to add to the Constructors' and Riders' titles. He posed happily with Jorge Lorenzo wearing specially prepared 'Triple Crown' T-shirts, but Lorenzo's smile seemed to be one of relief that the season was over, rather than elation at the team's achievements.

After a dismal year that saw him lying 19th in the points table ahead of the final round, Jorge Lorenzo had called a press conference ahead of the last race of 2019 to announce his retirement. He would not be honouring his two-year contract with HRC; it was over. With three MotoGP titles and two 250cc world titles, Lorenzo was one of the greats, and his departure was met with a great deal of sadness. But it did present an opportunity: there was now a vacant seat in the factory Repsol Honda team and, as the newly crowned Moto2 world champion, Álex Márquez would be invited to fill it. In 2020, Marc and Álex Márquez would be teammates in MotoGP. It was a perfect scenario; Marc could help his brother learn the ropes in MotoGP, and being in the same team and on the same bike would make this process infinitely easier. Neither brother could know that disaster lay just around the corner, in more ways than one – 2020 was going to be a nightmare.

CHAPTER 11

PANDEMIC

'I REALLY TURN INTO AN ANIMAL THAT NO POWER
IN THE WORLD COULD CONSTRAIN.'
Marc Márquez

It spread so fast it was frightening. Within months it had spanned the globe: the pandemic that would ultimately cost millions of lives and change our world forever.

With the rapid spread of Covid-19, people around the world were forced to live their lives very differently. Many countries had forced lockdowns, meaning only essential workers could leave their homes, social distancing measures were put in place to keep the virus from spreading, and the wearing of facemasks became compulsory. Hospitals couldn't cope with the sheer number of casualties, foreign travel was all but impossible, and most public events were cancelled or postponed. Everything and everyone were affected by the coronavirus, and MotoGP riders were no exception. Marc Márquez spent two months in lockdown, bored and frustrated, like so many others. '2020 is a very difficult year due to the pandemic that has had a huge impact on everyone's lives, and we the athletes have not been an exception,' he said. 'Being isolated at home for more than two months was challenging, but since we knew there was no other option, we adapted to this strange situation the best we could, and I think we have handled it pretty well. I spent a lot of time with my brother, playing on the PlayStation, doing some indoor cycling, and watching some series.'[118]

For a while, it looked like racing would be impossible. The opening round of the 2020 season in Qatar was cancelled – although the smaller classes raced as they were already at the circuit for testing before travel bans came into place – and the FIM got their heads together to see what could be done.

The end result was a much-delayed start to the season and a shake-up of the calendar in a way that had never been seen in the long history of Grand Prix motorcycle racing. In order to reduce travel, two races would be held at several circuits, one week apart. This doubling up would also make up for all the races which had to be cancelled. Jerez would hold two back-to-back rounds, as would the Red Bull Ring, Misano, Catalunya, Aragón and Valencia. That meant eight Grand Prix races in Spain in one year, but it was better than no racing at all. To avoid confusion, these back-to-back races would be given different names so, while the first race at Jerez would be known as the Spanish Grand Prix, the second would be the Grand Prix of Andalusia. Some races were run in front of empty grandstands, as spectators were not permitted to attend. It was the strangest of times.

Riders and teams would be restricted to their own 'bubbles' to reduce contact with others, and regular Covid tests were carried out on all. The MotoGP paddock was much, much quieter than normal as only key staff were permitted to attend. The number of

TV presenters, photographers and reporters was vastly reduced, as were all other staff deemed to be non-essential.

As a result of all the chaos, and the ever-changing situation globally, the MotoGP riders didn't get their first race until 19 July, some four months later than had been originally planned. And there, at Jerez in southern Spain, a much more personal disaster struck Marc Márquez – one that would prove to be a watershed in his career.

The first 20 laps of Marc Márquez's 2020 season were, not unusually, dramatic. After saving a monster slide that no one else in the world could have saved, he got his head down and sliced his way through the pack from 19th to third place. It was a staggering display, and Márquez made the best riders on the planet look like club racers.

As his Repsol Honda teammate, Álex Márquez could now look at his brother's data, and even he was astonished by what he saw after the race. 'If you show Marc's data from today, everyone would be destroyed,' he said. 'He was unbelievable.'

He was. Until it all went wrong.

It had been noted for years how lucky Márquez had been to have crashed so often yet always to have walked away without any serious injuries. For some, it was inevitable that he would eventually get hurt and at Jerez, on 19 July, he finally did.

It was by no means a life-threatening injury, but it was a serious one all the same, and painful enough for Márquez to be seen screaming in pain as he removed his helmet; something he had never done before.

On paper, it didn't sound too bad: a broken humerus in his right arm with potential damage to the radial nerve. Márquez had been thrown violently from his bike after clipping a white line and the front wheel of his Honda RC213V smacked into him hard as bike and rider tumbled through the gravel trap.

Márquez crashed on the Sunday and had an operation on his arm on the Wednesday. Famed Grand Prix surgeon, Xavier Mir, inserted a titanium plate and 12 screws into Márquez's arm and assured his relieved patient that there was no damage to the radial nerve.

Immediately after the surgery, Márquez reported feeling fine and wanted to prove to Dr Mir that he was fit enough to race in the second Jerez race, one week after the first. 'I did a few push-ups in my hospital room right after surgery and it felt good,' he said. 'When we riders see the slightest chance of being able to compete in the race, we take it. You couldn't think any other way; at least, I couldn't. I really turn into an animal that no power in the world could constrain.'[119]

Two days after surgery, Márquez stunned everyone by turning up at Jerez, fully intending to ride. He completed 29 laps during Free Practice 3 and Free Practice 4 before finally conceding defeat. The injury was too painful, and so much fluid had built up in his right elbow that he couldn't move it. He also had no feeling in the fingers of his right hand. He was forced to withdraw from the Grand Prix and headed home to rest and heal.

Then a strange thing happened. So strange that many doubted the truth of it. Two days after returning home, it was announced that Márquez had broken the titanium plate in his arm while opening a sliding glass door in his house. 'I prised open a sliding door – I felt a crack and said, "Damn!"' Márquez later explained. 'I looked at it, and it had a bump. I said, "What is going on?" I woke up (my physio, Carlos J. Garcia) and my brother. That's when I started getting dizzy. I lay down on the bed and he said, "Let me see." I said, "I doubt I broke the metal implant." He grabbed my bone and it went "crack". He went pale and said, "Let's go." We went straight to hospital.'[120]

It was such an unusual claim that it could only be true, but cynics thought Márquez had been out training on a motocross bike too soon and had broken the plate that way. Even *Motocourse* called it a 'tall story' and called upon Márquez to 'pull the other one'. Yet, what reason did he have to lie? He would have been no less thought of if he had broken the plate while training. People might have thought him foolish for pushing himself too soon, but that wouldn't exactly be a first in Grand Prix racing.

The Repsol Honda team came under fire for allowing Márquez to even try riding at the second Jerez Grand Prix, but team boss Alberto Puig defended his decision to let his rider go out in practice, and blamed poor medical advice for the situation. 'The doctors were okay [for him] to return to Jerez, and they never informed us that the plate could have broken. If we had this info, probably he wouldn't have gone, and Honda would not have given him the chance to ride.'

Márquez later clarified the situation. He explained that the surgery had gone perfectly, so doctors were shocked that he had broken the arm again. In their experience, he said, titanium plates did not break, but Márquez had been training so hard he had weakened the plate and the simple act of pulling a sliding door open had been enough to finally snap it.

Three years after the fact, Márquez admitted it was the decision to race in Jerez so soon after the initial operation on his arm that had led to all the complications that followed. Had he waited until he was fully fit before attempting to race again, his arm would have healed in a relatively short space of time, and complications would not have set in. He didn't, and he openly admitted that had been entirely his fault. 'It was my mistake – I have no problem admitting it,' he said. 'I have a racer, killer, winner mentality: "Ignore my arm; I want to compete and win this year."'

Márquez had also continued training, straight after surgery, which compounded the problem. His right arm was a fragile ticking time bomb, just waiting to snap again.

A second operation was carried out on 3 August, and this time it didn't go so smoothly. A fragment of bone had to be replaced with a form of bone cement, but that procedure led to intense and painful inflammation, and on 3 December, he underwent a third surgery on his tortured right arm. It simply wasn't healing, and the pain never decreased. 'I was afraid I would not have a normal arm (again),' he said. 'There was one point in October/November when I was not able to take a bottle of water; I was straining to eat; I was not able to move the arm in a normal way. I was afraid.'

This third operation was an attempt to correct the pseudarthrosis – a disease that occurs when a broken bone fails to heal – which was affecting Márquez's arm. The procedure involved grafting some bone from his hip into his humerus in the hope that it would stimulate bone growth. The arm had been drilled into so many times by now that it was no longer strong enough to be able to heal itself. An artery from his knee was also removed and transplanted into the arm.

Márquez's doctors at the Hospital Ruber Internacional in Madrid were not entirely confident this third procedure would be successful, and they warned Márquez that, if it didn't work, then the only alternative was to have an external cage fitted, and that would require 18 months of rehabilitation. Even if the operation was successful, he was told it would take six months to fully recover.

The procedure also ran the risk of damaging the radial nerve in Márquez's arm, which could, in turn, leave him with permanently restricted movement. What had at first appeared to be a simple broken arm had turned into a nightmare. Márquez's racing career was hanging by a thread. The operation appeared to have worked but, in reality, it hadn't. No one realised it at the time, but the procedure had left Márquez's arm crooked. It was no fault of the five specialist surgeons; his humerus had been so badly infected that they simply didn't have the correct points of reference to be as accurate as they would have liked in setting the bone. Further complicating matters was the ongoing pain and lack of movement from the right shoulder operation Márquez had undergone at the end of the 2019 season to tighten the muscles and sinews to prevent his shoulder from continually dislocating. Following the surgery, Márquez was kept in hospital for ten days then sent home to recover, but that third operation would prove to have far-reaching consequences.

With Márquez absent, MotoGP was thrown wide open and there was a different winner at almost every round. Fabio Quartararo, Brad Binder, Andrea Dovizioso, Miguel Oliveira, Franco Morbidelli, Maverick Viñales, Danilo Petrucci, Álex Rins and Joan Mir all took turns on the top step of the podium. No one could put a consistent title campaign together, and so it came down to a battle of consistency, which Joan Mir would eventually win. He would take the title for Suzuki, despite winning just one race all season. With that, Suzuki walked away from the championship, meaning there was one less manufacturer on the grid. The reason cited was the sheer cost of MotoGP racing, but it was a body blow to the championship to lose a company that had such a long and proud history in the sport dating back to the early 1970s.

Márquez's crash also meant he didn't get to enjoy having his brother as a teammate. The two only competed in one race together – the fateful Jerez race in which Marc crashed out. Left as the sole Repsol Honda rider (although test rider Stefan Bradl was brought in to replace Marc), Álex Márquez faced an uphill struggle, but he responded well, the highlights of his season being second places in Le Mans and Aragón. He would finish the championship in 14th place, one place in front of the beleaguered Valentino Rossi, who was struggling on the Yamaha. The Italian superstar would lose his seat in the factory team at the end of the season.

At the sixth round of the championship in Austria, HRC announced that Marc Márquez would be out for at least two or three months, with the earliest possible comeback perhaps being at the penultimate pair of races at Aragón in mid-October.

Forced to watch the racing at home on TV, Márquez struggled with boredom and frustration. 'About the physical side, now I am in a good moment,' he said in September. 'But of course, I am still far from my normal level. It's true that, last week, I started to do some running and cycling. From the cardio side, the legs, and the left arm, my condition is quite good. But about the right arm, still I need to make some big steps, but now we are starting to do more exercises. I am looking forward to starting to push a little bit more in the gym. But, at the moment, we must respect the timings and just be patient.'

He also had to battle his inner demons, which chiefly stemmed from boredom. 'From the mental side it was hard in the beginning. Because you know, there was nothing to do at home, the days and even the hours were very, very long, but now we have a plan for each day. We do two sessions of physio and then we also train in the gym with my trainer – the left arm, the legs, along with some cardio. So now the mental side is feeling much better. The moment where I suffer the most is during the race weekend because you are watching the race, all the practice sessions from the TV, and it is not easy. Aside from this, we can say that I'm happy now. I'm happy because I already feel that we have made some steps forward.'

He began training when the doctors said he could and gradually increased his regime with the assistance of a carbon fibre casing to protect his injured arm. Unable to push himself on track, Márquez began to do it in the gym, working out more and more as the arm healed, and doing everything he possibly could to get back to fitness and back to racing. Running, physio, cycling, gym work, more physio . . . Márquez needed so much work on his arm to get movement back into it that his physio moved into the house with him, just to be on hand 24 hours a day. The dedication, focus and commitment Márquez had always shown on track was now being mirrored in his training regime: he would leave no stone unturned to get back to racing. The difference now was that he had learned his lesson and had no intention of getting back on a bike until he was truly capable of riding it properly. There were to be no shortcuts: trying to race at Jerez two days after the initial operation on his arm had taught him that much. Patience was key; patience and an increasingly gruelling training regime that would see him spending months pushing through the pain barrier.

Márquez's crash didn't just hurt him, it also hurt Honda. Without him being there to develop the bike, the RC213V was performing poorly in the hands of others. The highest Honda finisher in the 2020 championship was Takaaki Nakagami in tenth place, and the firm didn't take a win all year. What's more, the longer Márquez was out, the more Honda seemed to lose its way.

Álex Márquez was a rookie and could not be expected to lead development in his first year, Takaaki Nakagami would retire at the end of the 2024 season without ever winning a Grand Prix, and test rider Stefan Bradl hadn't been a serial winner when he was a full-time racer, never mind several years after the fact as a stand-in rider. Marc Márquez had been flattering the RCV for some time, but no one else could seem to ride it anywhere close to his level, and the fewer results the bike got, the less the top riders were likely to sign for the Japanese firm. It was a classic catch-22 scenario, and it would only get worse.

Márquez made a brief return to the paddock at Catalunya in late September to catch up with his team and update them on his ongoing recovery. At that point, he was still hoping to race in the final rounds of the championship at Valencia and Portimão, but in early November he announced he would sit them out and focus on getting fully fit for the 2021 season.

As stated previously, on 3 December he underwent a third eight-hour operation on his arm, this time to replace the titanium plate and to undergo a bone graft from his hip to promote bone growth in the humerus. More recovery time, more agonising physio, more gruelling training. On and on and on, never wavering in his determination to get back on a bike and start winning again.

It would have been so easy to retire from the sport. By that point in his career, Márquez had made more millions than he could ever spend and had eight world championships to his name. He had changed the face of MotoGP forever and had nothing left to prove. But his millions couldn't buy him the one thing he craved most; the feeling that he valued above all others; the sheer euphoria of winning.

In pursuit of that feeling, Márquez decided to race in 2021, despite still being in considerable pain and having a severe lack of mobility in his right arm and shoulder. He was forced to sit out the first round in Qatar to allow himself more time to heal, but turned up in Portugal for round two in a desperate attempt to resurrect his career.

In a bizarre move by Honda, Álex Márquez had been moved from the factory Repsol team to the satellite LCR Honda team, although he still had a factory bike and a contract with HRC. The move had been announced before Álex had even made his MotoGP debut for the Repsol team in 2020, with team boss Alberto Puig saying, 'We were aware that, for a rookie – depending on what your career has been like – Repsol Honda is sometimes not the best place to start, in the sense that you have a lot of pressure and you have to get results from day one. Racing alongside a person like Marc Márquez, whether he is your brother or not, is difficult for anyone.'[121]

Álex was replaced by Pol Espargaró, but all eyes were on Marc Márquez as he returned to MotoGP after 265 days away. He was nervous. 'I will not be the same Marc,' he said before practice commenced. 'I have some butterflies in my stomach, that aren't normal for me.'

As things got under way, it was clear to see Márquez was uncomfortable on the bike and didn't have the mobility he needed in his right arm and shoulder, but he managed to qualify in sixth place and rode through the pain barrier to claim a heroic seventh in the race, before slumping exhausted into his pit box chair, emotionally and physically drained. It was more than he could have hoped for, and more than most riders in his condition could have achieved, but the effort had utterly drained him. No amount of training in a gym can prepare a rider for the forces he has to contend with while riding a MotoGP bike. Those forces can only be replicated by riding and Márquez hadn't ridden a MotoGP bike for eight months. In preparation for his return, he had twice ridden Honda's road-legal RC213V-S version of its MotoGP bike, but even that didn't come close to muscling a 300bhp, 220mph factory MotoGP around a roller-coaster circuit like Portimão.

As well as being exhausted, Márquez and his team were also highly emotional after the race. He had proved he still had the speed, still had the desire and willingness to risk everything – even a crash that could end his career, should his arm be further damaged.

Márquez was visibly emotional during the post-race press conference, at one point having to take a few moments out to fight back tears. 'Of course, emotions is the correct word,' he said when he was able to speak. 'I'm a person who likes to keep the emotions inside, but when I arrived in the box with all my mechanics I just exploded, and I couldn't control the emotions.

'It has been a very long time that I've been dreaming about today – finishing a MotoGP race – and it's the biggest step in my rehabilitation, my recovery, and to feel again being a MotoGP rider was my dream, and it's what I did in Portugal. So, when I arrived in the box, of course I was tired, and I was exhausted. But it was the explosion of emotion that I couldn't control – but was very nice.'

Márquez went on to explain that he didn't even feel like he deserved to be in the race at first. 'Maybe the hardest thing was the first laps because I was not in my place,' he said. 'You know in school, when you play football with the older guys, they overtake you where they want? So, in the first laps I didn't feel in my place – I didn't have the pace, I didn't have control of the bike, and then everybody started to overtake me.

'The last six laps I was just sitting on the bike trying to finish the race. But the most important thing is to finish the race. And then if we check, to finish the race only 13 seconds behind Quartararo (the race winner), this is something incredible.'

Despite making a massive effort over the winter, Honda's new RCV still lacked grip and, in a desperate attempt to regain some of the feeling he used to get from the bike, Márquez ended up running a hybrid 2019/20 machine. Honda hated going backwards; it was an admission of defeat, but the simple truth was the new RCV just wasn't competitive, and the team was having to try anything it could to regain a competitive edge. Honda had won races every year since entering the premier class in 1982, but in 2020 they failed to win a single one. As unthinkable as it was, the biggest motorcycle manufacturer on earth was in trouble. It did not bode well for the future.

Márquez passed another test at Jerez: after crashing at 140mph and slamming hard into an air fence, he proved his arm was at least strong enough to withstand a major crash, although, obviously, it's sheer luck how a rider's body is thrown around in a crash, and it could very easily have ended differently. As a result of his fall, Márquez failed to make it through to Qualifying 2 and had to start the race from 14th place on the grid. Once again, he rode bravely to ninth, one position ahead of his teammate Pol Espargaró.

For the first time in his career, Márquez then entered a run of three races in which he didn't score a single point. In France, he crashed no fewer than four times on the Saturday in treacherous conditions. He wasn't alone; the constantly changing track surface led to 117 crashes over the weekend.

He started from sixth on the grid and, when the heavens opened on lap four, entered the pits to change to his wet weather bike. On exiting the pit lane, he took the lead and, by the end of the seventh lap, had carved out a 1.5-second advantage. Riding in the wet is far less physical than riding in the dry, so the conditions were in Márquez's favour as he was still a long way from being fully fit. He estimated that some of his muscles were at 80 per cent strength while others were only at 50 per cent. The pain was mostly coming from the back of his right shoulder, and that made right-hand corners particularly painful to deal with. In left-handers he felt 'normal', but would then overcompensate and try to make up too much time in those corners, leading to further crashes.

Jerez was a right-hand, clockwise circuit but, in wet conditions, it didn't pose the same problems it would have done in the dry, and for three glorious laps it looked like Marc Márquez was going to win his first Grand Prix in over a year. He hadn't even led a GP for 302 days, but he was master of dry/wet, flag-to-flag races, having taken six wins from the seven flag-to-flag races that had been run between 2014 and 2017.

The dream only lasted for three laps, however. On lap eight he lost the rear of his Honda in the final corner and was thrown off. Uninjured, he remounted and made his way through the field from 18th place to 11th place before crashing out yet again. This time, his bike was too badly damaged to continue. It was his sixth crash of the weekend.

The Italian Grand Prix at Mugello was overshadowed by the tragic death of 19-year-old Swiss Moto3 rider, Jason Dupasquier. He had crashed heavily during qualifying on Saturday and, just as the Moto2 grid was lining up to race on the Sunday, it was announced that he had succumbed to his injuries.

A minute's silence was held ahead of the MotoGP race. It was obviously well intended but, for riders about to go out and risk their own lives, it was a difficult process to endure, and a harsh reminder of the risks they were all about to take; cruel, almost. Francesco Bagnaia, Aleix Espargaró and Danilo Petrucci all felt the meeting should have been abandoned, as had happened following Marco Simoncelli's death at Sepang in 2011.

Márquez very nearly withdrew from the race, not because of the tragic fatality, but because his arm and shoulder had proved to be terribly painful during practice and qualifying. In the end, he did race, but not for long; he only lasted two laps before crashing out yet again.

The once dominant Marc Márquez, the man who had repeatedly destroyed the greatest motorcycle racers on earth, was lying in 18th place in the 2021 championship standings with just 16 points to Fabio Quartararo's 105. And things would get even worse.

At Catalunya, he failed to make it through to Q2 again, and only lasted ten laps of the race before crashing out for the third race in a row. If he wasn't at rock bottom, he was very near it. The other Honda riders didn't fare any better, and all were having to override the RCV to even keep the other riders in sight. 'In acceleration, we cannot get the grip,' Márquez said, 'and in the entry, we cannot stop the bike. Two different problems, in two different areas, but I think the solution is going in the same way. So, we are braking late, and when you're braking with a lot of banking, these things [crashes] happen.'[122]

Of the other Honda riders in the Catalunya race, Pol Espargaró also crashed out, while Álex Márquez finished 11th and Takaaki Nakagami was 13th out of the 15 finishers. In Marc Márquez's absence, Honda had lost its way, and the RCV was no longer a competitive MotoGP bike. It meant that, injured and restricted though he was, Márquez was having to ride harder than ever, repeatedly pushing beyond the limits just to stay in touch, therefore increasing the risk of crashing and further damaging his already battered body. It started to seem like Márquez would never win another race. He needed a more competitive bike, but he had signed a four-year extension with Honda in 2020, so he was trapped: the greatest rider of his era was having to ride what was, by now, the most uncompetitive bike in the field.

Then came the Sachsenring.

Márquez had always performed miracles on the anticlockwise circuit, the predominance of left-hand corners perfectly complementing his dirt track riding style. In dirt track racing, every corner is a left-hander, and Márquez had won the last ten races at the Sachsenring. Left-handed circuits were also much less painful for him to ride as they put less stress on his injured right arm and shoulder. He might, at last, be able to salvage a result. After three crashes in a row, even a top ten could be considered a result. But then, Marc Márquez never raced to score top ten positions.

In the German Grand Prix, he was running much closer to the front and, when there was a brief shower mid-race, Márquez used his superior feel, aggression and skill to pull away from the pack and win the race by 1.6 seconds from Miguel Oliveira. It had been 581 days since his last win and, under the circumstances, it must be considered one of his greatest ever victories. His win was instantly hailed as one of the greatest comebacks from injury ever seen in Grand Prix racing, right up there alongside Mick Doohan and Barry Sheene's astounding returns to form after very serious injuries. (In 1992, Doohan had both legs sewn together so the blood flow from the good leg could feed the mangled one. The procedure saved him from amputation, and he came back to win five successive 500cc Grand Prix championships. Sheene had twice returned from near fatal crashes in 1975 and 1982.) Márquez had spoken at length with Doohan ahead of the German race and took great inspiration from the tough-as-nails Australian's advice and encouragement.

After the race, Márquez revealed that his injuries were so bad the previous year that he had considered quitting the sport rather than be left permanently disabled. 'In September, October and November, I was scared about more than not winning again,' he confessed. 'I was thinking about my arm, my life, not about racing.' And yet, here he was, back on the top step of the podium at a MotoGP race, having just beaten the best riders in the world, on the worst bike on the grid, with no pre-season testing, while also being handicapped by his injuries. It was nothing short of miraculous.

It was a huge moment for both Márquez and his Honda team. 'This is one of the most important, and hardest, moments of my career,' he said afterwards. 'Today I knew there was a great opportunity to do something. When I crossed the line, I just enjoyed it, and then arriving with my whole team there, emotional, it helps a lot after such a difficult situation. It's impossible to come back alone, you need people, you need a good team, a good team of doctors, a physio, Honda . . . Honda respect me a lot. Alberto Puig, Emilio Alzamora, my family, they helped me a lot. Now it's time to enjoy this weekend. We were looking for a petrol station but now we found one and the fuel tank is full again. It's extra motivation for me, for Honda, for the engineers, for the team, and let's see what the future brings. When I saw some drops of rain on lap four or five, I said, "It's my race!" I started pushing at this point and then, when it started to rain harder, I pushed even more, and then the second race with [Miguel] Oliveira began. He pushed so hard and was very fast, it was hard to keep concentrated because all the memories – everything I have lived over the last year – came into my mind. But we did it. We will do it again.'[123]

We will do it again. Márquez still clearly had confidence that Honda could turn things around with its RCV, but team boss Alberto Puig urged caution. 'Sunday was an important day because we could manage a victory,' he said in the week following the race, 'but we do not believe that our problems are fixed.'

He was right to be cautious. At Assen, Márquez's bike's electronics failed in Free Practice 2, and he was brutally thrown from the bike yet again, and was extremely lucky to escape injury. As a result of the crash, he could only qualify in 20th place – third last.

Seventh place in the Assen race was followed by an eighth in the first of two encounters at the Red Bull Ring in Austria, and things got even worse in the second Austrian race (due to the ongoing Covid-19 pandemic, the 2021 season again saw back-to-back races at certain circuits, often with no spectators present in the interests of social distancing). In a flag-to-flag race which would normally have suited Márquez and his uncompetitive Honda, he pitted and changed to his 'wet' bike but crashed out due to his tyres not being up to temperature. He remounted and finished 15th and last, a shadow of his former self.

Yet he claimed his motivation never waned. 'My motivation is higher than before, because it is the first time that I have a very hard moment in my career,' he said mid-season. 'In the hard moments you need to show your potential. In the good moments everybody is happy and smiling and quick – in the hard moments you need to fight. The easiest way would be to stop and come back when I feel ready in one or two years. But that's not my style. My style is to try to suffer to improve and come back. And to enjoy it on the bike. Now I am not enjoying it, now I am suffering.'[124]

The misery continued at Silverstone where he crashed at 170mph in Free Practice 1 then collided with Jorge Martin on the first lap of the race, causing both riders to crash. It was Márquez's 16th crash of the year – more than any other rider. Tellingly, his teammate Pol Espargaró stood second in the rankings with 15 crashes. The Honda was all but unrideable, despite having a new chassis. After 12 rounds (although he missed the first round), Márquez had accumulated just 59 points and was languishing in a lowly 12th position in the championship.

But just as it seemed that the dream was over and only an endless nightmare remained, Márquez pulled a rabbit out of the hat again at Aragón – one of his beloved left-hand circuits which he could ride in more comfort.

Another significant side effect of Márquez's lack of upper body strength was that he no longer had the ability to save crashes on his elbows and knees; he simply wasn't strong enough to haul the bike back upright and, as a result, he crashed even more often. 'The word "save" is not in my dictionary any more,' he bemoaned. With both rider and bike below par, Márquez was having to try harder than ever but, no matter how hard he tried, the results just weren't coming.

So, Aragón came as a huge relief. After qualifying in a respectable fourth place (despite another two crashes in practice), he took the fight to rising Italian star Francesco 'Pecco' Bagnaia. The pair engaged in a fierce fight throughout the race, with no fewer than seven overtakes in the last two laps. Bagnaia had shown pace before but had made too many mistakes under pressure and had yet to win a MotoGP race. There would be no mistakes in Aragón though, and every time Márquez pushed past, the Italian responded, eventually winning by less than a second. It was Bagnaia's first premier class win; it would not be his last.

After such a dismal run since the Sachsenring, a close second place must have felt like a win for Márquez. Honda had brought another new chassis to Aragón – the third different chassis in five races – and, while Márquez confirmed it was an improvement in some areas, Honda still seemed to be all at sea, with the other Honda riders preferring a different chassis and Márquez pursuing his own development path. There was no cohesion and no clear route forward for HRC. Neither Márquez nor the designers and engineers could figure out what direction they needed to go in to improve the RCV. The confusion was evident in a comment made by Pol Espargaró at Aragón: 'We are trying to improve the low grip on the edge [of the tyres], floating on entry, spinning with the bike straight . . . trying to get more grip, or applying force on the rear tyre in a different way.' It was clear there wasn't just one issue holding the Honda riders back – there were many.

While the RCV wasn't getting any better, nor were Márquez's injuries. Despite being so competitive at Aragón, he later admitted he had been suffering all weekend, and even had Alpinestars make him a new set of leathers with additional room at the right shoulder. 'At Aragón, I was suffering with a lot of pain in the shoulder,' he admitted after the event. 'I don't feel comfortable. I can't slide the bike and turn – one of my strong points. Now I go in (to the corner) like the others. In left corners, I can push with the left, but in right corners I have understeering. For this reason, I crash many times about the front, and I cannot save with the elbow.'[125]

From the outside, to the casual viewer or spectator, it might have appeared that Marc Márquez was simply past his best, and his lack of results was merely a reflection of this. Nothing could have been further from the truth as Repsol Honda team boss Alberto Puig acknowledged. 'I don't know if people really understand the level of the rider that he is,' he said. 'Marc's comeback has been more difficult than expected, due to the injury and what happened, and what he's doing currently in his situation, it's really amazing. He's riding with – I will not say one arm – but let's say with one-and-a-half arms. I think only one guy can do this, and it's him.'[126]

After taking fourth place at Misano, Márquez and the MotoGP circus moved on to the left-handed Circuit of the Americas (COTA), where he could be confident of a better result.

His opening salvo was promising – third position in qualifying saw him start a race from the front row of the grid for the first time since his return to racing. His performance in the race was even more astonishing; he led every corner of every lap for the entire race and crossed the finish line with the biggest winning margin of the year, 4.67 seconds ahead of Fabio Quartararo.

Honda finally appeared to be making some progress with its RCV as the second race to be held at Misano that year saw Marc Márquez and Pol Espargaró take the team's first one-two since 2017. Significantly, Misano is a right-hand circuit, so the result also boded well for Márquez's injured arm, although damp conditions over the whole weekend also played in his favour as the riding element was less physical.

Espargaró felt the team had turned a corner, saying, 'It feels like we have been able to break this wall,' but both he and Márquez benefitted from Francesco Bagnaia's crash on lap 22. The Italian had been leading the race when he fell and handed the Repsol team a one-two instead of second and third places. Bagnaia's crash also meant the end of his championship charge: Fabio Quartararo now had an unassailable points lead of 65 points with just two rounds and 50 points left up for grabs.

Márquez's run of form had hoisted him up to sixth place in

the championship, but Misano would be the last time he raced in 2021. He withdrew from the Portuguese Grand Prix, the reasons shrouded in mystery at the time. The official line was that he had suffered a concussion during a dirt bike training accident, team boss Alberto Puig saying it was a 'precautionary measure'. Many were sceptical, including Aleix Espargaró, the brother of Márquez's teammate Pol Espargaró. 'If it's a head concussion, it must be hard,' he said. 'If it wasn't, Marc would be here racing for sure. I don't know if concussion is the right word. I think it's something bigger.'

Espargaró was proven correct a week later when Márquez announced he would not be racing in the final round of the championship at Valencia either. He had, in fact, suffered another bout of diplopia following the dirt bike crash. The double vision problem had almost ended his career back in 2011 and he was now facing more complex and delicate surgery to correct his eye and, once again, there was no guarantee the operation would be a success. And this was on top of the ongoing arm and shoulder problems Márquez was still suffering from.

It meant he was facing yet another winter of surgery, rehabilitation and uncertainty. It would be the fourth winter in succession that he'd had to deal with such a long and painful process. To make matters worse, Márquez would also have to miss the crucial test at Valencia following the final race of the season. Without him being present to lead development of the 2022 RC213V, Honda's chances of building a more competitive bike took another blow. At that point, it wasn't even certain that Márquez would be fit enough to take part in the Sepang test in February. Development of the new bike would fall to Pol Espargaró, and once he had settled on an engine specification, the engines would be sealed for the duration of the 2022 season, as

MotoGP regulations dictate. His decision would be crucial and Marc Márquez could play no part in it. He was at the mercy of whichever specification Espargaró favoured, and would just have to race the bike, come what may. If, indeed, he was passed fit to race in 2022: he still had the threat of blindness hanging over him again. Márquez was not in a good place.

With Valentino Rossi having bowed out of MotoGP racing after the Valencia round, it seemed a changing of the guard was inevitable. One giant of the sport had retired, the other was uncertain if he would ever be able to race again. Another winter of discontent fell upon Marc Márquez.

CHAPTER 12

TO HELL AND BACK

'THERE WAS A MOMENT IN THE SEASON WHEN I TURNED MY HEAD OFF AND SAID THAT I CAN'T TAKE IT ANY MORE.'

Marc Márquez

Marc Márquez had finished the 2021 MotoGP season in seventh place, having taken three race wins. His brother Álex, riding the same bike, but for the satellite LCR Honda team, finished in 16th place with a season best of eighth place in the penultimate round in Portugal.

As Marc continued to struggle with his injuries, so too Honda continued to struggle with its RC213V. For the 2022 season, the team rolled out an all-new version of the bike: new chassis, new bodywork and very different exhausts. The Japanese engineers had worked hard, no one could deny that, but would the bike work?

At first, Pol Espargaró seemed to think so. He finally felt he had the grip he needed and seemed to prove it by setting fast lap times and race simulations on the bike in pre-season tests. But, as Marc Márquez later pointed out, it was a false impression. After days of testing at any particular circuit, so much rubber is laid down from spinning tyres that good grip is practically a foregone conclusion. Tests are the only times during the year when this is the case, however. When riders and teams turn up at every other circuit during the season, that kind of grip just isn't there, as the Honda teamsters discovered once racing began. It was this kind of insight that HRC had missed, with Márquez being injured so repeatedly in recent seasons.

By the time the racing started, every Honda rider complained about practically every aspect of the bike: it seemingly had no redeeming features or strong points at all. The riders were experiencing a 'floating' feeling from the rear when they braked, they were getting no 'feel' from the front end of the bike on corner entry, the bike wasn't turning as it should – which then made corner exits more difficult – and they all complained of a lack of edge grip through the corners and on corner exits. And, to top it all, the bike's acceleration and top speed were also way behind the opposition. It was, in fact, the worst version of the RC213V that Honda had ever built. The once dominant company was hopelessly lost.

Things got even more desperate and confusing as the season progressed, and HRC explored every possible avenue to improve its machine. Up to eight different chassis variations were tried over the season, as well as endless changes and experiments with the aerodynamic 'wings' that other manufacturers had long since perfected. Honda even took the drastic step of seeking outside help when they asked Moto2 chassis specialists Kalex to build an aluminium swinging arm for the RCV.

Still in great pain, and still very restricted in his movements even after three operations on his right arm, Marc Márquez lined up in Qatar to race a bike he knew he had no chance of winning on. Yet still he fought, still he pushed, still he refused to give up.

Unsure whether he could take part in the pre-season tests in Malaysia and Indonesia, due to ongoing problems with double vision, Márquez was finally given the all-clear at the last minute and tentatively took part in both tests before heading to Qatar for the season opener. Somehow, he managed to qualify in third place and then took an encouraging fifth place in the race.

It was a performance that flattered the RCV, and it was only at the second round in Indonesia that the bike's true nature was revealed. Márquez crashed three times during practice and qualifying, including twice within seven minutes during Qualifying 1. That prevented him from progressing to Qualifying 2, and meant he would start from 15th place on the grid. Or, at least, he should have done, but the crashing wasn't over; during Sunday morning warm-up, he suffered the biggest crash of his career, and one of the biggest ever seen in MotoGP. The built-in sensors in Márquez's high-tech Alpinestars leather suit showed he had experienced a 27.9g impact, followed by five further impacts ranging between 20 and 25g as he was repeatedly slammed into the tarmac at 115mph. A normal human being loses consciousness when subjected to a sustained 4–5g force; fortunately for Márquez, his exposure to such enormous forces was brief, but he still lost consciousness. 'Some crashes you remember everything – everything,' he said later. 'Indonesia? I remember just before [the] crash. When I start to fly – from that point to the end, when I arrive in the box [pit garage] – I don't remember anything. This was because I was unconscious.'[127]

Márquez had been somersaulted off the Honda and slammed into the tarmac repeatedly, his bike cartwheeling end over end and destroying itself. The impact was enough to rip the rear tyre off his RCV and to all but destroy the bike. It was such a terrifying crash that, for the first time, Márquez admitted he didn't want to get back on a bike. 'After a crash like Indonesia? It's true that we are humans, and you don't wanna ride again.'

Whether he wanted to or not, Márquez was a professional and knew he had to get back on his RCV as soon as possible or he might not have the nerve to get back on again. Despite everything, he wanted to race, but his brother talked him out of it. Álex Márquez had seen how violently Marc had hit his head in the crash and feared a return of the diplopia he had suffered in 2011. He was right to be concerned: although it didn't happen straight away, Marc began to suffer the symptoms again and knew his brother was right: it would be far too dangerous to race, either in Indonesia or at the next round in Argentina. His nightmare had become even darker: Márquez now had double vision to deal with as well as his mangled arm. He had never been so low.

More doctors, more specialists, more gruelling hard work to recover, using a special optical device to help train his eyes to focus and to 'fuse' his vision. Fortunately, this time the diplopia cleared relatively quickly, but the interaction between his ongoing injuries and his uncompetitive Honda started playing out. When he returned to race at the Circuit of the Americas, he revealed that he had been fit enough to race in Argentina but felt it simply wasn't worthwhile. 'I didn't feel motivated to take the risk,' he said.

To test his vision while riding a bike, Márquez took a Honda CBR600 and an RC213V-S (Honda's road-legal MotoGP replica) to the Alcarràs circuit in Lleida, some 50 miles to the west of Cervera, ahead of the American Grand Prix. He looked drained after the session; he was suffering from constant headaches due to the diplopia and was having difficulty sleeping. Lasting a full race distance on a MotoGP bike was clearly not going to be easy.

If ever proof were needed of how poor the 2022 Honda RC213V was, the American Grand Prix at COTA provided it. Márquez had won seven out of the last eight races at the left-handed circuit and was only denied a 100 per cent record when his electronics failed him in 2019. He had even won there with his injured arm in 2021, but there was to be no fairy tale this time around. Suffering from a constant headache all weekend, a lowly ninth in qualifying was followed by sixth place in the race, after he had suffered yet another problem with the RCV.

With a new swinging arm fitted to the bike, a Repsol Honda mechanic had inadvertently knocked a sensor out of place when removing the tyre warmers. With the sensors being in unfamiliar places due to the shape of the new swinging arm, it was an easy mistake to make, but it served to underline the mess that the Repsol team was in; nothing was going right for them. The end result was that the affected sensor played havoc with the electronics and left Márquez floundering on the start line as the other riders took off into the distance. The bike eventually righted itself, but it was too late, and sixth place was the best Márquez could salvage from the situation. He had, however, overtaken most of the field to achieve that sixth position, so the speed was still there, on left-handed circuits at least. Despite all the negatives, Márquez was still prepared to risk everything to get a result. 'I said to myself, "I will give everything,"' he explained after the race. 'I knew riding at 100 per cent I might not finish in a good way, and with five or six laps left my body said "That's it," and I just tried to finish.'[128]

He achieved the same results in Portugal – ninth in qualifying and sixth in the race – but it was a worse sixth place than in America. This time, he hadn't been left dead last on the line, and yet he could still finish no higher than sixth, and it appeared that he was on the verge of giving up. The fire was no longer there, and the optimism in Honda's new bike – which had been evident earlier in the year – had now completely evaporated. The bike was a dog. 'It's not only me, not only the bike; it's everything,' Márquez said, clearly deflated and at an absolute loss to see a way forward. 'Obviously, I'm not in my sweet moment and I need help from the bike. My target is not to be the first Honda – my target is to fight for the top positions.'[129]

That wasn't going to happen on a bike that no longer allowed him to push the front end – one of Márquez's strongest points. Yet he soldiered on, clawed his way to fifth on the grid at Jerez, then took the best result of his season so far in the race with fourth place. More significantly, perhaps, was that he managed to save one of his massive trademark slides for the first time in over two years. He credited the home crowd with giving him the strength to right his crashing RCV.

Márquez would later make a worrying comment on his injury woes of 2021 and into 2022, revealing where his mind had been at. 'I don't even know how I managed to win three races in 2021,' he said. 'But it's even less clear to me how I was able to finish fourth in Jerez at the beginning of the 2022 season, because I didn't have my head in the competition; neither the head nor the physique.'[130]

This was worrying, because a rider who is not fully committed and fully focused can be a danger to themselves and others. Any distraction at 200mph can lead to disaster. Things couldn't carry on as they were. Not only was racing no longer fun; it was now a hideously painful experience too. 'What comes out of me when I win is partying, celebrating and laughing with my family,' Márquez explained. 'Well, then it went the other way, and it was because of the pain; the pain that I constantly suffered in my arm, which I couldn't forget.'

After taking sixth place in France, Márquez headed for Mugello where he made a decision that would change everything, for better or for worse: he announced he was withdrawing from racing to have yet another operation on his arm; the fourth. There was nothing Márquez or the team could do in the short term about his bike, but he could at least try to fix his body. Marc Márquez wasn't a rider who would ever be content battling for top ten positions, so he made the difficult decision to end his season after eight rounds of 20 to go under the surgeon's scalpel once more.

'There was a moment in the season, when the Grands Prix of Portimão and Jerez arrived, when I turned my head off and said that I can't take it any more,' he admitted. 'And that's when I go, just before Portimão, to my doctors in Madrid and I tell them, "There's something wrong with this arm here."'[131]

Márquez and his team of specialists had known for some time that his upper arm had got twisted due to the accumulated displacement over the last three operations that had been performed on it. They had no way of knowing just how badly the arm had rotated, but specialists estimated it to be between ten and 15 degrees. Márquez had considered having surgery the previous winter, while he was still struggling with diplopia, but the surgeons had insisted his humerus wasn't strong enough to withstand another operation at that time.

The problem might have started with a broken humerus, but it had spread to other parts of the body over time. To compensate for the humerus injury, Márquez used his right shoulder more, and that became very painful. The painful shoulder then led to a painful right arm. He wasn't sitting properly on the bike either; his whole body contorted to compensate for the weakness of his elbow. He couldn't continue in such a condition, and many people felt he should retire, including his beloved grandfather, Ramón.

Marc Márquez had always been extremely close to his grandfather. He had been partly raised by his grandparents and had formed a bond in childhood that never diminished. Don Ramón watched every Grand Prix on television to see his grandsons, Marc and Álex, beating the greatest motorcycle riders on earth. He was so proud of their achievements that he would set an alarm and get up in the middle of the night to watch far-flung races from Malaysia, Japan or Australia. He would work himself into a great state of excitement, shouting at the television and beating his hands on the sofa, as deeply involved in the races as the boys themselves. If either of them won, Don Ramón would set off fireworks in the middle of the night to celebrate. Even into his nineties, he insisted on watching every race, despite his wife Sole's insistence that he was getting too old to be working himself into a frenzy in the middle of the night. But Ramón was committed; nothing was more important to him; the boys were his pride and joy. 'If my armchair could talk . . . for that armchair has seen me do all sorts,' he said. 'It's seen me leap in the air – even though I no longer have the strength to jump – it's seen me cry and suffer, it's heard me insult one or two people's mothers . . . Yes, that armchair could cause quite a drama.'[132]

Even Marc Márquez himself tried to discourage his grandfather from staying up all night and getting so worked up and excited, though he knew Don Ramón wouldn't listen to him. 'He just ignores me,' he said. 'He suffers terribly if he doesn't watch them.'

After every Grand Prix, the first thing Marc Márquez did upon his return to Cervera was to go round to see his grandfather to assure him he was okay and to tell him about the latest race in detail. So, when Don Ramón told Marc he should stop racing, Marc listened. 'My grandfather told me: "Leave it now; you have enough to live on, what you've done is done. Leave it."'

A deal was struck between the two: Márquez would undergo one final operation and, if that didn't work, he would call it a day. 'I told him: "Grandpa, I promise you that this will be the last operation. Let me try, because there is a solution, and they are giving it to me. Let me try it."'

Now, it was time to tell the world of his decision. On the Saturday of the Italian Grand Prix at Mugello, the Repsol Honda team called a press conference to announce that Márquez would take part in the race then step away from the sport to try to fix his ruined body. It was a make-or-break decision: everything or nothing. If the operation was a success, Márquez might hope to regain his fitness and once again be a force in MotoGP (assuming, of course, that Honda could also fix its RC213V). If it failed, Márquez's career would most likely be over. But, in his mind, that was a better option than struggling to make it into the top ten. He wasn't interested in being an also-ran.

With his humerus so badly rotated, Márquez was simply unable to ride a MotoGP bike. 'I could not ride as I liked,' he confessed. 'I didn't have the rotation so, on the straight, I have the arm more open than normal. Then, in left corners, I'm with the elbow completely up to compensate. In all races, I had arm-pump (where the membrane that encases the forearm muscle can't expand any further, causing numbness and pain). Then the pain in the shoulder arrive. I needed to ride really smooth – that is not my style.'[133]

After finishing in a dispirited tenth place at Mugello, Márquez took a flight to America and checked into the famous Mayo Clinic in Rochester, Minnesota, where he was treated by renowned specialist Dr Joaquim Sanchez-Sotelo. Two days after the Italian Grand Prix, on Tuesday, 31 May, Márquez went under the knife, and Dr Sanchez-Sotelo finally discovered just how badly his patient's arm was rotated: it was an incredible 34 degrees out of place. As Márquez later said, 'A 20-degree rotation would basically render you incapable of conducting your day-to-day life. In my case, the arm had rotated a full 34 degrees! No wonder I could barely ride in MotoGP with it.'[134]

The solution was brutal: Dr Sanchez-Sotelo had to literally saw Márquez's right arm in half. He then rotated the humerus outwards through 34 degrees, inserted two metal plates, and attached everything with around 40 screws. For the rest of his life, Marc Márquez's right arm would look like it had been savaged by a great white shark.

The operation took three hours and was declared a success, but the truth would only reveal itself once Márquez got back on a MotoGP bike, and that wasn't going to happen anytime soon. His sense of humour never left him, however. While still very groggy as the general anaesthetic wore off, Márquez was asked if he could feel the fingers on his right hand. He couldn't. This was perfectly normal, Sanchez-Sotelo assured him, but Márquez's instinctive racer's response was 'I can't brake!'

Dr Sanchez-Sotelo estimated the recovery process would take four to six months, which meant Márquez would miss the next six Grands Prix, but the plan was to come back before the end of the season to see how he felt on the bike.

Although the 'mechanical' problem (as Márquez referred to it) had been fixed in his arm, and he felt an improvement straight away, there were other issues to deal with too. Having been unable to use his right arm correctly for almost two years, many of the muscles had wasted away.

At the end of August, Dr Sanchez-Sotelo gave his patient the all-clear to start regular training again, and Márquez's life became an endless round of physio and training, blood, sweat and tears, to rebuild the muscle and regain full movement of his upper body. But at last he was now wise enough to wait until he had the full all-clear to begin training; not a practice he had always observed: 'When I try coming back too soon from injury, I need the good professionals around me to stop me,' he admitted. 'But I say to them: "When I'm injured, I'm like an animal inside a jail." I also say to the doctor: "When you open this jail, I'm an animal that wants to be out, and I will run!" So, don't open this jail before you think I'm ready to go.'[135]

Márquez's attitude played a big part in getting him through the dark days, weeks and months with his injuries. His 'never give up' philosophy was just as important off the track as on it. 'If I see a wall, I go through it,' he said. 'It doesn't matter how many goes it takes, or how hard I hit my head; I won't stop until I've got through that wall.'[136]

In the last week of August, Marc Márquez broke through the wall and rode a motorcycle for the first time since the Italian Grand Prix at Mugello back in May. Not a MotoGP bike, and not on a proper circuit; instead, he used a much less powerful Honda CBR600 road bike and stuck to a local go-kart track, just to get an idea of how he felt. The results were encouraging. He might not have set any lap records, but he felt relatively comfortable on the bike. 'The important thing is I have an acceptable level to ride a bike, but not like I want,' he said of the test. 'I still have a long way to go.'

With the arm operation being a success, Márquez shelved the

idea of retirement, and ignored those who said his time was up. 'People at home, sitting on the sofa, are saying, "It's time to retire, blah, blah, blah . . ." It's not going to happen.'

What *was* going to happen was a change of management. During his time away from racing, Márquez announced that, after 18 years, he would no longer be employing Emilio Alzamora as his manager. Álex Márquez (also managed by Alzamora) also decided to part company with the former 125cc world champion.

It was a significant move. Marc Márquez had worked with Alzamora since he was 12 years old and had won eight world championships under his guidance; Álex had added another two. The joint statement from the pair read:

> The Márquez brothers thank Emilio for the work he has done over the years and his dedication throughout this time where we have achieved great triumphs. After discussing it among the three of us, we have decided that the time has come to take different paths and start a new stage.

Emilio Alzamora also released a statement, and it too revealed nothing about the reason for the split:

> An important stage of my life is coming to an end with the Márquez brothers and, first of all, I want to thank the trust that their parents, Roser and Julià, placed in me. During this long relationship we have worked side by side with Marc and Álex to achieve great and unforgettable successes.
>
> I have no words to describe this story that we started when Marc was 12 years old, and in which I have humbly contributed all my knowledge. Together, we have had

unforgettable and incredible moments, but also very hard moments, such as injuries. I have no doubt that in this new stage that Marc begins he will return to the top to continue making history and, above all, the most important thing, to enjoy his passion.

It was only after a year had passed that Marc Márquez offered some insight about why the brothers brought the relationship to an end. 'It didn't happen overnight,' he explained. 'For a couple of years, we could feel something was missing. When the love is gone, you start arguing over [nothing]. The arguing turns to suspicion, which leads to misunderstandings. All of that builds up until you ask yourself: "What do I want for my sports career?" I want to win again. And for that, the sea has to be calm.'[137]

Alzamora had been absent from two races in 2022, sparking rumours that all was not well. He claimed his absence was due to contracting Covid-19, but the whispers continued. Alzamora later claimed the split was caused by 'others' without specifying who. 'He's been very important to me,' he said of Marc. 'In these situations, you either stick together or split. At this point, we were separated by others.'

MotoGP rider manager and former Aprilia team boss Carlo Pernat believes the split was forced by Honda. 'When a relationship breaks down after [nearly] 20 years, there is always a big problem,' he said. 'In my opinion it was not money, but after that period of chaos he got in the way of Honda, who no longer accepted him. [Honda] could accept Marc, but not Alzamora, so they put [an ultimatum] on Marc. In the middle there were millionaire contracts.'[138]

The Márquez brothers chose former professional wakeboarder Jaime Martinez to represent them. He had been the head of motorsport marketing at Red Bull, and with both Márquez brothers having long-standing sponsorship deals with the energy drink brand, they had worked with him many times. He seemed a natural fit. At 34, Martinez was younger than Alzamora and had a raft of new plans to promote the brothers on a whole new global level. 'After his experience at Red Bull, he knows perfectly the world of motorsport, and sport in general, and offers a new strategic vision that we believe will bring us a lot,' Marc Márquez said. Red Bull was also the second biggest sponsor of Honda's MotoGP effort after Repsol, so Martinez was also a perfect fit within the team. Márquez had clearly treated his enforced break as the perfect time to clean house and make all the changes he thought he needed to get back to his former glory.

His first time back on a MotoGP bike was at the Misano tests in the first week of September, and it seemed the operation had been a success as he set the fastest time of any Honda rider.

Two weeks later, he made his racing comeback at MotorLand Aragón, and it was suitably dramatic. First, he managed to perform one of his miraculous saves during Free Practice – a feat he had rarely managed with his badly rotated humerus. He then crashed out of FP3 and proved that his arm could withstand a fall. The crash ruined his qualifying chances and he started the race from 13th on the grid, then set about creating the drama that he was now famous for. After overtaking seven riders in the first two corners, he accelerated out of Turn 3 too aggressively and had to back off the throttle to avoid a highside. In doing so, he left Fabio Quartararo with nowhere to go, and the reigning world champion collided with the rear of Márquez's Honda and crashed out of the race.

The drama wasn't over yet. A piece of Quartararo's Yamaha had got lodged in Márquez's rear ride-height device (MotoGP bikes by that point had rider-activated devices to lower the rear end of the bike coming out of corners to prevent wheelies and promote acceleration), and when Márquez activated it, his bike slewed and veered off to the left. This time it was Takaaki Nakagami's turn to run into Márquez; the hapless Japanese rider having no chance to avoid the Spaniard's wayward bike.

While Márquez stayed upright, his bike was too badly damaged from the Quartararo collision and he was forced to retire from the race, but it had been encouraging. His arm still needed a lot of physio and a lot of training, but it was at least working in the way it should.

It certainly worked at Motegi in Japan where, in just his second race back from a potentially life-changing operation, Marc Márquez put his beleaguered Honda RCV in pole position in front of all his Japanese bosses. It was his first pole in 1,071 days; the last time he had qualified fastest was way back in 2019 at the same circuit. The strain on his wasted upper body was reduced due to the wet conditions, but it was still a huge encouragement, both to himself and to Honda. Early days it may have been, but it looked like Márquez's racing career had been saved, and that, in time, he might even return to his former glory.

Following the race, he offered an insight into what it was like to race with the injuries he had. 'There are still symptoms – my left arm was like a stone because I probably compensated with my left arm. But my right arm finished well, and, above all, I didn't feel the pain that goes to your head, which even the adrenalin doesn't make up for.'[139]

Fourth place in the race was further encouragement. It was Márquez's 150th MotoGP start, and the first time he had proved he was strong enough to last a full race distance.

The Thai Grand Prix at Buriram was held in near-monsoon conditions and, after qualifying eighth and starting the race cautiously, Márquez eventually finished in fifth, just 2.9 seconds off the win. The signs were good, and they got a whole lot better in the dry Australian Grand Prix.

Because he had missed six races and was well out of the championship hunt, Márquez was treating these lasts few races of the 2022 season as testing for 2023. In Australia, his Honda had new aerodynamic sidepods and fins, similar to those developed by Ducati. He noted a slight improvement, but his results at Phillip Island were down to the man, not the new aero package. With every race, Márquez was getting stronger, both physically and mentally. After qualifying in second place, he was right in the hunt for the race win and looked set to have a last lap lunge at Suzuki's Álex Rins, but by then he was exhausted (the frantic dry race had been hard on his still recovering body) and he settled for second place, just 0.18 seconds behind the winner. It was Márquez's 100th MotoGP podium and it gave his father Julià more joy than any of his race wins because it proved the operation had been a success, and that his son's career could continue.

Phillip Island is a circuit where a rider can make the difference, but the long straights at Sepang in Malaysia meant Honda was always going to struggle against the super-fast Ducatis. Márquez stunned his team by qualifying on the front row in third place, but the best he could manage in the race was seventh, his bike hopelessly underpowered. 'I feel a slow bike all weekend, then you are pushing more in the corners,' he explained. 'For a single lap, you can do it. For a race distance, you're pushing more the tyres, and, in the end, I had zero grip.'[140]

Márquez was now in better shape than his bike, and team boss

Alberto Puig was once again astonished by his rider's performance, saying, 'We are struggling for grip, with a lack of power, a lack of grip . . . We don't really understand how Marc put those laps together to be so competitive. We're talking about a super rider.'[141]

As a measure of just how super, the next best Hondas were Álex Márquez in 14th place and Pol Espargaró in 17th. Marc Márquez had once again proved he was by far the best Honda rider, and that the only thing holding him back now was the RC213V.

The final round of the 2022 championship at Valencia proved this point again. Márquez was able to post a single flying lap fast enough for second on the grid, but he was forced to push his RCV too hard in the race and eventually crashed out on the tenth lap, just trying too hard to make up for his bike's shortcomings.

With that, the toughest season in Marc Márquez's Grand Prix career was over. Despite missing six rounds, he finished the championship in 13th place. It was won by Francesco Bagnaia on the factory Ducati, which was now the best bike on the grid by a long way. So good that, in 2023, there would be no fewer than eight of them on the grid. The Desmosedici was clearly the bike to be on, but Márquez was still under contract to Honda: he had no option but to soldier on.

There were positives, however. For the first time in three years, he could go into the off-season without facing further surgeries and long, painful rehabilitation. He could train in a normal way, build on his strength, take part in all pre-season tests, and be as ready as he could for the 2023 season. It was up to Honda to provide a bike worthy of his talents. If they couldn't, they stood to lose him. Marc Márquez needed to win, and if he couldn't win on a Honda, he would win on something else.

CHAPTER 13

BREAKING POINT

'WITH THIS BIKE, WE CAN'T WIN A CHAMPIONSHIP.'

Marc Márquez

After the final operation on his right arm in 2022, Marc Márquez needed a lot of aftercare from his team of specialists in Madrid and made the decision to finally move away from Cervera for the first time in his life. Such was his commitment to winning in MotoGP, he was even prepared to move away from his beloved home town, and his family and friends, to give himself the best chance of being competitive again.

He decided to buy a house with his brother in Madrid, so he could be closer to his specialists – particularly traumatology specialist Ángel Ruiz-Cotorro – and so the pair bought a mansion worthy of two brothers with ten world championships between them and, together with their two beloved sausage dogs, Stitch and Shira, they moved in.

'I love the dogs,' Marc told *British GQ* magazine. 'It's a special relationship with the dogs – like, when you go out shopping for a few minutes, and when you come back, they act like they've been waiting for you for four or five days! That's nice. It helps me relax, to walk around the city with the dogs. They're like friends to share those moments with.'[142]

The Márquez brothers paid over €10 million for the former mansion of Real Madrid player Mariano Diaz in La Finca, the most exclusive residential area of Madrid. With seven bedrooms, and covering an area of 1,350 square metres, it was the last word in luxury, but no one could deny that the brothers had earned it, especially Marc, after the trauma he had been through.

But while Marc Márquez continued to make progress, Honda's RC213V didn't. After trying the 2023 bike for the first time at the end-of-season test at Valencia in 2022, Márquez declared, 'With this bike, we can't win a championship.' It was a brutal assessment. It's not that Honda wasn't trying; no manufacturer worked harder over the winter season, bringing three different chassis to the pre-season tests (they would try four in-house chassis during the season, as well as a Kalex-made one) and a host of different aero packages in a bid to try to find grip and 'feel', but nothing worked. It was clear there was no easy fix for the RCV, nor even a harder fix; to get back in the game it appeared that Honda needed an all-new bike, and that wasn't going to happen overnight. It was unlikely to happen for 2024 either (Márquez's last year of contract with HRC) since MotoGP regulations were changing in 2027 and every manufacturer was making plans to build new bikes to that deadline – an interim bike would not be financially feasible, and it would also take time to develop; again, not worth the effort since the rules were set to change in 2027.

Marc Márquez gained a valuable insight into the deficiencies of the Honda from his brother Álex in those pre-season tests. He had parted from Honda at the end of 2022 and signed to ride a Ducati Desmosedici for the satellite Gresini team. The family-owned team was one of the smallest in MotoGP, and the younger Márquez was riding a year-old bike, but his pace during testing confirmed just how superior the Italian machines were compared to the Honda. He had finished a lowly 17th on the Honda in 2022 but was on the podium in just his second race on the Ducati. If Álex Márquez could turn his fortunes around so dramatically by switching bikes, what could Marc do? He had always been superior to his brother on the Honda, so it seemed reasonable to assume that he could do even better than his sibling on a Ducati.

Honda had failed to take a win in 2022 and had, embarrassingly, finished last in the constructors' championship. In desperation, the firm fired technical chief Takeo Yokoyama and replaced him with former Suzuki technical manager, Ken Kawauchi. After winning the final two races of the 2022 season, Suzuki had opted to withdraw from MotoGP, so the HRC team also signed Joan Mir – who had won the 2020 title for the firm – as Márquez's teammate.

For Márquez and his team, the 2023 season was an unmitigated disaster. Whenever he tried to push the RCV, it flicked him violently over the highside, the consequence being that he didn't see the chequered flag in a Grand Prix until the tenth round in Austria.

The RCV was so unrideable that Joan Mir would fall into a deep depression as the season progressed, and would seriously contemplate retirement, despite being just 26 years old. A world champion just two years previously, Mir didn't finish a single race on the Honda between Portimão in March and Catalunya in September.

The season saw a major change with the introduction of MotoGP

Sprint races. Held on Saturdays after qualifying, the races were half distance and offered half points. It meant a lot more work, and a lot more risk, for the riders, but the Sprint races ramped up the entertainment value of MotoGP and, after some objection from traditionalists, most people quickly came out in favour once the racing began. For Marc Márquez and the other Honda riders, it meant they had to suffer the frustration of riding the worst bike on the grid in even more races, putting them at even greater risk of injury.

Still able to grit his teeth and put a single fast lap together, Márquez flattered the Honda by taking third position on the grid at the season opener in Portugal. Then came the first ever Sprint race; a 12-lap free-for-all where riders didn't need to worry about tyre life or race strategies; they could just ride as fast as they dared. The format suited Márquez's all-action style and he once again flattered the Honda by taking third place behind Francesco Bagnaia and Jorge Martin.

The main race was another matter altogether. With poor edge grip, poor acceleration and lacking top speed, Márquez had to rely on hyper-aggressive braking as the only way to keep the RCV in the fight and, on the third lap, he paid the price. So did Miguel Oliveira on the Aprilia. Márquez locked the front wheel of his Honda, clipped Jorge Martin's leg, then lost control and smashed into the side of Oliveira's bike. It was the Portuguese rider's home race, and he had the crowd on its feet as he made a bid for the lead of the race just before Márquez smashed into him. Both he and Márquez crashed out, the Portuguese rider suffering a major haematoma on his right leg that ruled him out of the next Grand Prix.

Race Direction was not impressed and handed Márquez a double long lap penalty (where riders have to complete an additional loop added on to the circuit, thereby losing time), to be served at the next round in Argentina. But there was the crux: Márquez had broken a bone in his right hand when he crashed out, so was going to miss the Argentine round anyway, meaning he would not be punished. The stewards quickly revised their wording of the penalty which was now to be served 'at the next race in which he will be able to participate'.

Since there was no legal precedent for this kind of delayed penalty, the Repsol team protested it and, after a whole month of legal wrangling, they won their case. It was finally agreed that Márquez missing the Argentine Grand Prix would be penalty enough.

As things turned out, he would not only miss the Argentine Grand Prix, but also the American Grand Prix (where, against all expectation, Álex Rins won on a Honda, though it was a freakish, track-specific, one-off result in a race that nine riders crashed out of) and the Spanish Grand Prix. It seemed extreme for a broken finger, but it was a measure of how careful Márquez was being to avoid further injury to his right arm. At Jerez, he explained in a press conference that he had consulted three specialist teams who had all agreed that further injury to his right arm might result in permanent damage. 'The main risk was not crashing, only with the pressure of the handlebar,' he explained. 'It's a very small crack, but it gives stability to the most important finger, especially when you brake.'

The subtext was that the Honda was so uncompetitive, and so prone to spitting him off, that it simply wasn't worth the risk. If he couldn't win races on the RCV, why risk permanent damage battling for sixth place?

If there was any happiness for Marc Márquez during the 2023 season, it was in his personal life, rather than his professional one. He had always kept his private life very private, but in May 2023 he took to Instagram to reveal he was in a relationship with 26-year-old Catalan model and influencer, Gemma Pinto. 'On a professional level, it is one of my hardest moments,' he said, 'but the personal level is compensating for it, which is one of my best moments . . . It is there where the balance is being offset a bit, and that will surely give me the strength to keep pushing. But it helps a lot that I am in one of my best moments on a personal level, and that is what is saving me.'

In earlier years, Márquez had focused exclusively on racing and felt that a girlfriend would be a distraction. And, while he did have relationships from time to time, they were always kept very low key; he was never a rider who turned up at races with a girl on his arm. In his 2023 book *Being Marc Márquez: This is How I Win My Race*, he revealed that, 'I've had two relationships: one when I was 19/20, with a girl from my home town, and I also had a girlfriend during my best season, 2019. Maybe my attitude will change, and maybe I just haven't met the right partner yet but, to be honest, I haven't yet felt ready to commit to something longer term. I hate compromise. I love my job, my profession, and I'm the same in my private life: it's all or nothing.'[143]

The girlfriend from 2019–20 he referred to was Spanish model Lucia Rivera Romero, whose father, Cayetano Rivera Ordóñez, is a famous bullfighter, and whose mother, Blanca Romero, a famous actress, singer and model.

There had been rumours that Márquez had been dating Spanish actress Maria Pedraza, after she had enjoyed Repsol Honda hospitality and cheered for Márquez at the Portuguese Grand Prix in 2021. Márquez denied the rumours and pointed out that Pedraza had simply attended the race with fellow stars of her Spanish TV show *Toy Boy*.

Márquez has also stated that, in the past at least, he was too spontaneous to hold down a long-term relationship and prefers doing things on the spur of the moment, rather than planning nights out at a restaurant, or going to the cinema with a girl. 'If I had a girlfriend, I'd have to compromise and worry whether she was happy,' he said. That attitude clearly changed when he met Gemma Pinto, and the pair seemed blissfully happy as the 2023 season unfolded, despite the dire results on track.

As happy as he was with Pinto, Márquez had to force himself to return to his depressing professional career, and when he did return to racing at the French Grand Prix, he had a new chassis to try. Breaking with long-held tradition, Honda had employed German engineering firm Kalex to build a swinging arm for the RCV in 2022 and now upped the stakes by outsourcing the building of an entire chassis to the same firm.

Márquez felt the Kalex chassis was a slight improvement on Honda's version and managed to put the bike in second place on the grid in France behind Francesco Bagnaia. He was in the hunt in the Sprint race but ran wide at one point and finished fifth. The main race saw Márquez's best ride since he broke his arm the previous year, but then the Honda let him down again. While fighting Jorge Martin for the lead, he crashed out with just two laps remaining, blaming the nature of the bike. He had lost the front end tipping into a corner because he'd had to slow up slightly as Martin passed him. It was enough to cause a crash because he needed to slide the RCV into corners and, at slightly reduced speed, he couldn't slide the bike and crashed out as a result. He wasn't alone: fellow Honda riders Joan Mir and Álex Rins also crashed out of the race.

It was the same story at Mugello, where Márquez was again the best Honda rider by a considerable margin, and was clearly still fast enough to be running at, or near, the front, but was having to ride too far over the edge to make the RCV competitive. After qualifying second to Bagnaia again, he finished seventh in the Sprint but crashed out of the main race while desperately trying to stay with the leaders. Always unfailingly loyal to Honda and his team, Márquez's frustration was now beginning to show. After crashing, he stared at his RCV with arms outstretched in a gesture of disbelief and exasperation. It had thrown him again. His body language spoke volumes: something had to be done.

Crisis talks began in earnest at Mugello with HRC president, Koji Watanabe, and Shinji Aoyama – the vice president of the entire Honda Motor Company, who very rarely attended MotoGP races. With such heavyweights present, things were clearly getting serious, and Márquez was looking for rock-solid reassurances that Honda could fix its wayward motorcycle. Throughout his career, Márquez had been confident and courageous on whatever he rode, but that confidence was now taking repeated knocks. Confidence, once lost, is a difficult thing to regain, and the longer Márquez spent having his confidence knocked by the unpredictable RCV, the harder it would be to get it back.

Once again, he wasn't the only Honda rider to crash. Mir and Rins both crashed out again, and both suffered injuries; Mir injuring a finger, and Rins breaking his right tibia and fibula. Rins would be out of racing for four months.

With such dire results and little prospect of the RCV being suddenly turned into a competitive machine, rumours first began to circulate at Mugello that Márquez was looking elsewhere for a ride. He was contracted to Honda for the following year, but contracts can be broken (though usually at huge expense), and it was the retired Jorge Lorenzo who first predicted that Márquez would be on a Ducati in 2024. Márquez batted these rumours aside, insisting he still had faith that Honda could turn the situation around, but he didn't entirely close the door on the rumours of a move. 'Honda will always be my Plan A,' he said, 'but I will always look for a winning project. It doesn't matter the colours, the names . . .'[144]

The RCV clearly wasn't a 'winning project', but Ducati's Desmosedici certainly was. Heading into the Italian Grand Prix, the bikes had won four out of the previous five races, and at Mugello the Italian bikes would have locked out the top five places in both the Sprint and the main race, had Álex Márquez not crashed out of third place in the latter. The conversations between the Márquez brothers back in their shared house in Madrid must have been interesting as the two compared their respective mounts.

The final straw came at the Sachsenring in Germany. At a circuit where he had been unbeaten since he first raced a 125cc machine there in 2009, Márquez suffered no fewer than five crashes in three days and, although unhurt, he decided to withdraw from the race. At the one track where he should have achieved a result, everything fell apart.

The weekend started well, with Márquez posting the second-best time in Practice 1, but then came the first crash in P2. He then crashed out of Qualifying 1 but had already posted a time fast enough to make it through to Q2. Then it all went wrong again as he slid off the RCV in the final corner. He was running back to the pits to retrieve his second bike before his crashed one had even stopped tumbling through the gravel. There was still one last shot at qualifying on the front row of the grid, but that prospect too was scuppered when he crashed at the first corner, his bike smashing into Johann Zarco's fast-travelling Ducati. It was a terrifying incident, and Zarco was hugely fortunate to escape without injury. With the session being red-flagged because of the debris, Márquez then ran back to the pits, hoping to be allowed back out on his other bike. The problem was, there was no other bike; he had crashed so often his team was unable to put a bike underneath him.

Having tried so hard to publicly defend Honda as the situation deteriorated, Márquez's frustration finally outed in Germany. After the RCV tried to spit him off yet again – this time as he entered the notorious Waterfall section during Practice 2 – he flipped the bird at the onboard camera facing him. He couldn't have made his feelings towards the bike any clearer.

And all this before the racing had even begun. Márquez started the Sprint race from seventh on the grid, but it was a very different Márquez who lined up for the German Grand Prix. For the first time in his career, he admitted to throttling off and dropping to a miserable 11th place. He had, in short, given up. The RCV was all but unrideable, and a serious accident was going to happen sooner or later if Márquez continued to push it.

Incredibly, worse was to come on the Sunday of the main race. On just the third lap of morning warm-up, Márquez crashed for a fifth time, this one a vicious highside at the fast Turn 7. Enough was enough. He hadn't even been pushing, yet the RCV still spat him off. 'If you are pushing and crash, you accept it,' he said, 'but I was not pushing – still at a slow pace.'

Márquez was the picture of dejection after his fifth crash, leaning against the guard rail looking 'mentally and physically broken' as respected journalist Mat Oxley observed.

Dejected, frustrated, angry and at his wits' end, Márquez withdrew from the race. It was an unprecedented scenario. He wasn't injured, he had been passed fit to race by the circuit doctor, and he had a bike to ride, so to *not* ride was tantamount to breach of contract, but he'd simply had enough. Racing a MotoGP is dangerous enough; racing a violently unpredictable one was just asking for a hospital bed, but withdrawing from a race because your bike feels too dangerous to ride was unheard of – especially since Márquez was being paid millions to ride the RCV.

His withdrawal from the race – and the continued absence of the injured Álex Rins and Joan Mir – meant that only one Honda rider took part in the German Grand Prix. Takaaki Nakagami finished in a lowly 14th place, then vividly described the issues with the RCV. 'There is no grip, and the front end is always closing mid-corner,' he said, 'and, on [corner] exit, the rear grip is really bad, so the bike is moving a lot. Mainly, we're losing acceleration. In the traction area, the bike is shaking a lot – it's really difficult to keep the pace.'[145]

Including the German Grand Prix, there had been 14 Sprint and main races in the championship by this point, but Marc Márquez had scored just 15 points and lay 19th in the championship. For arguably the greatest MotoGP rider of his age – indeed, one could argue, of all time – these were sobering statistics. He was 30 years old and hadn't won a world title for four years. It was beginning to look like he might never do so again.

Márquez's season from hell continued at Assen, where he once again withdrew from the main race, this time citing an accumulation of injuries. He had suffered another two demoralising crashes in practice and clearly gave up in the Sprint race, trailing home in 17th place, completely demoralised: a broken man. 'Injury aside, this is the worst moment of my sporting life,' he said before announcing that he would not be competing in the main race. There seemed no point.

At a two-day test at Misano, Honda's test rider Stefan Bradl had been puzzled that Honda had brought no new parts for him to try and, instead, he spent the two days working on the bike's electronic settings. Had Honda also given up? It certainly appeared so, unless the firm believed the bike's multitude of problems were all down to its electronics.

By now, the whispers about Márquez breaking his Honda contract were growing louder and becoming more public. Even Repsol Honda team boss Alberto Puig – always intensely guarded when speaking to the media – could no longer hide from the issue. While saying he expected Márquez to stay with Honda in 2024 because he had signed a contract, he also acknowledged that his rider might have other ideas, saying, 'Every person is free to do what he wants in life, and Honda is not a company that wants to have people that are not happy being in Honda.'

After suffering five crashes in Germany, and a further two in Assen before withdrawing from the feature race, Márquez refused to be drawn on his future, his mind a turmoil of emotions. 'I'm in a very deep moment and I cannot think about this,' he said, on what was race day for everyone else, but not for him. 'You cannot decide things in that condition. I need to rebuild my body, my mental side.'[146]

The downward trajectory continued at Silverstone as the British race marked a deliberate change in strategy for Márquez. He explained he was no longer willing to push the bike beyond its capabilities, and to risk further injury, for a meagre top ten finish. Instead, his plan was to treat the race like a test session, to try to understand what was so fundamentally wrong with the RCV. There was to be no more riding over the limit. 'The objective for this second part of the season is to be maybe less explosive – not looking for results,' he said, 'but with the aim of trying to continue growing with the project and, above all, regaining confidence in myself and race pace.'[147]

After qualifying in 14th position at Silverstone, he even admitted slowing down in the Sprint race so he could sit behind his teammate, Joan Mir, to watch what the RCV was doing from behind. The eight-time world champion finished in 18th place, one position behind Mir.

While Marc Márquez was making up the numbers in 18th place, his younger brother Álex took his first premier class win on the Gresini Ducati. It may 'only' have been a Sprint race win, rather than a full Grand Prix win, but it was still a victory against the best riders on the planet and, while Marc was naturally delighted for his brother, it was yet another lesson in the superiority of the Ducati Desmosedici: Álex Márquez had never won a race on a Honda.

Álex Rins, whose victory in the 2023 American Grand Prix had been Honda's only win in two years, left the sinking ship first. It was announced at the British Grand Prix that the Spaniard had exercised a clause in his contract to leave the LCR Honda team and join the factory Yamaha team. He, for one, had had enough. How much more could Márquez take?

The main race at the British Grand Prix was another disaster for Márquez. He lost the right-hand aerodynamic wings early on after clashing with Franco Morbidelli, then crashed out after tagging the rear of Enea Bastianini's Ducati. No points. Again.

At the Red Bull Ring in Austria, Márquez toured round in the Sprint race, his focus solely on preserving life and limb, and crawled home in tenth place, though, by now, simply getting a finish was a bonus. A 12th place in the main race netted him four points, taking his season total to 19. The Catalan Grand Prix was no better: 12th in qualifying, 11th in the Sprint and 13th in the Grand Prix proper.

On the Thursday before the Misano race, Márquez finally admitted he was looking elsewhere for a ride, and the press began speculating that he would be joining his brother in the Gresini Ducati team for 2024. Álex's 2023 teammate, Fabio Di Giannantonio, was fighting for his job, having not achieved the kind of results expected of him. His seat in the team, many believed, was vulnerable, and should he lose it, the door would be open for Marc Márquez, who added fuel to the fire when he tweeted 'Things are happening'.

When questioned at Misano about a possible move, Márquez refused to be drawn but did, significantly, admit that he simply wasn't enjoying racing any more. How could he? Serial world champions are never going to be happy lying in 19th place in the championship: he desperately wanted to be competitive again.

Honda tried hard to convince their rider to stay. More Japanese top brass began appearing at races, trying to figure out what needed to change, and Alberto Puig was finally given permission to hire European technicians and engineers as all the successful teams were now doing. Puig had argued this case before, but Honda – firmly rooted in its traditions – had insisted it could fix any problem with its own Japanese staff. With very few exceptions, it was the way the firm had always worked, but that model was no longer effective. European manufacturers like Ducati, Aprilia and KTM hired the best men and women for each respective job; their nationality was of no importance, nor was blind loyalty to any particular firm. Those European manufacturers were also able to respond to problems much faster than Honda and Yamaha (the only other Japanese manufacturer left on the grid, and also struggling to make its bike competitive). Those firms could manufacture new parts and utilise their European testing teams to assess them in a matter of weeks, rather than months. Honda's approach had always been about very slow evolution and endless miles of testing before approving new parts. It simply wasn't working any longer; it was an outdated way to go racing, and Honda bosses had finally seemed to accept this, however reluctantly, and however belatedly.

Yet, even with a new willingness to try a different approach, it was clearly going to take time to implement such major changes, and to make them work. Marc Márquez was 30 years old; he didn't have time to wait. But even if he might have been encouraged by Honda's new approach, any new-found optimism vanished at the post-race tests at Misano.

After qualifying ninth, finishing the Sprint race in tenth and the main race in seventh, Márquez and the other Honda riders tested the first prototype of the 2024 RC213V. Márquez was wholly unimpressed: he felt it was even worse than the current bike.

By the time of the first ever Indian Grand Prix in late September, the Márquez rumour mill was in full flow, the latest juicy titbit coming from Ducati's sporting director, Paolo Ciabatti. Referring to the satellite Gresini Ducati team, he said, 'It looks like they have this opportunity, and they are waiting for Marc's decision.' For his part, Márquez remained tight-lipped.

Results picked up for the Honda riders in India. The track was new to everyone (so new that it was only officially homologated on the eve of the race) which acted as something of a leveller, and Márquez perhaps tried harder to prove to any prospective new employers that he still had what it takes. The quirky nature of the Indian circuit also played in his favour – he still had a greater level of feel than most of his rivals and, despite his earlier statement that he was no longer willing to take risks on the RCV, he went back on his word as soon as he saw the opportunity to secure a result. He was, after all, still Marc Márquez, however browbeaten and downtrodden.

He took third place in the Sprint race – his first podium since the Sprint race at the opening round in Portugal. It hadn't come easy though, and Márquez admitted to taking 'huge risks' on the last five laps to secure the result.

He rode just as hard, and took just as many risks, in the main race, but this time he didn't get away with it and crashed out on lap six. Rejoining in 16th place, he again rode superbly to carve his way up to ninth place by the end of the race. He could still ride a MotoGP bike; that much was clear.

After qualifying seventh in front of his Honda bosses in Japan, Márquez also took seventh in the dry Sprint race at Motegi and was then aided by rain in the main race to take third place; his first podium in a feature race all year. He had also been helped by the race being stopped after 12 laps due to even heavier rain. A restart was attempted, but then abandoned, as conditions deteriorated, and it became too dark to race.

Then, on the Sunday night following the race, Ducati Racing General Manager, Gigi Dall'Igna, dropped a bombshell live on Sky Italia. Márquez had remained tight-lipped all weekend about any progress being made with Ducati, but Dall'Igna displayed no such reticence, saying, 'Marc is one of the strongest riders in history, so the fact he strongly wants to get on a Ducati can only be pleasing. He's decided to leave Honda for an unofficial Ducati.'

While excited to see what Marc Márquez could do on a Ducati, Dall'Igna was also aware of the tension that might create amongst the other Ducati riders. 'That is one of the concerns; one of the challenges,' he admitted. 'We have to be good at managing strong riders, with strong characters. Beyond Marc, there is already a concentration of champions in Ducati (Francesco Bagnaia, Enea Bastianini, Jorge Martin, Marco Bezzecchi, Franco Morbidelli, Álex Márquez and Fabio di Giannantonio would all be Ducati-mounted in 2024). We will add one who is perhaps more cumbersome, having won many titles, but it's a job we know how to do.'[148]

Dall'Igna admitted he had been approached by Honda to switch camps in an 11th-hour bid to keep Márquez in the Repsol team, but he didn't take the bait. 'I feel good at Ducati,' he said. 'I've worked so hard to get to a situation where Ducati is considered a reference for everyone else, so to leave at this time would not have been logical.'[149]

A few days later, Honda released a statement that read:

The Honda Racing Corporation and Marc Márquez have mutually elected to end their four-year contract prematurely . . . With a year still remaining . . . both parties agreed it was in their best interests to each pursue other avenues in the future.

Márquez had decided on the Tuesday following the Japanese Grand Prix that his time at Honda was over. Meetings with the big Japanese bosses had failed to convince him that he should stay and, following the meetings, heads began to roll. Honda had lost the greatest rider of his era because they couldn't provide him with a bike that his talents deserved. It was a serious loss of face, and the first to go was HRC director, Shinichi Kokubu; more would follow.

It was only at the Indonesian Grand Prix, two weeks later, that Márquez finally broke his silence and spoke openly of his decision to leave the team he had been with since first competing in MotoGP back in 2013. It had been the 'toughest decision of my career' he admitted, and 'hard from the emotional side'. Every member of the Repsol team was like family to Márquez. They had been hand-picked and, for the most part, had worked with him for 11 years in MotoGP, with some of the team having worked for him even back in his Moto2 days. 'Sometimes you need to go out of your comfort zone,' Márquez said, 'and my comfort zone was Honda.'

The most important factor, he insisted, was enjoyment. Riding a crash-prone motorcycle in the bottom half of the top ten (or worse) was no fun for an eight-time world champion; he wanted to enjoy his racing again, and he could only do that on a competitive bike. 'The last four years, I've been suffering a lot – not enjoying,' he admitted. 'I made a change to enjoy again on the racetrack, because, if not, there's no meaning for me to continue.'

It was another week before the Gresini team made the official announcement that they would be running two brothers in 2024 – Álex and Marc Márquez. After 11 years on a factory bike in a factory team, Márquez would be riding a year-old Ducati Desmosedici for one of the smallest satellite teams on the grid. There was no possibility of taking his beloved Honda crew with him either; he didn't want to make Honda's situation even more desperate, nor did he want to see anyone lose their job at Gresini.

As a compromise, Márquez would take only one trusted team member with him – tyre and fuel technician Javi Ortiz. Márquez's right-hand man, Santi Hernández, would stay at Honda and Márquez would inherit a British crew chief in the shape of Frankie Carchedi, who had taken Joan Mir to the 2020 world championship for Suzuki, and had been working with Fabio di Giannantonio since then. It was the most sensational signing in MotoGP since Valentino Rossi left Honda to join Yamaha in 2004, and now it was official.

While some pundits felt Márquez was past his best and wouldn't be a threat, even on a Ducati, others retained their faith in him, including former Honda rider Cal Crutchlow. He had seen Márquez's data when they were both Honda riders and couldn't believe the things he was doing on the bike. Nobody knew better than Crutchlow just how hard he had been riding it, despite not getting results. 'I think it took some massive balls for Marc to leave,' he said. 'It shows how much of a winner he is, and how much of a winner he wants to be. He wants to prove he's still the best rider on the grid. I believe he's the best rider, and that is no disrespect to the others.'[150]

But amidst the media frenzy, there was still the rest of the 2023 season to deal with, and while Ducati riders, Francesco Bagnaia and Jorge Martin, fought it out for the championship, Márquez's misery continued. He lasted just one lap of the Sprint race in Indonesia before crashing out, and seven laps in the main race before taking another fall when he wasn't even pushing. It must have felt like confirmation that he had made the right decision.

Honda wasn't the only manufacturer struggling to field a competitive bike. Yamaha had lost its way too and, after the Sprint race in Australia was cancelled due to high winds and heavy rain, Márquez found himself fighting Yamaha-mounted Fabio Quartararo for 14th place. The Frenchman had won the world championship for Yamaha in 2021, but the Japanese firm was struggling against the new breed of Ducatis, Aprilias and KTMs. After so many years of Honda and Yamaha dominance, it was puzzling and disheartening to see riders of the calibre of Márquez and Quartararo fighting it out for a single point. In the end, Quartararo prevailed, leaving Márquez in 15th place, with one single point. How the mighty had fallen. The Japanese dominance of MotoGP was at an end; at least for now.

Fourth in the Thai Sprint race and sixth in the main race was a marked improvement for Márquez, but it was just a blip, and the Malaysian Grand Prix was another disaster. After crashing out of the Sprint race, remounting and finishing 21st, Márquez could only manage a dispirited 13th in the main event, meaning he only took away three points from the whole weekend. By contrast, his brother took his first double podium, with second in the main race after winning the Sprint. Bizarrely, Álex put his results down to breaking four ribs earlier in the season; that, he said, had forced him to ride the Ducati much more smoothly, and suddenly everything clicked. He had been riding the Ducati aggressively, as the Honda had needed to be ridden, and it had taken him time to adapt to the Ducati. But information like that was gold dust to his older brother: Marc Márquez had an inside line on how the Ducati needed to be ridden before he even threw a leg over it.

A brace of 11th-place finishes was the best he could muster in Qatar, so it must have been a huge relief to get to the final round in Valencia to end his season from hell. It would prove to be an emotional weekend as Márquez worked with his old team one last time before starting a new chapter in his career. Results were mixed: a microcosm of the entire season. Desperate to end his Honda career with a dignified result, Márquez rode his heart out to take third place in the Sprint race, but in his final appearance for Repsol Honda, he was viciously highsided off his bike in the main race. And, with that, it was over. His 11-year career with Honda in MotoGP ended in the gravel trap, where he had spent so much time during the 2023 season. For once, it hadn't been the bike, or Márquez's fault; he was hit by an impatient Jorge Martin, who was desperately fighting for a world championship. Martin had fought a tremendous battle all season with Francesco Bagnaia and it had all come down to the final round, but after barging into Márquez, Martin also crashed, automatically handing the title to Bagnaia and making him a double MotoGP world champion.

Márquez had given his all in the final round of the season, approaching his Honda swan song 'like I was fighting for the championship . . . fully concentrated, all the laps, all the race, all the practice'. It was enough to gain him what he called a 'romantic' podium in the Sprint, and he felt he could have achieved the same in the main race had Martin not taken him out.

While Márquez accepted the crash as a racing incident, another Ducati rider, Marco Bezzecchi, lashed out at him after being taken out by him in just the third corner of the first lap of the main race. 'It was very, very dirty,' Bezzecchi complained, 'but they didn't even show the replay [on TV]. Nobody does anything to him, because it's Márquez. He's the dirtiest rider.'[151]

Having not had to worry about Marc Márquez for the last few seasons, the Ducati riders knew things could be very different in 2024 when he would be mounted on a similar bike to them. And he would get the chance to test it the day after the Valencia race.

Márquez had a genuine love and respect for his Honda team

after so many years together, both good and bad. He had given Honda so much success and kept on trying and trying, when even Honda knew its bike was totally uncompetitive. For that reason, the love and respect were mutual, and a sure sign of this was Honda's gracious decision to allow Márquez to ride the Ducati at the test sessions following the final round in Valencia, while he was still under contract to Honda. It's common for manufacturers to prevent their riders from testing other bikes until the new year begins and contracts have expired, and it was a clear sign that Honda respected Márquez's talents and didn't want to hold him back. There was no point in burning bridges after all; if Honda could build a competitive bike within the next few years, there was a chance, however slim, that Márquez might one day return to the Honda fold.

For that to happen, however, Honda would have to build a far better bike. During the 2023 season, Márquez crashed more than any other rider – 29 times in total, despite missing three full Grand Prix weekends and a further two Sunday races due to injury. Proving that it wasn't all his fault, Márquez's teammate Joan Mir was second on the list with 24 crashes. He too had missed three weekends and two partial weekends; the crash tally for both could have been even higher had they participated in all rounds. Mir's previous record had been 12 crashes in a season.

During his career with Honda, Marc Márquez had won six MotoGP world championships, 59 races, and taken a total of 2,626 points. He had also taken 101 podiums, set pole position 64 times and set 59 fastest laps. He had been Honda's most successful rider in terms of premier class race wins. During this period, he also crashed 182 times.

He was sad to be leaving. After his final race with the Japanese company, he said, 'Of course it was a super emotional Sunday, honestly a super emotional week, and it was hard at some points to contain the feelings. Sadly, we didn't finish the race today. I was feeling really strong, and I honestly think a podium was possible – even maybe more. It wasn't our mistake, and I don't push against [Jorge] Martin because he was in attack mode. It happens when you're fighting for a championship. But the most important thing today is to remember all of the incredible times I have had with HRC and the Repsol Honda team – they will be the team of my life. We have written an incredible story together and they have become more than just my team; they have become my friends and my family.'[152]

And with that, Marc Márquez changed out of his Repsol Honda leathers for the last time and got ready to ride a Ducati.

CHAPTER 14

PHOENIX

'NOT MANY ATHLETES IN THE PAST HAVE SPENT THREE YEARS INJURED AND WERE ABLE TO COME BACK.'

Marc Márquez

There was a price to pay for riding a Ducati and, in Marc Márquez's case, it was a heavy one. Back in 2020 he had signed a four-year contract extension with Honda, said to be the most lucrative in MotoGP history. It was rumoured to have been worth €100 million, equating to €25 million per season. To ride a Ducati, Márquez had to break that contract. Whether he had to pay a heavy penalty for doing so was never made public. On top of that, the Gresini team is one of the least well-funded teams in MotoGP and certainly couldn't come anywhere close to matching the wages Honda had paid Márquez. It's believed he had to take a 98.5 per cent pay cut, with Gresini only offering a salary of €300,000. Again, this was never confirmed or denied.

But money wasn't Márquez's motivation; being competitive again was. Whatever penalty he may have had to pay to buy himself out of his Honda contract, Márquez was still wealthy enough and was prepared to take the hit. It was a gamble, but if he could prove he was still competitive, Márquez could negotiate for a higher salary in 2025. To that end, he signed a one-year deal with Gresini, rather than the more usual two-year deal. It was a shrewd move: if he didn't get results and wasn't enjoying racing, he could simply walk away after one year; if he did get results, he could aim for a factory ride and much higher wages for the 2025 season.

While Honda had graciously allowed Márquez to test the Ducati in November 2023, he wasn't permitted to speak about it. Even so, the media swarmed all over the Gresini garage at that first Valencia test, eager to record such a historical moment in MotoGP – Marc Márquez's first ride on anything other than a Honda.

In the end, there was no need for quotes from Márquez: one look said it all. As he sat down in his pit box after his first stint on the bike, he removed his helmet, looked at new crew chief Frankie Carchedi and gave him a huge grin. It was clear in just that one moment that he knew he had made the right choice; learning to ride a Ducati after 11 years on a Honda would take time, but he realised the potential was there from that first tentative ride. 'That smile was one of tranquillity after 11 years riding the same bike,' he later revealed. 'I was restless and nervous and, after getting off the Ducati, I felt some relief. I knew that from that moment on, I was starting a new chapter in my career, and I felt reassured that everything had gone well, and it was time to roll up my sleeves. Obviously, every change requires adaptation and requires time, effort and, above all, learning a lot of new things.'[153]

There was even more reason to smile later in the day when Márquez topped one of the sessions: an incredible achievement, given the circumstances. He would eventually finish the tests in fourth place overall.

After such a solid start, Márquez knew he could build and improve, but he needed to keep expectations realistic: being in a satellite team was going to be a massive change for him. Factory riders lead development of the bikes, they receive all the latest parts and upgrades before satellite team riders, they have more staff, more back-up, and the direct support of the factory itself. Throughout his MotoGP career, Márquez had been a pampered factory rider, but no longer. He would be riding a second-hand bike for the lowest team in the Ducati pecking order: of the four teams running Ducatis (the official Lenovo team, the Pramac team, the VR46 team, and the Gresini team), the Gresini outfit received the least support from the factory.

But there were also benefits. First and foremost was having his own brother as a teammate. The pair had been teammates at Repsol Honda in 2020, but Marc had been injured in the first race of the season (when he broke his arm) and never really got the chance to share a garage with Álex. The Gresini team was also much smaller than the Repsol Honda outfit and the atmosphere was relaxed and friendly. It had been owned and run by former 125cc world champion Fausto Gresini since 1997, and after Gresini passed away from Covid-19 in February 2021, his wife, Nadia Padovani, decided to run the team herself. It was a hugely emotional moment for the entire MotoGP paddock when Enea Bastianini gave the Gresini outfit its first victory under Padovani's guidance at Qatar in 2023. It was the ultimate tribute to the late Fausto Gresini, and it meant the world to the small, tightly knit team. Although he didn't yet know the individuals well, it was clearly the sort of team set-up that would suit the family-orientated Marc Márquez.

As he began a new chapter in life, Márquez set out his goals. 'The first target is try to enjoy it, and for that reason I choose the

Gresini team, because it's a big family,' he said. 'They have the best bike now on the grid [albeit a year-old version], and there is my brother there. It will be a big change in all the aspects, and what I'm looking for is to enjoy it; smile in the helmet. If I smile, everything will come.'[154]

The smile came the first time he rode the bike, yet he was under no illusions about the scale of the challenge he was facing. 'Not many athletes in the past have spent three years injured and were able to come back,' he admitted. 'I want to come back and be competitive again and fight for championships.'[155]

After the third and final pre-season test in Qatar, Márquez was satisfied with his progress. 'I've taken the pre-season very calmly, but always from less to more,' he said. 'In both the Malaysia and Qatar tests, I started a bit too far from my rivals, but on the second day I was closer, and so on. Now we will see if in the Grand Prix we can be a little bit closer from Friday practice. Throughout the winter testing we've been discovering things about the bike. It's helped me a lot to go to a team that already knew the bike and knows what it needs, and this helps to have a more solid base.'[156]

At the official Gresini team launch in January 2024, Márquez played down his expectations for the coming season, saying, 'I feel I have the chance, and level, for the top five places. I can't say I'll be fighting for the championship, but the top five, yes.'

As well as getting to know his new team, Márquez also had to learn how to ride the Ducati Desmosedici after 11 years on the Honda RC213V. 'It's a completely different riding style,' he said after the Sepang test in February. 'Basically, I was used to riding a lot with the front, and massive pick-up with the Honda. But, with the Ducati, you are using more the rear, and the way to use the rear tyre is different.'[157]

He adapted steadily, finishing the test in sixth place overall, but testing also showed that Ducati had made a big step up with its 2024 bike and would continue to improve on it throughout the season. Márquez, on a year-old bike, was clearly going to be at a disadvantage.

While everything was coming together with his new team, the Márquez family was privately grieving. On 4 February, Marc and Álex posted a joint statement on social media announcing that their beloved grandfather, Ramón, had passed away at the age of 92. Don Ramón had been their biggest fan, and a constant source of comfort and support since their childhoods. He had encouraged them on two wheels and watched all their races on television, right up to the end. It had been Ramón who had tried to persuade Marc to retire when his arm injury was at its worst. Marc had promised his grandfather that, if the fourth operation on his right arm didn't work, he would retire. Now his arm was fixed, and he had a competitive bike again but, sadly, his grandfather would not live to see just what his grandsons could achieve together as Gresini Ducati teammates.

In the same month that Ramón Márquez passed away, Prime Video aired the first episode of a five-part miniseries, *Marc Márquez: All In.* Having his own documentary series was an honour not even granted to Valentino Rossi in his prime. The series covered all of Márquez's career but focused heavily on his arm injury and his brutal struggle to get back to full fitness. It was the first time Márquez had allowed such access to his private life and inner circle.

'This is the other side of an athlete,' he said of the series. 'Normally, when athletes have success and good results, that's when you open your house and have the cameras showing that you are happy. But then, when you have a difficult moment, normally you go into more of a protective period and the cameras don't go in with you.'[158]

The series exposed Márquez's vulnerabilities and self-doubts, particularly when dealing with his decision to retire or to keep on taking risks and gathering more injuries. The opening scenes depict him questioning his very career. 'Is it worth it or not?' he asks. 'This suffering isn't necessary.'

This was not the happy-go-lucky Marc Márquez fans saw at races. Nor was it the superhero they saw doing impossible things on a MotoGP bike. This was the Márquez who had been through more pain than most people could imagine, and who was desperately trying to decide if it really was worth it. It was a revelation and showed a much more human side to Márquez than anyone other than his family and inner circle had previously seen.

Márquez's popularity had suffered greatly when he started regularly beating Valentino Rossi. The Italian was by far the most popular rider in MotoGP, and therefore had the support of the vast majority of race fans. Both he and Márquez had made harsh moves on each other over the years, but Rossi fans (which meant almost everybody) painted Márquez as the bad guy. It was unfair. When two titans of any sport clash, it's going to get ugly; blows will be struck and moves will be made that are right on the edge of acceptability. Such was the case with Rossi and Márquez: they were as guilty as each other, but Márquez was deemed to be the guilty party by most fans.

As well as beating Rossi regularly, Márquez had also been the man standing in the way of the Italian winning an elusive tenth world championship, when time was not on the Italian's side. It was another reason for the legions of Rossi fans to hate Márquez and to boo him. Yet Márquez maintained a quiet dignity throughout, never resorting to bad-mouthing Rossi in the media, and never making personal attacks on him. To be presented with a cup of faeces on his own doorstep by the Italian media showed just how far some Rossi 'supporters' were prepared to go to in the hope of belittling Márquez.

Marc Márquez: All In finally allowed MotoGP fans to see the real man, at home, at work and at play. It also allowed them to see the incredible struggle he had been through in recent years, and to see the unflinching determination to give everything to the sport he loved. The end result was that Márquez's popularity soared as people realised they might have been wrong to paint him as a pantomime villain. He is now the most popular rider in MotoGP, and the Prime Video miniseries contributed in no small way to that turnaround.

To launch the series, Márquez rode his Honda RC213V MotoGP bike down the closed-off streets of Madrid in front of thousands of fans, and at the head of 350 bikers who had paid for the privilege of being in the parade. The tickets sold out within hours. With the show being free to view for Amazon Prime members (and Red Bull TV then making it free to watch globally four months later), the series guaranteed Márquez a worldwide audience.

The world premiere of the first episode was held on a giant screen in Gran Via in Madrid, where Márquez also addressed the crowds and thanked everyone for their continued support. 'It has been a unique experience – as I like them!' he said after the event. 'Normally, movie premieres tend to be in theatres, something quiet, but I wanted it to be different and to be able to be close to my fans. I am very grateful that it was possible, and that so many fans have accompanied me on an important day.'[159]

With the miniseries having been seen by millions, Marc Márquez took part in his first race for Ducati with much greater support from MotoGP fans. The first round of the 2024 season was held, as usual, at Doha in Qatar and, at the end of the second practice session, he was the fastest rider on track. He was helped by the damp conditions (which meant the 2024 Ducatis could not use their power and edge grip advantage), but it was still a hugely encouraging start. Opinions had been split over winter as to how well Márquez would do on the Ducati. Some felt he would destroy everyone straight away when finally handed a more competitive bike than the Honda, while others felt he would continue crashing, simply because he had crashed so often when trying to make up for the deficiencies of the uncompetitive Honda. Yet others felt he would take time to adjust to the Desmosedici and would always be at a disadvantage to the 2024 Ducatis, but would still be able to take race wins when conditions – and/or particular circuits – favoured him. Finally, there were those who believed that Márquez would never be able to beat the young guns like Francesco Bagnaia and Jorge Martin. He was 31 by the time the season started; he was past it, many thought, and, once he discovered he couldn't beat the new breed of riders, even on a Ducati, he would simply walk away from the sport and retire to enjoy his millions. How Márquez would perform on a Ducati had been the talk of the off-season, and his debut on the bike was hugely anticipated.

He eventually lined up for his first race (the Sprint) on a Ducati in sixth place and was immediately competitive, battling for a podium spot before running wide at Turn 14 on lap eight and dropping back to fifth place over the line. Top five: exactly where Márquez, at the Gresini team launch, predicted he would be if all went well. It *had* gone well, and there was much more to come, as he later explained. 'Every day I improve my riding style; every day I change a few things that help a little bit. Still, I believe that I don't arrive on the limit of the bike.'

In his first full-length race for Ducati the following day, Márquez was again in contention and, for the first time, he had to contend with a young Spanish rider who was already being heralded as Márquez's natural heir.

Pedro Acosta was making his debut in the premier class at just 19 years old, having won the Moto3 title in 2021 and the Moto2 crown in 2023. He had already broken several of Márquez's records, (including becoming the youngest ever rider to win a race in Moto2), and he was keen to measure himself against Márquez in his debut MotoGP race. Mounted on the satellite GasGas Tech 3 KTM, brimful of confidence and as aggressive as Márquez in his approach to racing, Acosta slipped past him to take fourth place on lap 12. It only took two laps for Márquez to re-pass, but it was a hint of things to come; it would not be the last battle between the old master and the young pretender.

Márquez finished the race in a strong fourth place, behind Francesco Bagnaia, Brad Binder and Jorge Martin. His brother Álex finished two places behind him in sixth. Both Ducatis in front of Marc Márquez were 2024 models, but he never used this as an excuse, instead explaining that he was simply outridden on the day. 'They are faster,' he said of Bagnaia and Martin specifically. 'One is the world champion, and the other one is second [in the championship in 2023].'

He was pleased with his efforts, nonetheless. 'First Grand Prix for Ducati, of course it was a solid weekend, like I did in the pre-season,' he said. 'Solid days, trying not to exaggerate, trying not to make any mistakes, trying to be calm in all situations, don't be crazy . . . I want to be patient this year, I want to enjoy again, I want to fight for the top five positions, and it's what I do this weekend. But yeah, I enjoyed it.'[160]

In just his second Grand Prix with Ducati, Márquez put his Desmosedici on the podium with second place in the Sprint race. With only Aprilia's Maverick Viñales in front of him, he also finished as top Ducati rider, beating both title favourites, Bagnaia and Martin. And this despite crashing during qualifying (he accidentally activated the rear ride-height device too early through a corner) and only starting from the third row of the grid in eighth place. 'I'm super happy for that Sprint race – first podium,' he said afterwards. 'But we did a big mistake in qualifying, starting from eighth position penalise [me] a lot. But I have the speed – I show the speed, and I feel more comfortable, even for overtake, than in Qatar.'

The main race saw the first Ducati-on-Ducati clash involving Márquez – something that many had predicted ahead of his move to the marque. Unable to reach a podium position, Francesco Bagnaia made a desperate lunge inside Márquez in an attempt to take fifth place, but Márquez, who was slightly wide, came back on to his line and both riders crashed out. It was deemed a racing incident, but it looked more like two Ducati riders trying to establish who was boss. Bagnaia was by now a double world champion, and was fully aware of how big a threat Márquez would become once he was truly at home on the Ducati.

Márquez laid the blame for the incident firmly at Bagnaia's doorstep, arguing that the move was far too aggressive, given that they were only fighting for two points. 'In the last laps, if you're fighting for the victory, maybe you can be aggressive but, today, I don't think it was the moment to be like this. But okay, he decided to do it and, for sure, he'll learn.'[161]

With the riders on 2024 Ducatis complaining of chatter [vibration] problems at the American Grand Prix – as they had done from the start of the season – Márquez qualified in third and took another second place in the Sprint race at a circuit that had always favoured him. In the main event he scythed his way through the pack to lead a race for the first time on a Ducati, but then crashed out when his brakes failed. 'When I pulled the front brakes, there was no pressure,' he said, before seeing the positive side of the weekend. 'The important thing for me is that I crashed while leading the race. I'm proving I'm still competitive and am calm about this.'

At Jerez – scene of the crash that almost ended his career four years previously – Márquez made another step, taking his first pole position for Ducati. He then backed that up by leading the Sprint race before crashing out on lap seven of 12. He rejoined the race and carved his way through to fifth place, again showing he had speed, but was later docked one position for making a harsh move on Joan Mir as he fought his way back through the pack.

The main race saw him put in his best performance yet on the Ducati as he fought tooth and nail with the reigning world champion, Francesco Bagnaia, the pair continually dive-bombing each other until Bagnaia made a decisive move, forcing Márquez to lift his bike up and allow the Italian through for the win.

It was a magnificent performance on a year-old bike, racing against Ducati's number one rider, revered for his precision and smoothness. It looked like the Márquez of old was back, and that he had shaken off the nightmare of the last four years. 'Sometimes mental injuries weigh more than physical ones,' he said of his struggle. 'Physically, I had a very serious one, but this also causes a mental injury that you have to heal, little by little. It was my bet this year. It was risky, but I gave it that courage that sometimes an athlete has to put in to face openly whatever comes.'[162]

It seemed a first Ducati win was imminent, yet problems kept arising to prevent it. It was how Márquez dealt with those problems that showed his true pace, however. In France he struggled to find a good setting on the Ducati and qualified in a lowly 13th place. It didn't deter him: when the lights went green, Márquez got a flyer from the fifth row of the grid and overtook nine of the world's fastest riders to grab fourth place.

With Aleix Espargaró having to serve a long lap penalty and Marco Bezzecchi crashing out, Márquez then found himself in second place behind Jorge Martin and held position to the chequered flag. As outrageous as it was to take second place from 13th on the grid, Márquez then went out in the main race and did exactly the same thing again.

Within striking distance of Jorge Martin and Francesco Bagnaia as they entered the last lap of the feature race, he squeezed past the reigning world champion to take second, just four-tenths of a second behind championship leader Jorge Martin. Once again, Márquez was fighting it out with the two top Ducati riders on the very latest bikes, and easily outperforming every other rider on a 2023 Ducati (including his brother Álex, who finished 14th in the Sprint at Le Mans and tenth in the feature race).

Two podiums from the fifth row of the grid meant Márquez was now being considered a title contender – something even he had never expected to be. After five rounds he was just 39 points behind Martin and, while a win had so far eluded him, he acknowledged that he mustn't become obsessed with the only piece of the puzzle that was still missing. 'I trust that my first victory will come, but it must not become an obsession,' he said, realising the dangers of pushing too hard against superior machinery in a desperate bid to tick the 'win' box. Gaining consistent podiums – with the possibility to fight for a win when conditions favoured him – was a far more sensible approach.

Five rounds into the championship, Marc Márquez was already making noises about wanting a 2025 bike for the 2025 season, even if it wasn't a Ducati. In his hands, there seemed no reason why a KTM or an Aprilia couldn't be more competitive. Both manufacturers' machines were slightly behind the Ducatis in terms of performance, but a rider like Márquez might be able to make the difference, as he was already showing on his second-hand bike. He was sending an early warning to Ducati bosses that he intended to be in a factory team. 'In 2025 I don't care about the brand or the colour of bike, because if you want to fight for the world championship, you have a better chance of succeeding.'

Riders also have a better chance of succeeding if they start a race from the first two rows of the grid. Márquez took two second places from 13th on the grid at Jerez, a feat practically unheard of in modern MotoGP racing; if he could qualify nearer the front of the grid, he knew he had the pace to win races.

It was the same story at the Catalan Grand Prix, where he failed to make it through to Qualifying 2 and had to start from 14th place. The problem was down to a lack of data; Márquez had no base settings from the previous year for the way he rides a Ducati at each circuit and, with limited time to work not only on a race set-up, but also on a one-off, fast lap set-up (two very different things), he quite often just ran out of time. Márquez also felt the 2024 Michelin tyres, and his tendency to still ride the Ducati like he rode his Honda, were other factors affecting his qualifying times.

The 2024 Ducati had been built around the 2024 Michelin tyres, whereas Márquez's 2023 bike had not.

'One of my strong points is going in [to the corners],' he explained. 'When I put on a new tyre – that going in? I cannot do it, because the rear is pushing more to the front. So, we need to understand the set-up we are using; we need to understand all these things to take advantage of the tyre. With Honda, I was used to riding like this for years, especially on the fast lap. Go in, and then you will go out. But with this bike, it is a bit different.'[163]

Six rounds into the 2024 championship, Márquez sat third in the points standings. But to be a genuine title contender, he knew he needed to improve in qualifying. 'We are third in the championship after six races already, but we are third and it is our real position, because there are two guys that are a bit faster. If we want to fight with them, we need to improve the qualifying practice.'[164]

There could no longer be any doubting Márquez's race pace though, nor his willingness to take risks, nor his determination to win again. He had even regained his ability to save massive slides and still wasn't afraid of crashing, despite his years of injury hell.

At Catalunya, he performed miracles again from 14th on the grid, taking another two podiums: second in the Sprint and third in the Grand Prix.

There had been so much doubt surrounding Márquez over the last four years as to just how competitive he was. Had it really just been the Honda, or had his injuries permanently affected his ability to challenge for race wins? Had he lost the desire to push as hard as was necessary to win Grand Prix races? Was he, in short, past it? His results in the first six races of 2024 had put an end to any such doubts, but they also created a big problem for Ducati.

For many, Marc Márquez was still the best rider on the grid, and deserved a full factory bike. Part of the reason he signed a one-year deal with the Gresini team was so that he could try to get a factory bike for the 2025 season, should his 2024 results be good enough. They were good enough, but Jorge Martin's were even better.

Martin was in his fourth year with Pramac Ducati, and he was armed with the latest Desmosedici, unlike Márquez, but it was still a satellite team (though higher up the pecking order than Márquez's Gresini team) and Martin felt Ducati should have chosen him for the factory team in 2023. Instead, Ducati opted for Enea Bastianini. Martin felt slighted, and his results in 2023 showed why. He had run Francesco Bagnaia extremely close for the world title, while Bastianini had finished the year in a lowly 15th place, hampered by injuries and a subsequent lack of confidence.

After six rounds of the 2024 season, Martin was leading the championship by 39 points from Bagnaia. He was beating Ducati's number one factory rider while riding for a satellite team, so was surely at the front of the queue for a seat in the factory Ducati team.

With Bastianini's factory contract expiring at the end of the 2024 season, Martin felt he would finally get the call-up to join the number one team. He had done everything to earn the seat, and no one believed otherwise. But there remained one single problem – Marc Márquez.

As one of the greatest riders in the history of MotoGP, Márquez not only possessed outrageous riding talent (as he had shown by taking podiums and battling for race wins on a year-old bike), but he also had a massive global fan base, meaning his marketing potential was huge. He was still the most famous rider in MotoGP by a long way and, armed with a current bike in the factory Ducati team, he would surely be a challenger for the 2025 title. Ducati had a decision to make – Martin or Márquez.

If Martin was overlooked by Ducati again, it seemed likely he would leave the Ducati fold altogether and ride for a rival manufacturer. If Márquez wasn't offered a seat in the factory team, he would most likely do the same. Both Aprilia and KTM had good bikes and, with Martin or Márquez on board, they might just be able to turn them into serial race winners. With Bagnaia's seat safe, Ducati was going to have to let one of its top riders go, and whichever rider they dropped would make a fearsome opponent in 2025.

Opinion was split as to whom should be awarded the factory seat. Martin was five years younger than Márquez and was leading the championship in a satellite team. Many fellow riders believed he was the fastest man on the grid, when all else was equal. Márquez was doing things on a year-old bike that really shouldn't be possible and was only going to get stronger as he learned how the Ducati needed to be ridden. He would also be much stronger with a factory bike.

Jorge Martin had his supporters too, though. 'He deserves the official Ducati,' Aleix Espargaró said of Martin. 'There is no one who merits that bike more . . . What else does he have to do?'

Ducati rider Marco Bezzecchi was also in the Martin camp. 'Martin's the one that deserves this more, because last year he fought for the championship and this year he's leading by a good amount of points.'

TNT Sports presenter Suzi Perry favoured Márquez. While acknowledging that Ducati was in 'an impossible situation', Perry said, 'Unless you can convince Márquez to take a satellite bike, he's going to go to another manufacturer. And you do not want that now that he's found his form again.'

For Ducati race boss Gigi Dall'Igna, deciding who should have the second factory seat was clearly a tough decision, but respected MotoGP journalist Mat Oxley pointed out that the Italian boss had access to data that outsiders didn't have, and that this could have helped him come to a decision. 'Dall'Igna examines the data streams from all his riders, and ever since Márquez first threw a leg over his Gresini GP23, it's been very obvious that the six-time MotoGP king makes magic, even on a second-hand motorcycle.'[165]

The debate raged on as the MotoGP circus rolled into Mugello for the Italian Grand Prix. By then, there were strong rumours that Martin was the chosen one and that a deal for him to race in the factory Ducati team was all but signed. If Márquez wanted to stay with Ducati, it would need to be in a satellite team. At Mugello, he publicly announced he would not accept a seat in the Pramac Ducati team, which was, in effect, saying he would leave Ducati altogether if they signed Martin to the factory team.

Amidst all the rumours and counter-rumours, there were still races to attend to. Francesco Bagnaia dominated the Italian Grand Prix, winning both the Sprint and feature races, while Márquez took second and fourth places respectively; another solid weekend.

The following day, Jorge Martin dropped a bombshell: he had signed for Aprilia. Marc Márquez's public statement that he would not join the satellite Pramac Ducati team had forced Ducati's hand; they simply couldn't lose the biggest name in MotoGP, the last of the 'aliens', and a rider who was back on form and showing so much potential on a Ducati. In 2025, Marc Márquez would ride for the official factory Ducati team, with the very best equipment and back-up, as teammate to Francesco Bagnaia. Jorge Martin had been overlooked by Ducati for a second time.

Márquez had played his cards perfectly to secure the most coveted seat in MotoGP, but race fans were divided, with many feeling that Martin had more than earned the seat. Questions were immediately asked of how Márquez and Bagnaia would get along within the Ducati team. Bagnaia is a protégé of Márquez's old enemy, Valentino Rossi, and many insisted that, while he might be a laid-back character, he wouldn't take kindly to Márquez coming into the team and trying to take charge. Márquez was Márquez, and he had always been the number one rider in whichever MotoGP team he was in. Trouble was predicted as soon as the signing was announced.

The signing also affected Enea Bastianini who announced that, having been dumped by the factory Ducati team, he would be joining the Tech 3 KTM satellite team. Another Ducati rider, Marco Bezzecchi, also jumped ship, this time from Valentino Rossi's VR46 team to join Jorge Martin at Aprilia. Rossi, still full of loathing for Márquez, was furious about Ducati's tactics. 'Ducati had set up an interesting system with a pyramid, allowing young riders to progress and dream of one day joining the official team,' he said. 'That's how Pecco (Bagnaia) climbed the steps up the ladder, and how Martin and Bezzecchi also hoped to get there. Then, all of a sudden, Ducati decided to put Márquez in red on the factory bike. It's normal for young riders who have been loyal to the brand for years to feel betrayed.'[166]

Márquez's signing also had a knock-on effect within the Pramac Ducati team who, after 20 years of loyalty to the Italian manufacturer, announced that they would become a satellite Yamaha team in 2025. Ducati had hinted that Rossi's VR46 team might be the recipient of a current factory bike in 2025, meaning the Pramac team would have year-old bikes. Team owner Paolo Campinoti opted out.

At least Marc Márquez was happy with how things turned out.

'I am very happy to be able to wear the red colours of the factory Ducati team in MotoGP next season,' he said after signing a two-year contract. 'Basically, from the first contact with the Desmosedici GP, I enjoyed riding it and adapted well straight away. From that moment on, I knew that my goal was to continue this path, to continue to grow, and to move to the team where Pecco Bagnaia has been the world champion for two years in a row. I am happy to be able to take this big step in 2025 and grateful for the trust Ducati has placed in me. Finally, I want to thank Nadia, Carlo, Michele and the entire Gresini Racing family for opening the door of their team to me at a delicate time in my career. Now, we will continue to have fun and give it our all in what remains of the current season, which is my priority right now.'

At the same time, Ducati supremo Gigi Dall'Igna explained the reasons for Ducati's choice. 'Deciding on Bagnaia's new teammate in the Ducati Lenovo Team was not easy as we had a list of very strong riders to choose from,' he said. 'In the end, our choice fell on an unquestionable talent like Marc Márquez. In just a few races, he has managed to adapt perfectly to our Desmosedici GP and his innate ambition pushes him to grow continuously. In the box, we will have two riders who together hold 11 world titles, and being able to count on their experience and maturity will be invaluable for our growth as well.'

With so much hype surrounding all the moves, it was easy to forget there was still racing to be dealt with, but Assen wasn't kind to Marc Márquez. Starting from seventh on the grid after crashing in qualifying, he was up to fifth place in the Sprint race before clipping a kerb on the second lap and crashing out again.

There was more misery to come in the feature race. He finished in a respectable fourth place behind Bagnaia, Martin and Viñales, but was then handed a 16-second time penalty for a tyre pressure infringement and dropped down to 11th place.

New – and hugely controversial – minimum tyre pressure rules for 2024 meant riders now had to maintain more than 1.8 bar of pressure in the front tyre for 60 per cent of the race or face being penalised. Márquez's Ducati failed the random inspection. For many, it was a farcical situation. Tyre pressure is greatly affected by a rider's position on track during the race. If he is fighting in a pack, tyre pressures can rise, if he is out front alone, there will be no such issue. Clearly, riders cannot predict what's going to happen in races, no matter how well educated their guesses might be. 'It's guesswork,' respected MotoGP journalist Michael Scott wrote in a scathing attack on the rule. 'Nobody knows whether they will be alone or in a pack, making it very easy to fall foul of the rule.'[167]

At Assen, it was Márquez's turn to fall foul of the rule, but he wasn't the first, and he wouldn't be the last. He had tried desperately to keep his tyres within the permitted pressure range – even going so far as to wave another rider past so that he could tuck in behind him and get more heat (and therefore pressure) into his front tyre, but it wasn't enough to avoid a penalty.

The need for the rule – which many claimed was ruining the sport – was down to Michelin's front tyres not being up to the job of dealing with the increased stresses on its tyres caused by aerodynamics and ride-height devices. A new tyre was announced midway through 2024, much to everyone's relief, but it would not be ready until 2026, meaning another year of unfair penalties that could genuinely affect the outcome of a championship. It was far from being an ideal situation.

Márquez had been competitive all season on his second-hand Ducati and had taken podiums but not yet a win. His beloved left-handed Sachsenring offered perhaps his best chance of the year. He had won there 11 times across all classes, including eight times in the premier class, and he had even won there in 2021, on an uncompetitive Honda and with a crocked right arm. He was the undisputed king of the ring, and now that he was injury-free and on a much better bike than the Honda – even if it was still lacking compared to the 2024 Ducatis – all eyes were on Márquez to see if he could finally return to the top step of the podium.

It wasn't to be. He crashed during practice on the Friday and broke his left index finger as well as suffering bruised ribs. That meant he was unable to pass through to Qualifying 2 so he started from a lowly 13th place on the grid. He rode superbly through to sixth place, but it wasn't the result he had hoped for coming into the weekend.

There was reason to celebrate after the feature race, however. Not only did Márquez make it all the way from 13th on the grid up to second, but his brother Álex joined him on the podium in third. It was the first time the brothers had shared a podium in MotoGP and Marc was ecstatic. 'I promise you, I would exchange the victory to be with my brother on the podium,' he said afterwards. 'It's some feeling – amazing.'

He clearly had the pace to win the race, had qualifying gone better, but the consolation of sharing a podium with his brother kept the smile on Márquez's face. Jorge Martin was not so happy. He had made an unforced error and crashed out of the lead, handing the championship advantage back to race winner Francesco Bagnaia.

At the British Grand Prix at Silverstone, it was Bagnaia's turn to crash out, this time in the Sprint race. Márquez did too, sliding out of fourth position on the penultimate lap. He would at least finish a safe fourth in the main race, but as the 2024 Ducatis continued to develop, it seemed fourth was the best he would be able to achieve; a win seemed to be out of reach. The new, and superior, ride-height device on the 2024 Ducatis (which led to much better acceleration) was reckoned to be worth anywhere between 0.3 and 0.5 seconds per lap, depending on the circuit.

That didn't stop Márquez from trying, however. He was lying safely in second place in the Sprint race in Austria before crashing out again, once more pushing his GP23 Desmosedici past its limits.

More bad luck was to follow in the feature race. Starting from the front row, he was unable to engage his ride-height device on the grid and was swamped by riders flying past him before eventually joining the race in 13th place. Again, he showed race-winning pace by scything through the pack to fourth place, but he was going to need a clean weekend with no crashes, no technical issues, and no bad luck if he was to finally win a race for Gresini Ducati. He would need, he said, 'a perfect weekend'.

At MotorLand Aragón, he would get one.

CHAPTER 15

EL RETORNO DEL REY

**'WE WILL TRY TO BE THE SPECIAL ONE AGAIN IN THE FUTURE,
BUT WE HAVE TO AWAIT OUR MOMENT.'**

Marc Márquez

Situated in Alcañiz, in the north-east of Spain, just over 100 miles from Marc Márquez's home town of Cervera, the MotorLand Aragón circuit first appeared on the MotoGP calendar in 2010, when Márquez was still racing in the Moto3 class.

The layout used for MotoGP is 3.15 miles long and features seven left-hand corners and five right-hand corners. Márquez had always favoured left-handed circuits due to his dirt track background, having spent thousands of hours riding round left-hand oval circuits. He was a specialist.

Since first racing at Aragón in 2010, Márquez had won there seven times in Moto2 and MotoGP. If he was going to win a race in his first year with Ducati, the Spanish circuit offered one of his best chances. While the 2024 Ducatis had superior acceleration on to the kilometre-long back straight – and a faster top speed down it – Márquez's talent could make up for his older bike's shortcomings on such a track; his superiority through left-hand corners would, in theory, make him competitive.

Getting back to the sharp end of MotoGP again had been a tremendous struggle for Márquez; the injuries, the pain, the rehab, the humiliation of riding an uncompetitive and uncompliant motorcycle near the back of the field, the stress, the indecision about leaving Honda . . . it had all taken its toll. Ahead of the 2024 Aragón round, he finally confessed how close he had come to throwing in the towel; his body, mind and spirit battered almost beyond repair. 'One year ago, I was very close to retiring after Assen,' he admitted. 'That would have been a disastrous ending. But, luckily, after that race there was the long summer break and I had enough time to rebuild my body from different fractures, and to rebuild my mind. If I had retired then, I would've always had that question: "What if I tried a different bike?"'[168]

Winning the MotoGP title as a rookie in 2013 had given Márquez a skewed impression of the most elite motorcycling championship on earth: he *expected* to win, and he had often won easily. Between 2013 and 2019 he took six world championships and almost became blasé about winning. The years of struggle following his big crash in 2020 changed that outlook. 'I understand now that being first is not the normal thing,' he said of MotoGP. 'The normal thing is to be second, third, fourth, fifth, sixth . . . I mean, the one that's winning is the special one. We will try to be the special one again in the future, but we have to await our moment.'[169]

At Aragón, on 31 August 2024, Marc Márquez finally became the 'special one' again. He rode like he had done in his prime, not only beating his rivals, but annihilating them. He was fastest in every practice session (although he didn't go out for the damp Sunday morning warm-up as there was nothing to be gained and too much risk), fastest in qualifying by a massive 0.8 seconds (the largest margin in dry conditions since 2011), and he led the 11-lap race from lights to flag, carving out a four-second lead before slackening off to ensure the victory. It was vintage Márquez, and neither Francesco Bagnaia nor Jorge Martin could do anything about it.

It had been 1,042 days since Márquez had won a race, and it was his first ever Sprint race win (Sprint races were only introduced in 2023). He had last tasted victory at Misano, back in 2021 and was understandably elated. 'When I crossed the finish line, it was an amazing feeling,' he said. 'My first thought was all the people who helped me in these very hard moments. I'm alone on the racetrack, but behind me there is a very nice team, very nice people, a very nice family.'[170]

It was a win, but it wasn't a full Grand Prix win, so Márquez didn't get too carried away. 'I feel super good,' he said after the race. 'It was a very good weekend until now, but the race always is the race, and you cannot do any mistakes. I started a little bit stiff on the first lap, but then we started to ride in a better way, and we controlled the race but, of course, the most important day is tomorrow. Today we celebrate, because it's a Sprint race, but it's really important for us – the first victory in the Sprint – and I am looking forward for tomorrow, in front of these amazing people.'

As Márquez pointed out, the following day was more important. While half points are awarded for them, Sprint races do not count as official MotoGP victories, only feature races do, so there was still one last box to tick before Márquez could really claim to be back at the very top of his game: he had to win a full-length MotoGP race.

One day later, he did. Leading the race from start to finish, he crossed the line some five seconds ahead of Jorge Martin to take his 60th MotoGP win. From the first practice session on Friday, right through to the end of the MotoGP race, Márquez had been fastest. He had not been led at any point, in any session or race, and all on a year-old bike, operating out of a satellite team. This was Márquez the Merciless of old: one of the greatest motorcycle racers of all time was back on top. After such a long, gruelling struggle, the relief was intense. 'It was difficult to control the emotions in the last few laps,' he admitted. 'And, when I crossed the line, I felt like I lost three or four kilos.'

Since he had first ridden the Ducati at the end of the previous year, Márquez knew a win was coming; he didn't know when, only that it was. 'During the Valencia test I realised this day will arrive,' he admitted. 'I understood that, sooner or later, it will arrive.'

Key to Márquez's Aragón success had been learning to focus on his 2023 bike, rather than trying to set it up like the 2024 model. 'We were looking a lot at the 2024 bikes, but they're different,' he explained. 'We need to ride with *our* set-up, with *our* performance, and believe in ourselves. Our technicians, our team, is doing a very good job, and step by step I start to ride smoother, and by instinct, so this makes the difference.'

Even his rivals were in awe of Márquez's abilities. World champion Francesco Bagnaia had seen the data downloaded from Márquez's bike (Ducati riders all have access to each other's data) and had pointed out that the Spaniard was leaning over four degrees more in left-hand corners than any other Ducati rider at Aragón. 'When he tells me his secret in the right corners, I will tell him the secret to the left ones!' Márquez joked. 'Each rider has their strong points. Unfortunately for me, most of the circuits are on the right, [but] on the left corners I feel super-good.'

During the feature race at Aragón, Álex Márquez inadvertently affected the championship standings when he clipped the rear of Bagnaia's bike and caused both riders to crash out of the race. With no points scored, Bagnaia fell 23 behind Jorge Martin in the points table. Marc Márquez's double victory saw him overtake Enea Bastianini for third place in the championship.

Third-place finisher in the feature race, Pedro Acosta, was impressed by Márquez's dogged, never-give-up attitude. 'He is one of the few who, after being injured, had no need to go back to racing,' he said. 'He could have gone home, but what he has done defines him as a person.'[171]

Márquez had gone from the heights of ecstasy to the troughs of despair; he had undergone four operations on his right arm – during the last one his arm was literally sawn in half – he had walked away from a multi-million-euro contract, and he had taken a chance on a year-old bike and a modest satellite team to get back to the top in MotoGP, and back to the ecstasy of winning that every motorcycle racer lives for. It was one of the greatest comebacks in MotoGP history and it cemented his legend. Media outlets around the world covered the inspirational story. What he had done to secure those victories in Aragón had never been done in racing before: his was a unique achievement.

He might have had a one-off victory at Misano in 2021, but Márquez hadn't been a genuine podium and race-winning contender since he barrelled into the gravel trap at Jerez way back in 2020. As well as being his 60th win in the MotoGP class, the Aragón victory was his 86th across all classes, and it moved him to fourth in the all-time winners' list, just five short of Ángel Nieto in third place, and behind Valentino Rossi (115) and Giacomo Agostini (122). It should be noted that both Nieto and Agostini often raced in two championships in the same season, so had more chances to collect wins.

After the Aragón weekend, Márquez sat 70 points behind championship leader Jorge Martin, but he insisted he was too far behind to fight for the title. 'One weekend will not change our life,' he said. 'Of course, it will help our life, but will not change. We are too far to fight for the championship this year, but let's see if we can fight to be in the top three positions. That's a realistic goal.'[172]

Márquez had never expected to fight for the title in 2024. He had always intended for it to be a foundation year, getting used to the Ducati and regaining his confidence with more competitive results. It was also intended as a year to showcase his talents and prove that he deserved a factory ride. He had achieved everything he set out to do and had done everything he needed to do to set up a full title assault in 2025. His master plan was working out perfectly.

One week after his Aragón win, Márquez did it again. After crashing in qualifying and starting from ninth place on the grid, he finished fifth in the Sprint race, but Sunday's main race was twice as long, giving him more time to slice his way through the field. He was also assisted by a brief rain shower and used his superior skills in low grip conditions to register his second win in a week, crossing the line ahead of factory Ducati men, Francesco Bagnaia and Enea Bastianini. Jorge Martin rode straight into the pit lane to change bikes when the rain came, but it was only the briefest of showers and he had to pit again to change back to slick tyres. His race was ruined. Martin's blunder meant his lead over Bagnaia was reduced to just seven points, with Márquez a further 46 behind.

Márquez's back-to-back wins came at two very different circuits, and in totally different circumstances, proving that he still had the talent that had taken him to six MotoGP titles. 'After the mistake in qualifying, when the [rain] drops came, I knew it was my only chance – it was time to attack,' he said after his opportunistic win.

The victory was even more poignant as it happened at Valentino Rossi's local circuit, where he and his VR46 Academy riders (including Bagnaia) had spun countless thousands of laps in training. Despite being on an Italian bike, and despite that bike being painted in tribute colours to the late Gresini team owner, Fausto Gresini (also Italian), a certain element of lingering Valentino Rossi fans booed Márquez on the podium. Other MotoGP riders, including Bagnaia and Martin, were quick to condemn such behaviour and to support Márquez. 'For me, we are giving our 100 per cent,' Martin said. 'Our life is a gamble, because we can die out there. For me, there should be a bit more respect and this booing makes no sense.'[173]

Márquez's former team boss, Livio Suppo, was also disgusted by the lack of respect. 'It has been going on for a long time; even now when he races in Italy, stupid people boo him. But I think now Marc doesn't care any more, especially after what happened in 2020 with his injury. That was his real hell, and it really changed his perspective of what is important.'

Yet, while Rossi continued to attack Márquez in the press, three years after retiring, Márquez didn't appear to hold any grudges. When asked if he was especially delighted to win in Rossi's backyard, he answered, 'I'm not interested in this. I don't need psychological blows against anyone, but a good booster for myself, to improve my confidence, which I have been losing year after year in the last three seasons.'[174]

In November 2024, after Rossi had once again attacked Márquez – this time in an interview for Spanish media outlet AS – MotoGP boss Carmelo Ezpeleta urged the Italian to let bygones be bygones. 'I think it would be better to let it be,' he said. 'It's been a while. That was many years ago. Obviously, I'm not the one to tell Valentino what he has to do or not do, but I don't think it helps much to say that now.'[175]

At the same time, Ezpeleta praised Márquez for refusing to respond to Rossi's remarks, saying, 'It seemed good to me that Marc did not comment on his statements.'

Márquez's decision to leave Honda had another knock-on effect at Misano. After 30 years of loyal support and with 15 world titles in the bag, Repsol announced it would no longer be sponsoring the factory Honda team in MotoGP. The Spanish energy giant was accustomed to winning; the highest Honda finisher at Misano was Johann Zarco in 12th place. It was not what Repsol executives had signed up for. Honda had not only lost its greatest rider, but also its title sponsor of the last three decades.

With the Kazakhstan Grand Prix having to be cancelled because the circuit hadn't been built, Misano staged another Grand Prix the following week, acting as a stand-in venue. After taking fourth place in the Sprint race, Márquez took yet another podium in the main event, this time behind Enea Bastianini and Jorge Martin. With Bagnaia crashing out, Martin's championship lead was extended to 24 points, while Bastianini took third place in the standings by a single point from Márquez. The young Italian had finally found his form after a difficult period, and it was now a matter of some pride to take third in the championship from Márquez; after all, Bastianini was in the factory Ducati team, and it wouldn't look good to be beaten by a year-old bike being run out of a satellite team. Márquez would also be taking Bastianini's ride in 2025, so the motivation for the Italian to beat him was strong.

Bastianini narrowly beat Márquez into third place in the Indonesian Sprint race and, with Martin crashing out, Bagnaia halved the Spaniard's championship lead. Márquez had been hounding Bagnaia for a podium position in the main race until his engine blew up, bursting into flames as he coasted to a halt. In a bid to make Márquez's bike work better with the super grippy 2024 Michelin rear tyre, the Gresini team had been running a lighter fly wheel in the Desmosedici. In theory, it should have reduced engine inertia into corners, but the experiment failed in the most dramatic fashion and the team reverted to the standard fly wheel for the remainder of the season.

The GP23 was almost completely destroyed in the fire, with only the frame being salvageable but, while he was disappointed, Márquez remained philosophical about the incident. 'It's true that it's something that's not in our hands,' he said, 'even not in the hands of our team, but it sometimes happens in the races and today it happened to me. We can say that we were super unlucky, but with Ducati and my team and me, we win together, so we lose together.'[176]

Márquez took another two podiums in Japan, but with Enea Bastianini beating him to second place in the feature race, he lost third place in the championship by two points to the Italian.

But then came Australia, where Marc Márquez put in one of the greatest performances of his career to win the feature race. The Sprint had seen him turn the tables on Bastianini, this time beating him to second place, but it was Márquez's performance in the main event that truly impressed.

In a freak incident, he disposed of a tear-off visor on the grid and the Phillip Island wind blew it underneath his bike, just in front of the rear tyre. Riders usually have a gentleman's agreement not to dispose of tear-offs on the grid – to avoid just such dangerous situations – but as Márquez had rolled up to his starting position, his vision became obscured by a squashed bug; he was unsighted and had to make an exception; the visor had to go.

Starting from second place on the grid (a huge boost after so many poor performances in qualifying), Márquez at least knew the visor was there, so it didn't come as a complete surprise when he launched his GP23 Ducati and spun up violently off the line, his bike slewing dangerously sideways, smoke pouring off the rear tyre as it spun wildly, trying to find grip. By the time it hooked up, half of the MotoGP pack had already passed Márquez, but it took him just two corners to move up from 13th place to sixth.

Phillip Island is the fastest and most flowing circuit on the MotoGP calendar, and tyre management is usually crucial. On this occasion, however, Márquez decided to throw caution to the wind. 'Here, you have to manage the tyres,' he said afterwards, 'but from the first lap I decided to use all the tyre, and let's see what happens.'

What happened was remarkable. Márquez destroyed the two title contenders, Francesco Bastianini and Jorge Martin, on his older bike, and rode so hard he broke his own lap record which had stood for 11 years. He also overtook 12 riders in an era of MotoGP when aerodynamic devices have made overtaking exceptionally difficult (due to the turbulence created by the aero devices as one rider tries to pass another). Márquez led Martin home by almost a second, with Bagnaia a further ten seconds adrift. It was one of the greatest rides of his career and it put him 14 points clear of Enea Bastianini in the championship standings. And this on a bike that was only seventh fastest through the speed trap. Bastianini's 2024 factory Ducati was clocked at 220.7mph while Márquez's GP23 was travelling at 217.2mph. With MotoGP races often being won by tenths – or even thousandths – of a second, such advantages can be crucial.

Given the speed advantage of the newer bikes, Márquez was forced to dive-bomb Jorge Martin on the brakes, knowing that both he and Bagnaia had to ride more cautiously as they were fighting for the championship: Márquez, on the other hand, could afford to throw caution to the wind. 'I don't know where I was in the first corner, but I overtook many riders, and I thought that one time was impossible to catch Martin,' he said after the race. 'Then, in lap five or six, I started to get the rhythm, and it was more calm. It was a bit stressful but I'm super happy.'[177]

Excepting the blip when his engine blew up in Indonesia, it was Márquez's sixth podium in a row, proving that he had really got to grips with riding the Ducati, and begging the question yet again of what he might be able to achieve once he had the latest version of the bike.

A lonely fourth place was the best he could manage in the Sprint race in Thailand, while his rival for third place in the championship, Enea Bastianini, took the victory. Álex Márquez finished one place behind his brother, but almost five seconds further back.

The feature race promised better for Márquez senior as he clearly had the pace to fight with – and perhaps even beat – both Bagnaia and Martin. He had been running in second place, attacking Bagnaia when he crashed out on lap 13, once again trying to force his older Ducati to do things it wasn't capable of doing. He remounted and finished 11th, one place behind his brother. Márquez blamed himself for the crash, saying, 'I was the fastest, but not the smartest.'

Bagnaia's victory meant he closed the points gap on Martin to

17 and, with Bastianini crashing out, Márquez's points advantage in third place was 11 with two rounds to go.

The Malaysian Sprint race saw him finish a strong second behind Martin but, more significantly for the championship, Bagnaia crashed out, giving Martin a 29-point lead. That gap was reduced to 24 points after Bagnaia dominated the feature race.

Márquez had been running in a strong third place in the main race before crashing out again, this time on lap seven. Third place for Bastianini meant Márquez now had just a single point over him in the battle for third in the championship. It would all come down to the final round at Valencia in Spain. Or at least, that had been the plan, but no one could have foreseen the devastation that was wreaked on the Valencia region by floods of biblical proportions.

They were the worst seen in decades and over 200 lives were lost. Thousands of homes in coastal areas of Catalunya – and many more in central Spain near Madrid – were without electricity, and both road and rail links were severed. Buildings were devastated, cars and bridges washed away, tunnels blocked by vehicles swept along by the deluge. Prime Minister Pedro Sánchez ordered the biggest ever deployment of Spanish troops in peacetime to help with the rescue and clear-up efforts. Central government approved a €10 billion relief package, and the Valencian regional government asked for a further €31 billion.

The Circuit Ricardo Tormo in Valencia – where the final race of the 2024 MotoGP season was due to be held in just two weeks' time – also suffered extensive damage, with access roads collapsing and trees and fences being torn apart. There was clearly no way to race there but, even if it had been possible, the MotoGP riders didn't want to. Marc Márquez led calls for an alternative venue, feeling it would be disrespectful to race in an area which was fighting a life-

or-death battle, and Francesco Bagnaia announced he would rather see the final round cancelled (and lose any hope of retaining his title) than race there. The riders were united: an alternative venue would be found, and they would race FOR Valencia, but not IN Valencia. The last round was to become a huge money-raising event for the victims of the floods.

It was eventually decided that the Circuit de Barcelona-Catalunya would host the season finale. On the same day as the Malaysian Grand Prix took place, Dorna's Chief Sporting Director, Carlos Ezpeleta, announced: 'We have been looking at all the possibilities we had. It's very challenging to organise an event in two weeks, but during the last 48 hours we've looked at all possible alternatives and we think that Barcelona is the best possible place, given the proximity to Valencia, given that a lot of people were already travelling through to get to the finale, and especially for fans – we think it's the best possible place for them. We also know we will be able to help the Community of Valencia from that location as well.'

Marc Márquez was understandably devastated by the floods; his home region of Catalunya being one of the most affected areas. Ahead of the announcement of a replacement final round he said, 'As a Spanish person, it's super-difficult to see this kind of images. I think all the facilities of the government, of Spain, need to go for those people that lost their house. We need to understand well the situation, but all the facilities need to go for those people. I mean, I see the damage of the circuit in Valencia, but it (makes no sense) to start to repair those things while having many people without a house. So, let's see what they will do.'[178]

Alex Márquez also realised how unimportant a MotoGP race was, in light of such a catastrophe. 'It's not the time, I think, to see if there will be a GP there or not,' he said about Valencia.

'Now, everything – and all the facilities – need to be with the people that are there, that don't have a home: many deaths, many losses. It's difficult. It's not easy for all the Spanish people, but especially for the Valencian people. So, we will see how it will be, but now we cannot just focus to try to put everything correct for the facilities of the track – more important is the people that don't have a home or lose family, than thinking if we have a GP there or not.'[179]

The final round of the 2024 MotoGP season would be held on the same date as the Valencia round had been planned (16–17 November) and would be officially dubbed 'The Solidarity Grand Prix of Barcelona'. It would be MotoGP's way of standing by the people of Spain and raising millions of euros to help with relief aid.

Starting the final Sprint of the year from third place on the grid, Marc Márquez made heavy contact with Pedro Acosta at Turn 3 on the first lap, damaging the younger rider's bike and forcing him out of the race. Márquez hung on to claim seventh place, but Acosta was not amused. 'I was in front!' he said of the incident. 'I didn't see anyone until Marc hit me. I was fully right on the inside, and he went in like it was a normal lap, as if no one was there. It was the third corner on the first lap . . . It was not necessary to go like this, but racing is racing. I was really in front.'[180]

Jorge Martin took a 19-point lead into the final feature race of the year and only needed to outscore Francesco Bagnaia by two points to claim the 2024 world championship. He rode cautiously to secure third place, and the title, while Bagnaia did all he could by winning the race. It wasn't enough, and the Italian was forced to relinquish the crown he had held for two years.

Marc Márquez rounded out his incredible year with a second place, which was enough to give him third in the championship ahead of factory Ducati rider Enea Bastianini. He hadn't been holding back, trying to protect future teammate Francesco Bagnaia's lead; he just couldn't match the Italian's pace on the day. 'We spent many laps behind Pecco, and I was trying to control the situation,' Márquez said after the race, 'but during those last five laps, I could not follow him. Every time when I was close to him the front tyre started to gain temperature, and today he was much faster than me.'[181]

In all, Márquez had taken three wins and ten podiums during the season. The next best rider on a GP23 Ducati was his brother, who finished the season in eighth place.

Márquez had far exceeded his goals for the 2024 season, but admitted that, even if he'd had a current bike, he would have struggled to win the championship because he had been injured and uncompetitive for so long. He had needed a season just to get back up to speed. 'Everything I had in my notebook this year, I've done it, and the rest has come as a gift,' he said. 'Had I written it down to be world champion? It wasn't realistic. I couldn't go from four years in hell to glory all at once.'[182]

It had been a transitional year; one to rebuild, relearn and gain confidence ahead of a full-on title assault in 2025. Perhaps most importantly, Márquez was enjoying his racing again, as his podium and victory celebrations proved. The sparkle was back, the injuries were healed, he was having fun, and the drive and determination had never gone away. He was once again the full package. 'My plan is already accomplished,' he said. 'When I came to Gresini, I had a plan. The priority was to see if I could become competitive again. The plan was to have the opportunity to be part of an official team – the best team and the best bike. That was the Ducati Lenovo. I needed to show speed, because you are worth what your last race is worth – not what you got in the past.'[183]

Two days after the final race of the 2024 season, testing began for the 2025 MotoGP world championship. The Barcelona test saw Márquez in red for the first time (and, since sponsorship deals were still being finalised, he was *completely* in red) as he made his debut on the full factory Ducati. He would finish fourth overall as he slowly got to grips with the new bike. 'The engine is better in the straights, as well as the character of the bike in the corners,' he said, 'but I have to figure out the limit.'[184]

Just as importantly, Márquez immediately gelled with the factory Ducati team. 'The feeling was super good, especially with the team,' he said. 'That is the most important on the first impression, and we work in a good way.'

There was a fond farewell from the Gresini team too. After the final race, team members had carried Márquez down the pit lane and deposited him in the factory Ducati garage. Then, during testing, he jokingly flipped the Gresini team the bird during qualifying as his brother had set the fastest time overall, just like the team had predicted (the 2025 Ducatis were at the beginning of their development, whereas Álex's 2024 bike was fully developed and race ready, giving him an early advantage). It was a good-natured send-off and Márquez remained hugely grateful to the Gresini team for helping him get back to winning ways.

Márquez's comeback year had played out even better than he had hoped, and he already had his eye on the future. 'From my personal point of view, for me the comeback I did from the last four years to now is already something that I'm proud of,' he said after wrapping up third place in the championship. 'So, let's see what we can do in the next two years in the official team.'

Marc Márquez had no need to write a letter to the Three Kings in January 2025. They had set him on his incredible journey

28 years ago with their gift of a small, child's motorcycle, and now he had the best racing motorcycle on the planet at his disposal. He had earned it the hard way, toiling through four years of pain, doubt and misery to prove what he was capable of, and to prove that he deserved a seat in the factory Ducati team. He was whole again, and now, as he faced the most important racing season of his life, Márquez had no doubts about how much effort he was prepared to put into regaining the MotoGP world championship after all he had been through. 'If you ask me, "What can we expect from Marc Márquez?"' he postulated. 'Everything.'

MARC MÁRQUEZ GRAND PRIX RESULTS, 2008–24

2008 MOTO3 WORLD CHAMPIONSHIP
Team: Repsol KTM
Bike: KTM FRR125

Losail, Qatar: (Too young to enter)
Jerez, Spain: (Too young to enter)
Estoril, Portugal: 18th
Shanghai, China: 12th
Le Mans, France: DNF
Mugello, Italy: 19th
Catalunya, Spain: 10th
Donington Park, Great Britain: 3rd
Assen, Netherlands: DNF
Sachsenring, Germany: 9th

Brno, Czech Republic: DNF
Misano, Italy: 4th
Indianapolis, USA: 6th
Motegi, Japan: DNF
Phillip Island, Australia: 9th
Sepang, Malaysia: DNS
Valencia, Spain: DNS
Final Championship Position: 13th

2009 MOTO3 WORLD CHAMPIONSHIP
Team: Red Bull KTM Moto Sport
Bike: KTM FRR125

Losail, Qatar: DNF
Motegi, Japan: 5th

Jerez, Spain: 3rd
Le Mans, France: DNF
Mugello, Italy: 5th
Catalunya, Spain: 5th
Assen, Netherlands: 10th
Sachsenring, Germany: 16th
Silverstone, Great Britain: 15th
Brno, Czech Republic: 8th
Indianapolis, USA: 6th
Misano, Italy: 4th
Estoril, Portugal: DNF
Phillip Island, Australia: 9th
Sepang, Malaysia: DNF
Valencia, Spain: 17th
Final Championship Position:
8th

2010 MOTO3 WORLD CHAMPIONSHIP
Team: Red Bull Ajo Motorsport Derbi
Bike: Derbi RSA125

Losail, Qatar: 3rd
Jerez, Spain: DNF
Le Mans, France: 3rd
Mugello, Italy: 1st
Silverstone, Great Britain: 1st
Assen, Netherlands: 1st
Catalunya, Spain: 1st

Sachsenring, Germany: 1st
Brno, Czech Republic: 7th
Indianapolis, USA: 10th
Misano, Italy: 1st
Aragón, Spain: DNF
Motegi, Japan: 1st
Sepang, Malaysia: 1st
Phillip Island, Australia: 1st
Estoril, Portugal: 1st
Valencia, Spain: 4th
Final Championship Position:
1st

2011 MOTO2 WORLD CHAMPIONSHIP
Team: Team CatalunyaCaixa Repsol
Bike: Suter

Losail, Qatar: DNF
Jerez, Spain: DNF
Estoril, Portugal: 21st
Le Mans, France: 1st
Catalunya, Spain: 2nd
Silverstone, Great Britain: DNF
Assen, Netherlands: 1st
Mugello, Italy: 1st
Sachsenring, Germany: 1st
Brno, Czech Republic: 2nd
Indianapolis, USA: 1st

Misano, Italy: 1st
Aragón, Spain: 1st
Motegi, Japan: 2nd
Phillip Island, Australia: 3rd
Sepang, Malaysia: DNS
Valencia, Spain: DNS
Final Championship Position:
2nd

2012 MOTO2 WORLD CHAMPIONSHIP
Team: Team CatalunyaCaixa Repsol
Bike: Suter

Losail, Qatar: 1st
Jerez, Spain: 2nd
Estoril, Portugal: 1st
Le Mans, France: DNF
Catalunya, Spain: 3rd
Silverstone, Great Britain: 3rd
Assen, Netherlands: 1st
Sachsenring, Germany: 1st
Mugello, Italy: 5th
Indianapolis, USA: 1st
Brno, Czech Republic: 1st
Misano, Italy: 1st
Aragón, Spain: 2nd
Motegi, Japan: 1st
Sepang, Malaysia: DNF

Phillip Island, Australia: 3rd
Valencia, Spain: 1st
Final Championship Position:
1st

2013 MOTOGP WORLD CHAMPIONSHIP
Team: Repsol Honda
Bike: Honda RCV213V

Losail, Qatar: 3rd
Circuit of the Americas, USA: 1st
Jerez, Spain: 2nd
Le Mans, France: 3rd
Mugello, Italy: DNF
Catalunya, Spain: 3rd
Assen, Netherlands: 2nd
Sachsenring, Germany: 1st
Laguna Seca, USA: 1st
Indianapolis, USA: 1st
Brno, Czech Republic: 1st
Silverstone, Great Britain: 2nd
Misano, Italy: 2nd
Aragón, Spain: 1st
Sepang, Malaysia: 2nd
Phillip Island, Australia:
Disqualified
Motegi, Japan: 2nd
Valencia, Spain: 3rd
Final Championship Position: 1st

2014 MOTOGP WORLD CHAMPIONSHIP
Team: Repsol Honda
Bike: Honda RCV213V

Losail, Qatar: 1st
Circuit of the Americas, USA: 1st
Termas de Río Hondo, Argentina: 1st
Jerez, Spain: 1st
Le Mans, France: 1st
Mugello, Italy: 1st
Catalunya, Spain: 1st
Assen, Netherlands: 1st
Sachsenring, Germany: 1st
Indianapolis, USA: 1st
Brno, Czech Republic: 4th
Silverstone, Great Britain: 1st
Misano, Italy: 15th
Aragón, Spain: 13th
Motegi, Japan: 2nd
Phillip Island, Australia: DNF
Sepang, Malaysia: 1st
Valencia, Spain: 1st
Final Championship Position: 1st

2015 MOTOGP WORLD CHAMPIONSHIP
Team: Repsol Honda
Bike: Honda RCV213V

Losail, Qatar: 5th
Circuit of the Americas, USA: 1st
Termas de Río Hondo, Argentina: DNF
Jerez, Spain: 2nd
Le Mans, France: 4th
Mugello, Italy: DNF
Catalunya, Spain: DNF
Assen, Netherlands: 2nd
Sachsenring, Germany: 1st
Indianapolis, USA: 1st
Brno, Czech Republic: 2nd
Silverstone, Great Britain: DNF
Misano, Italy: 1st
Aragón, Spain: DNF
Motegi, Japan: 4th
Phillip Island, Australia: 1st
Sepang, Malaysia: DNF
Valencia, Spain: 2nd
Final Championship Position: 3rd

2016 MOTOGP WORLD CHAMPIONSHIP
Team: Repsol Honda
Bike: Honda RCV213V

Losail, Qatar: 3rd
Termas de Río Hondo, Argentina: 1st
Circuit of the Americas, USA: 1st
Jerez, Spain: 3rd
Le Mans, France: 13th
Mugello, Italy: 2nd
Catalunya, Spain: 2nd
Assen, Netherlands: 2nd
Sachsenring, Germany: 1st
Red Bull Ring, Austria: 5th
Brno, Czech Republic: 3rd
Silverstone, Great Britain: 4th
Misano, Italy: 4th
Aragón, Spain: 1st
Motegi, Japan: 1st
Phillip Island, Australia: DNF
Sepang, Malaysia: 11th
Valencia, Spain: 2nd
Final Championship Position: 1st

2017 MOTOGP WORLD CHAMPIONSHIP
Team: Repsol Honda
Bike: Honda RCV213V

Losail, Qatar: 4th
Termas de Río Hondo, Argentina: DNF
Circuit of the Americas, USA: 1st
Jerez, Spain: 2nd
Le Mans, France: DNF
Mugello, Italy: 6th
Catalunya, Spain: 2nd
Assen, Netherlands: 3rd
Sachsenring, Germany: 1st
Brno, Czech Republic: 1st
Red Bull Ring, Austria: 2nd
Silverstone, Great Britain: DNF
Misano, Italy: 1st
Aragón, Spain: 1st
Motegi, Japan: 2nd
Phillip Island, Australia: 1st
Sepang, Malaysia: 4th
Valencia, Spain: 3rd
Final Championship Position: 1st

2018 MOTOGP WORLD CHAMPIONSHIP
Team: Repsol Honda
Bike: Honda RCV213V

Losail, Qatar: 2nd
Termas de Río Hondo, Argentina: 18th
Circuit of the Americas, USA: 1st
Jerez, Spain: 1st
Le Mans, France: 1st
Mugello, Italy: 16th
Catalunya, Spain: 2nd
Assen, Netherlands: 1st
Sachsenring, Germany: 1st
Brno, Czech Republic: 3rd
Red Bull Ring, Austria: 2nd
Silverstone, Great Britain: Race cancelled
Misano, Italy: 2nd
Aragón, Spain: 1st
Chang International Circuit, Thailand: 1st
Motegi, Japan: 1st
Phillip Island, Australia: DNF
Sepang, Malaysia: 1st
Valencia, Spain: DNF
Final Championship Position: 1st

2019 MOTOGP WORLD CHAMPIONSHIP
Team: Repsol Honda
Bike: Honda RCV213V

Losail, Qatar: 2nd
Termas de Río Hondo, Argentina: 1st
Circuit of the Americas, USA: DNF
Jerez, Spain: 1st
Le Mans, France: 1st
Mugello, Italy: 2nd
Catalunya, Spain: 1st
Assen, Netherlands: 2nd
Sachsenring, Germany: 1st
Brno, Czech Republic: 1st
Red Bull Ring, Austria: 2nd
Silverstone, Great Britain: 2nd
Misano, Italy: 1st
Aragón, Spain: 1st
Chang International Circuit, Thailand: 1st
Motegi, Japan: 1st
Phillip Island, Australia: 1st
Sepang, Malaysia: 2nd
Valencia, Spain: 1st
Final Championship Position: 1st

2020 MOTOGP WORLD CHAMPIONSHIP
Team: Repsol Honda
Bike: Honda RCV213V

* Due to the Covid-19 pandemic, some circuits hosted two races, one week apart
Losail, Qatar: No MotoGP race due to Covid pandemic
Jerez, Spain: DNF
Jerez, Spain: DNS
Brno, Czech Republic: DNS
Red Bull Ring, Austria: DNS
Red Bull Ring, Austria: DNS
Misano, Italy: DNS
Misano, Italy: DNS
Catalunya, Spain: DNS
Le Mans, France: DNS
Aragón, Spain: DNS
Aragón, Spain: DNS
Valencia, Spain: DNS
Valencia, Spain: DNS
Portimão, Portugal: DNS
Final Championship Position: 26th (no points)

2021 MOTOGP WORLD CHAMPIONSHIP
Team: Repsol Honda
Bike: Honda RCV213V

* Due to the Covid-19 pandemic, some circuits hosted two races, one week apart
Losail, Qatar: DNS
Losail, Qatar: DNS
Portimão, Portugal: 7th
Jerez, Spain: 9th
Le Mans, France: DNF
Mugello, Italy: DNF
Catalunya, Spain: DNF
Sachsenring, Germany: 1st
Assen, Netherlands: 7th
Red Bull Ring, Austria: 8th
Red Bull Ring, Austria: 15th
Silverstone, Great Britain: DNF
Aragón, Spain: 2nd
Misano, Italy: 4th
Circuit of the Americas, USA: 1st
Misano, Italy: 1st
Portimão, Portugal: DNS
Valencia, Spain: DNS
Final Championship Position: 7th

2022 MOTOGP WORLD CHAMPIONSHIP
Team: Repsol Honda
Bike: Honda RCV213V

Losail, Qatar: 5th
Mandalika, Indonesia: DNS
Termas de Río Hondo, Argentina: DNS
Circuit of the Americas, USA: 6th
Portimão, Portugal: 6th
Jerez, Spain: 4th
Le Mans, France: 6th
Mugello, Italy: 10th
Catalunya, Spain: DNS
Sachsenring, Germany: DNS
Assen, Netherlands: DNS
Silverstone, Great Britain: DNS
Red Bull Ring, Austria: DNS
Misano, Italy: DNS
Aragón, Spain: DNF
Motegi, Japan: 4th
Buriram, Thailand: 5th
Phillip Island, Australia: 2nd
Sepang, Malaysia: 7th
Valencia, Spain: DNF
Final Championship Position: 13th

2023 MOTOGP WORLD CHAMPIONSHIP
Team: Repsol Honda
Bike: Honda RCV213V

* The 2023 season saw the introduction of Sprint races which were half the distance of a feature race with half points being awarded.

Portimão, Portugal
Sprint race: 3rd
Feature race: DNF

Termas de Río Hondo, Argentina
Sprint race: DNS
Feature race: DNS

Circuit of the Americas, USA
Sprint race: DNS
Feature race: DNS

Jerez, Spain
Sprint race: DNS
Feature race: DNS

Le Mans, France
Sprint race: 5th
Feature race: DNF

Mugello, Italy
Sprint race: 7th
Feature race: DNF

Sachsenring, Germany
Sprint race: 11th
Feature race: DNS

Assen, Netherlands
Sprint race: 13th
Feature race: DNS

Silverstone, Great Britain
Sprint race: 18th
Feature race: DNF

Red Bull Ring, Austria
Sprint race: 10th
Feature race: 12th

Catalunya, Spain
Sprint race: 11th
Feature race: 13th

Misano, Italy
Sprint race: 10th
Feature race: 7th

Buddh International Circuit,
India

Sprint race: 3rd
Feature race: 9th

Motegi, Japan
Sprint race: 7th
Feature race: 3rd

Mandalika, Indonesia
Sprint race: DNF
Feature race: DNF

Phillip Island, Australia:
* Sprint race cancelled
Feature race: 15th

Buriram, Thailand
Sprint race: 4th
Feature race: 6th

Sepang, Malaysia
Sprint race: 21st
Feature race: 13th

Losail, Qatar
Sprint race: 11th
Feature race: 11th

Valencia, Spain
Sprint race: 3rd
Feature race: DNF

Final Championship Position:
14th

2024 MOTOGP WORLD CHAMPIONSHIP
Team: Gresini Ducati
Bike: Ducati Desmosedici GP23

Losail, Qatar
Sprint race: 5th
Feature race: 4th

Portimão, Portugal
Sprint race: 2nd
Feature race: 16th

Circuit of the Americas
Sprint race: 2nd
Feature race: DNF

Jerez, Spain
Sprint race: 6th
Feature race: 2nd

Le Mans, France
Sprint race: 2nd
Feature race: 2nd

Catalunya, Spain
Sprint race: 2nd
Feature race: 3rd

Mugello, Italy
Sprint race: 2nd
Feature race: 4th

Assen, Netherlands
Sprint race: DNF
Feature race: 10th

Sachsenring, Germany
Sprint race: 6th
Feature race: 2nd

Silverstone, Great Britain
Sprint race: DNF
Feature race: 4th

Red Bull Ring, Austria
Sprint race: DNF
Feature race: 4th

Aragón, Spain
Sprint race: 1st
Feature race: 1st

Misano, Italy
Sprint race: 5th
Feature race: 1st

Misano, Italy (second meeting)
Sprint race: 4th
Feature race: 3rd

Mandalika, Indonesia
Sprint race: 3rd
Feature race: DNF

Motegi, Japan
Sprint race: 3rd
Feature race: 3rd

Phillip Island, Australia
Sprint race: 2nd
Feature race: 1st

Chang International Circuit,
Thailand
Sprint race: 4th
Feature race: 11th

Sepang, Malaysia
Sprint race: 2nd
Feature race: 12th

Catalunya, Spain (second
meeting)
Sprint race: 7th
Feature race: 2nd

Final Championship Position:
3rd

Key

DNS: Did Not Start
DNF: Did Not Finish

ENDNOTES

1   Pérez de Rozas, 'A champion resulting from the euphoria of Wembley 92', www.elcorreodeburgos.com.

2   *Marc Márquez: All In*, A Fast Brothers Production A.I.E., Prime Video, 2023.

3   *Marc Márquez: All In*, A Fast Brothers Production A.I.E., Prime Video, 2023.

4   Scott, Michael, *Motocourse 2013–2014*, Icon Publishing Limited, 2013, p.20.

5   From an uncredited and undated interview on www.boxrepsol.com.

6   *Unconditional: Marc Márquez – A Mother's Story.* Director Myles Desenberg, 2019. www.dazn.com.

7   Pérez de Rozas, Emilio, *Marc Márquez, Dreams Come True: My Story*, Ebury Press, 2014, p.19.

8   *From Cervera to Tokyo: The Marc Márquez Story*, Director Sergi Sendra Vives, Dorna Sports SL/Red Bull TV, 2017.

9   *From Cervera to Tokyo: The Marc Márquez Story*, Director Sergi Sendra Vives, Dorna Sports SL/Red Bull TV, 2017.

10 'Fearless Kid Márquez Leaves MotoGP Legends Standing', Nicks, Mike, www.independent.co.uk, 30 August 2013.

11 Jessner, Werner and Márquez, *Being Marc Márquez: This Is How I Win My Race*, gestalten, 2023, p.124.

12 Pérez de Rozas, Emilio, *Marc Márquez, Dreams Come True: My Story*, Ebury Press, 2014, p.98.

13 'Marc Márquez's schoolteacher: he wasn't satisfied with a 9, he had to get a 10', www.cope.es, 11 November 2013.

14 Jessner, Werner and Márquez, *Being Marc Márquez: This Is How I Win My Race*, gestalten, 2023, p.129.

15 'Meet Emilio Alzamora – The Third Márquez', Paul Keith, redbull.com, 2 August 2016.

16 Pérez de Rozas, Emilio, *Marc Márquez, Dreams Come True: My Story*, Ebury Press, 2014, p.28.

17 *Marc Márquez: Story of a Trophy Collector*, Dorna Sports, S.L., 2015.

18 *Marc Márquez: Story of a Trophy Collector*, Dorna Sports, S.L., 2015.

19 Emmett, David, 'Introducing Marc Márquez: Repsol presents their 125cc representative', www.motomatters.com, 7 August 2010.

20 *Marc Márquez: Story of a Trophy Collector*, Dorna Sports, S.L., 2015.

21 *Marc Márquez: Story of a Trophy Collector*, Dorna Sports, S.L., 2015.

22 *Marc Márquez: Story of a Trophy Collector*, Dorna Sports, S.L., 2015.

23 Pérez de Rozas, Emilio, *Marc Márquez, Dreams Come True: My Story*, Ebury Press, 2014, p.72.

24 Dawe, Joseph Caron, 'What Makes Marc Márquez a MotoGP World Champion?', www.redbull.com, 27 November 2014.

25 'Márquez wins Moto2 at Le Mans', www.motoaus.com, 15 May 2011.

26 Scott, Michael, *Motocourse 2011–2012*, Icon Publishing Limited, 2011, p.184.

27 Cazeneuve, André, 'MotoGP Marc Márquez Honda', www.paddock-gp.com, 16 March 2019.

28 Rowles, Aaron, 'Márquez' Career was in doubt in 2011', www.gpextra.com, 15 October 2014.

29 McLaren, Peter, 'Marc Márquez Still; Recovering from Vision Problems', www.crash.net, 12 January 2012.

30 McLaren, Peter, 'Moto2: Marc Márquez Q&A', www.crash.net, 9 August 2012.

31 McLaren, Peter, 'Moto2: Marc Márquez Q&A', www.crash.net, 9 August 2012.

32 *Marc Márquez: Story of a Trophy Collector*, Dorna Sports, S.L., 2015.

33 Dawe, Joseph Caron, 'What Makes Marc Márquez a MotoGP World Champion?', www.redbull.com, 27 November 2014.

34 *Hitting the Apex*, Directed by Mark Neale, The First Movie Company LLC/ Universal Pictures, 2013.

35 Jessner, Werner and Márquez, *Being Marc Márquez: This Is How I Win My Race*, gestalten, 2023, p.79.

36 Jessner, Werner and Márquez, *Being Marc Márquez: This Is How I Win My Race*, gestalten, 2023, p.29.

37 Birt, Mathew, 'Cal Crutchlow hails "Special" Marc Márquez', www.motorcyclenews.com, 15 November 2012.

38 Pérez de Rozas, Emilio, *Marc Márquez Dreams Come True: My Story*, Ebury Press, 2014, pp.26–27.

39 *Marc Márquez: All In*, A Fast Brothers Production A.I.E., Prime Video, 2023.

40 'Marc Márquez Engineer Interview', www.fastbikesmag.com, 29 March 2013.

41 Scott, Michael, *Motocourse 2013–2014*, Icon Publishing Limited, 2013, p.74.

42 Pérez de Rozas, Emilio, *Marc Márquez, Dreams Come True: My Story*, Ebury Press, 2014, p.32.

43 Vyas, Hardik, 'Interview with 2013 Champion Marc Márquez', www.sportskeeda.com, 11 December 2013.

44 Pérez de Rozas, Emilio, *Marc Márquez, Dreams Come True: My Story*, Ebury Press, 2014, p.32.

45 'MotoGP Repsol Honda – Marc Márquez Interview', www.cycleworld.com, 1 August 2013

46 Tremayne, Sam, 'Rossi says Márquez/Lorenzo clash at Jerez a racing incident', www.autosport.com, 7 May 2013.

47 Jessner, Werner and Márquez, *Being Marc Márquez: This Is How I Win My Race*, Benevento Publishing, 2023, p.145.

48 *Marc Márquez: All In*, A Fast Brothers Production A.I.E., Prime Video, 2023.

49 Pérez de Rozas, Emilio, *Marc Márquez, Dreams Come True: My Story*, Ebury Press, 2014, p.45.

50 *Hitting the Apex*, Directed by Mark Neale, The First Movie Company LLC/ Universal Pictures, 2013.

51 *Hitting the Apex*, Directed by Mark Neale, The First Movie Company LLC/ Universal Pictures, 2013.

52 Pérez de Rozas, Emilio, *Marc Márquez, Dreams Come True: My Story*, Ebury Press, 2014, p.47.

53 Scott, Michael, *Motocourse 2013–2014*, Icon Publishing Limited, 2013, p.136.

54 Scott, Michael, *Motocourse 2013–2014*, Icon Publishing Limited, 2013, p.162.

55 *Hitting the Apex*, Directed by Mark Neale, The First Movie Company LLC/ Universal Pictures, 2013.

56 Vyas, Hardik, 'Interview with 2013 Champion Marc Márquez', www.sportskeeda.com, 11 December 2013.

57 *Hitting the Apex*, Directed by Mark Neale, The First Movie Company LLC/ Universal Pictures, 2013.

58 *Marc Márquez: Story of a Trophy Collector*, Dorna Sports, S.L., 2015.

59 *Hitting the Apex*, Directed by Mark Neale, The First Movie Company LLC/ Universal Pictures, 2013.

60 Pérez de Rozas, Emilio, *Marc Márquez, Dreams Come True: My Story*, Ebury Press, 2014, p.68.

61 Oxley, Mat, *MotoGP Season Review 2013,* Haynes Publishing, 2014, p.5.

62 *Hitting the Apex*, Directed by Mark Neale, The First Movie Company LLC/ Universal Pictures, 2013.

63 Mitchell, Scott, 'Marc Márquez has no flaws, say Jorge Lorenzo and MotoGP rivals', www.autosport.com, 11 November 2013.

64 Mitchell, Scott, 'Marc Márquez has no flaws, say Jorge Lorenzo and MotoGP rivals', www.autosport.com, 11 November 2013.

65 Mitchell, Scott, 'Marc Márquez has no flaws, say Jorge Lorenzo and MotoGP rivals', www.autosport.com, 11 November 2013.

66 Oxley, Mat, *MotoGP Season Review 2013*, Haynes Publishing, 2014, p.6.

67 Scott, Michael, *Motocourse 2014–2015*, Icon Publishing Limited, 2014, p.128.

ENDNOTES

68 *Hitting the Apex*, Directed by Mark Neale, The First Movie Company LLC/ Universal Pictures, 2013.

69 Jessner, Werner and Márquez, *Being Marc Márquez: This Is How I Win My Race*, Benevento Publishing, 2023, p.112.

70 *Marc Márquez: Story of a Trophy Collector*, Dorna Sports, S.L., 2015.

71 'Marc Márquez: Success Can Make You Uncomfortable, www.weare93.com, 15 January 2018.

72 Jessner, Werner, 'How Marc Márquez's Relentless Resolve Keeps Him Ahead of the MotoGP Pack', www.redbull.com, 14 July 2020.

73 *Marc Márquez: All In,* A Fast Brothers Production A.I.E., Prime Video, 2023.

74 'Márquez Q&A: You Want to Beat Your Team-Mates, Your Friends', www.motogp.com, 16 June 2016.

75 Guidotti, Maria, 'Marc Márquez: The Honda is Restless, Aggressive, Nervous', www.cycleworld.com, 1 April 2016.

76 Scott, Michael, *Motocourse 2016–2017*, Icon Publishing Ltd, 2016, p.108.

77 Morsellino, Tom, '2016 MotoGP Championship, Marc Márquez Writes a Page of History', www.paddock-gp.com, 17 October 2017.

78 Hawkins, Jonathan, 'Marc Márquez: Will MotoGP's Catalan King Wear the Crown in Spain?', www.edition.cnn.com, 9 November 2017.

79 Scott, Michael, *Motocourse 2016–2017*, Icon Publishing Ltd, 2016, p.108.

80 'Márquez Q&A: You Want to Beat Your Team-Mates, Your Friends, www.motogp.com, 16 June 2016.

81 'Marc Márquez Crowned 2016 World Champion at Motegi', www.weare93.com.

82 Bloom, Josh and Dawe, Joseph Caron, 'Marc Márquez: I Hope I Never Find My Limit', www.redbull.com, 2 August 2016.

83 Bloom, Josh and Dawe, Joseph Caron, 'Marc Márquez: I Hope I Never Find My Limit', www.redbull.com, 2 August 2016.

84 'Interview with Repsol Honda Team's Marc Márquez', The Wire, www. cycleworld.com, 14 March 2017.

85 'Interview with Repsol Honda Team's Marc Márquez', The Wire, www.cycleworld.com, 14 March 2017.

86 'Interview with Marc Márquez, 2017 MotoGP World Champion, www.boxrepsol.com.

87 Scott, Michael, *Motocourse: 2017–2018*, Icon Publishing Ltd, 2017, p.163.

88 Hawkins, Jonathan, 'Marc Márquez: Will MotoGP's Catalan King Wear the Crown in Spain?', www.edition.cnn.com, 9 November 2017.

89 Hawkins, Jonathan, 'Marc Márquez: Will MotoGP's Catalan King Wear the Crown in Spain?', www.edition.cnn.com, 9 November 2017.

90 'Interview with Marc Márquez, 2017 MotoGP World Champion, www.boxrepsol.com.

91 Ryder, Julian, *'MotoGP Review 2017'*, Motocom, 2017.

92 Richards, Avin, 'Marc Márquez is the 2017 MotoGP World Champion: An Interview', www.iamabiker.com, 14 November 2024.

93 Scott, Michael, *Motocourse 2017–2018*, Icon Publishing Limited, 2017, p.228.

94 Richards, Avin, 'Marc Márquez is the 2017 MotoGP World Champion: An Interview', www.iamabiker.com, 14 November 2024.

95 'Interview with Marc Márquez, 2017 MotoGP World Champion', www.boxrepsol.com.

96 de Menezes, Jack, 'Valentino Rossi claims Marc Márquez has "destroyed MotoGP" and says he's "scared" to race against world champion', www.independent.co.uk, 10 April 2018.

97 *Marc Márquez: All In*, A Fast Brothers Production A.I.E., Prime Video, 2023.

98 Scott, Michael, *Motocourse: 2018–2019*, Icon Publishing Ltd, 2018, p.152.

99 'MotoGP Riders Meet the Pope at the Vatican', www.motogp.com, 5 September 2018.

100 'MotoGP Riders Meet the Pope at the Vatican', www.motogp.com, 5 September 2018.

101 Lee, Sammy, '"Aragon was turning point," says Marc Márquez after winning 7th world title', www.redbull.com, 19 October 2018.

102 Lee, Sammy, '"Aragon was turning point," says Marc Márquez after winning 7th world title', www.redbull.com, 19 October 2018.

103 'Interview with Marc Márquez', www.amcn.com.au, 18 January 2019.

104 Scott, Michael, *Motocourse: 2018–2019*, Icon Publishing Ltd, 2018, p.152.

105 'Interview with Marc Márquez', www.amcn.com.au, 18 January 2019.

106 Jessner, Werner, 'How Marc Márquez's Relentless Resolve Keeps Him Ahead of the MotoGP Pack', www.redbull.com, 14 July 2020.

107 'Interview with Marc Márquez', www.amcn.com.au, 18 January 2019.

108 'Interview with Marc Márquez', www.amcn.com.au, 18 January 2019.

109 'Interview with Marc Márquez', www.amcn.com.au, 18 January 2019.

110 'Marc Márquez and Jorge Lorenzo have a love-hate relationship', www.bbc.co.uk, 23 January 2019.

111 Osbourne, John, 'Marc Márquez on his "almost-perfect" year', www.redbull.com, 9 October 2019.

112 Scott, Michael, *Motocourse 2019–2010*, Icon Publishing Limited, 2019, p.152.

113 Scott, Michael, *Motocourse 2019–2010*, Icon Publishing Limited, 2019, p.152.

114 Jessner, Werner, 'How Marc Márquez's Relentless Resolve Keeps Him Ahead of the MotoGP Pack', www.redbull.com, 14 July 2020.

115 Scott, Michael, *Motocourse 2019–2010*, Icon Publishing Limited, 2019, p.186.

116 Osbourne, John, 'Marc Márquez on his "almost-perfect" year', www.redbull.com, 9 October 2019.

117 Osbourne, John, 'Marc Márquez on his "almost-perfect" year', www.redbull.com, 9 October 2019.

118 'Marc Márquez – Locked Down', www.shoei-europe.com, 2020.

119 Jessner, Werner and Márquez, *Being Marc Márquez: This Is How I Win My Race*, gestalten, 2023, p.206.

120 *Marc Márquez: All In*, A Fast Brothers Production A.I.E., Prime Video, 2023.

121 Klein, Jamie, 'Honda: Moving Álex Márquez to LCR MotoGP is in his best interest', www.autosport.com, 14 July 2024.

122 Scott, Michael, *Motocourse 2021–2022*, Icon Publishing Limited, 2021, p.137.

123 'SachsenKING: Marc Márquez Wins Again', www.motogp. hondaracingcorporation.com,, 20 June 2021.

124 Richards, Giles, 'Marc Márquez: I was afraid I would not have a normal arm again', www.theguardian.com, 20 August 2021.

125 Scott, Michael, *Motocourse 2021–2022*, Icon Publishing Limited, 2021, p.200.

126 Richards, Giles, 'Marc Márquez: I was afraid I would not have a normal arm again', www.theguardian.com, 20 August 2021.

127 *Science of Survival*, MotoGP Films/TNT Sport.

128 Scott, Michael, *Motocourse 2022–2023*, Icon Publishing Limited, 2022, p.114.

129 Scott, Michael, *Motocourse 2022–2023*, Icon Publishing Limited, 2022, p.123.

130 Izquierdo, Hector, 'Marc Márquez: "Ganaba y me ponía a llorar, y era a causa del dolor", www.rivistagq.com, 24 January 2023.

131 Izquierdo, Hector, 'Marc Márquez: "Ganaba y me ponía a llorar, y era a causa del dolor", www.rivistagq.com, 24 January 2023.

132 Pérez de Rozas, Emilio, *Marc Márquez, Dreams Come True: My Story*, Ebury Press, 2014, p.19.

133 Scott, Michael, *Motocourse 2022–2023*, Icon Publishing Limited, 2022, p.146.

134 Jessner, Werner and Márquez, *Being Marc Márquez: This Is How I Win My Race*, gestalten, 2023, p.212.

135 McRae, Donald, 'Marc Márquez: Always attack, never defend; this is my killer mentality', www.theguardian.com, 12 June 2023.

136 Jessner, Werner and Márquez, *Being Marc Márquez: This Is How I Win My Race,* gestalten, 2023, p.144.

ENDNOTES

137   *Marc Márquez: All In*, A Fast Brothers Production A.I.E., Prime Video, 2023.

138   Dielhenn, James, 'Revealed: Honda's role in the Márquez-Alzamora split', www.crash.net, 14 January 2023.

139   Young, Colin, 'He's Back!', MCN, 29 September 2022, p.66.

140   Scott, Michael, *Motocourse 2022–2023*, Icon Publishing Limited, 2022, p.235.

141   Scott, Michael, *Motocourse 2022–2023*, Icon Publishing Limited, 2022, p.235.

142   Bugler, Daphne, 'At home with Marc Márquez: FIFA, dogs, and a whole lot of coffee', gq-magazine.co.uk, 19 June 2023.

143   Jessner, Werner and Márquez, *Being Marc Márquez: This Is How I Win My Race*, Benevento Publishing, 2023, p.112.

144   Scott, Michael, *Motocourse 2023–2024*, Icon Publishing Limited, 2023, p.125.

145   Scott, Michael, *Motocourse 2023–2024*, Icon Publishing Limited, 2023, p.132.

146   Scott, Michael, *Motocourse 2023–2024*, Icon Publishing Limited, 2023, p.132.

147   Garcia Casanova, Germán, 'Marc Márquez interview: On his injury recovery, Honda's MotoGP progress, and Eins', www.autosport.com, 2 August 2023.

148   Villanova, Leonardo, 'I expect Marc to fight for the championship', MCN, 11 October 2023.

149   Villanova, Leonardo, 'I expect Marc to fight for the championship', MCN, 11 October 2023.

150   Scott, Michael, 'Márquez confirmed at Ducati for 2024', MCN, 11 October 2023, p.63.

151   Scott, Michael, *Motocourse 2023–2024*, Icon Publishing Limited, 2023, p.237.

152   www.honda.racing, 26 November 2023.

153   Bueno, Pablo and Llurba, Lluís, 'How Marc Márquez plans to get back amongst the best in MotoGP', www.redbull.com, 7 March 2024.

154   Lamonato, Michael, 'Championship for sure: why everyone's a winner in Márquez's Gresini gamble', www.foxsports.com.au, 13 October 2023.

155   Bugler, Daphne, 'At home with Marc Márquez: FIFA, dogs, and a whole lot of coffee', www.gq-magazine.co.uk, 19 June 2023.

156   Bueno, Pablo and Llurba, Lluís, 'How Marc Márquez plans to get back among the best in MotoGP', www.redbull.com, 7 March 2024.

157   MCN, 14 February 2024., p.63.

158   Bugler, Daphne, 'At home with Marc Márquez: FIFA, dogs, and a whole lot of coffee', gq-magazine.co.uk, 19 June 2023.

159   'Marc Márquez launches his long-awaited documentary: Marc Márquez: All In', www.marcmárquez93.com, 21 February 2023.

160   Duncan, Lewis, 'Márquez not at limit of Ducati despite strong Qatar MotoGP debut', www.autosport.com, 14 March 2024.

161   Close, Josh, 'Battle lines are drawn', MCN, 27 March 2024.

162   Young, Colin, 'When I'm happy I'm fast', MCN, 1 May 2024.

163   'What is stopping Marc Márquez from being a serious title contender?', www.motogp.com, 28 May 2024.

164   'What is stopping Marc Márquez from being a serious title contender?', www.motogp.com, 28 May 2024.

165   Oxley, Mat, 'Expect Gigi to pick Márquez', MCN, 5 June 2024.

166   Turco, Michel, 'Pecco doesn't need Márquez in the garage to show he's the No.1', MCN, 25 September 2024.

167   MCN, 2 October 2024, p.60.

168   Weeink, Frank, 'We will try to be the special one again', *MCN*, 31 July 2023.

169   Weeink, Frank, 'We will try to be the special one again', *MCN*, 31 July 2023.

170   Rooke, Sam, 'Marc Márquez revels in Aragon MotoGP victory to break three-year winless run', www.tntsports.co.uk, 1 August 2024.

171   Puigdemont, Oriol, 'Why Marc Márquez's Aragon win has more implications than people might think', www.autosport.com, 2 September 2024.

ENDNOTES

172 Whitworth, Alex, 'Marc Márquez "too far to fight for the championship" despite Aragon win', www.crash.net, 3 September 2024.

173 Thukral, Rachit, 'MotoGP riders criticise disrespectful booing of Márquez at Misano', www.motorsport.com, 19 September 2024.

174 Guidotti, Maria, 'Marc Márquez speaks about his second win and the future', www.cycleworld.com, 11 September 2024.

175 Dielhenn, James, 'Valentino Rossi told "it doesn't help now" to hammer Marc Márquez', www.crash.net, 13 October 2024.

176 Mitchell-Malm, Scott, 'Márquez and MotoGP Track Mandalika at Odds Over Bike Fire Damage', www.the-race.com, 1 October 2024.

177 'Márquez wins in Australia as Martin extends title lead', www.bbc.co.uk, 20 October 2024.

178 Whitworth, Alex, 'Valencia MotoGP: Spain needs to help "people that lost their house", not circuit – Marc Márquez', www.crash.net, 31 October 2014.

179 Whitworth, Alex, 'Valencia MotoGP: Spain needs to help "people that lost their house", not circuit – Marc Márquez', www.crash.net, 31 October 2014.

180 Scaysbrook, Rennie, '2024 Solidarity MotoGP News and Results', www.cyclenews.com, 17 November 2024.

181 'New Chapter for Márquez', MCN, 20 November 2024, p.59.

182 Thukral, Rachit, 'Márquez: I wouldn't have won MotoGP title even with Ducati GP24', www.autosport.com, 2 December 2024.

183 'Ducati, Marc Márquez paws (sic): "The plan succeeded, now I have the right bike"', sportal.eu, 11 September 2024.

184 Guglielmetti, Riccardo, 'MotoGP Márquez: In red I was comfortable. The GP25? I have to study it better', www.gpone.com.

BIBLIOGRAPHY

Books

Márquez, Marc, and Pérez de Rozas, Emilio, *Marc Márquez Dreams Come True: My Story*, Ebury Press, 2014.

Márquez, Marc, and Jessner, Werner, *Being Marc Márquez: This Is How I Win My Race*, gestalten, 2023.

Scott, Michael (ed), *Motocourse 2008–2009*, CMG Publishing, 2008.

Scott, Michael (ed), *Motocourse 2009–2010*, Icon Publishing Limited, 2009.

Scott, Michael (ed), *Motocourse 2010–2011*, Icon Publishing Limited, 2010.

Scott, Michael (ed), *Motocourse 2011–2012*, Icon Publishing Limited, 2011.

Scott, Michael (ed), *Motocourse 2012–2013*, Icon Publishing Limited, 2012.

Scott, Michael (ed), *Motocourse 2013–2014*, Icon Publishing Limited, 2013.

Scott, Michael (ed), *Motocourse 2014–2015*, Icon Publishing Limited, 2014.

Scott, Michael (ed), *Motocourse 2015–2016*, Icon Publishing Limited, 2015.

Scott, Michael (ed), *Motocourse 2016–2017*, Icon Publishing Limited, 2016.

Scott, Michael (ed), *Motocourse 2017–2018*, Icon Publishing Limited, 2017.

Scott, Michael (ed), *Motocourse 2018–2019*, Icon Publishing Limited, 2018.

Scott, Michael (ed), *Motocourse 2019–2020*, Icon Publishing Limited, 2019.

Scott, Michael (ed), *Motocourse 2020–2021*, Icon Publishing Limited, 2020.

Scott, Michael (ed), *Motocourse 2021–2022*, Icon Publishing Limited, 2021.

Scott, Michael (ed), *Motocourse 2022–2023*, Icon Publishing Limited, 2022.

Scott, Michael (ed), *Motocourse 2023–2024*, Icon Publishing Limited, 2023.

BIBLIOGRAPHY

Websites

www.amcn.com.au, www.autosport.com, www.bbc.co.uk,
www.boxrepsol.com, www.cope.es, www.crash.net,
www.cycleworld.com, www.dazn.com, www.edition.cnn.com,
www.elcorreodeburgos.com, www.fastbikesmag.com,
www.foxsports.com.au, www.gpextra.com, www.gpone.com,
www.gq-magazine.co.uk, www.honda.racing, www.iamabiker.com,
www.independant.co.uk, www.marcmárquez93.com,
www.motoaus.com, www.motogp.com, www.motogp.
hondaracingcorporation.com, www.motomatters.com,
www.motorcyclenews.com, www.motorsport.com,
www.paddock-gp.com, www.rivistagq.com, www.shoei-europe.com,
www.sportal.eu, www.sportskeeda.com, www.theguardian.com,
www.the-race.com, www.tntsports.co.uk, www.weare93.com

Films

From Cervera to Tokyo: The Marc Márquez Story, Red Bull Films,
2019.

Hitting the Apex, Directed by Mark Neale, The First Movie
Company LLC/Universal Pictures, 2013.

Marc Márquez: All In, A Fast Brothers Production A.I.E.,
Prime Video, 2023.

Marc Márquez: Story of a Trophy Collector, Dorna Sports, S.L., 2015.

Rookie93 Marc Márquez: Beyond the Smile, Dorna Sports S.L., 2013.

Unconditional: Marc Márquez – A Mother's Story, Directed by
Myles Desenberg, 2019. www.dazn.com